W9-ALA-320

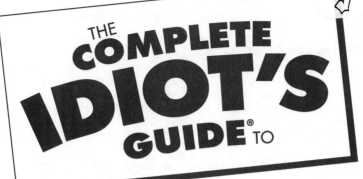

THE
COMPLETE
IDIOT'S
GUIDE® TO

Understanding the Amish

by Susan Rensberger

ALPHA

A member of Penguin Group (USA) Inc.

To Mark, for his love and support, and for making me laugh.

International Standard Book Number: 0-02-864470-0
Library of Congress Catalog Card Number: 2003102273

05   04   03   8   7   6   5   4   3   2   1

Interpretation of the printing code: The rightmost number of the first series of numbers is the year of the book's printing; the rightmost number of the second series of numbers is the number of the book's printing. For example, a printing code of 03-1 shows that the first printing occurred in 2003.

Printed in the United States of America

Note: This publication contains the opinions and ideas of its author. It is intended to provide helpful and informative material on the subject matter covered. It is sold with the understanding that the author and publisher are not engaged in rendering professional services in the book. If the reader requires personal assistance or advice, a competent professional should be consulted.

The author and publisher specifically disclaim any responsibility for any liability, loss, or risk, personal or otherwise, which is incurred as a consequence, directly or indirectly, of the use and application of any of the contents of this book.

Most Alpha books are available at special quantity discounts for bulk purchases for sales promotions, premiums, fund-raising, or educational use. Special books, or book excerpts, can also be created to fit specific needs.

For details, write: Special Markets; Alpha Books, 375 Hudson Street, New York, NY 10014.

Publisher: *Marie Butler-Knight*
Product Manager: *Phil Kitchel*
Senior Managing Editor: *Jennifer Chisholm*
Senior Acquisitions Editor: *Randy Ladenheim-Gil*
Development Editor: *Jennifer Moore*
Production Editor: *Billy Fields*
Copy Editor: *Jeff Rose*
Illustrators: *Abigail Falck, Jody Schaeffer*
Cover/Book Designer: *Trina Wurst*
Indexer: *Brad Herriman*
Layout/Proofreading: *Megan Douglass, Ayanna Lacey*

Contents at a Glance

Contents

Foreword

The Amish have become increasingly well known in the recent past. Their simple dress and austere life style have become the object of novels, movies, and even television commercials. Tourists by the millions flock to their rural settlements to gawk at these unusual people, buy their quilts and furniture, and gorge themselves on their sumptuous fare. The Amish are also becoming familiar to more and more Americans as land pressures in their older communities force them to branch out into parts of the country where they had never been before.

But how much do we know about these other-worldly folks beside what we see on the outside—beards, broadbrims, bonnets, and buggies? Why do they insist on going against the current of the American mainstream? Are they religious fanatics? Are they just ignorant of modern ways? Where do they get all their rules and regulations? Do they use some holy book besides the Bible? Susan Rensberger takes you behind the curtain of Amish life to explain the "why" of their beliefs and practices.

We learn that the Amish take the Bible very seriously and very literally. They earnestly try to put into practice the passage "be not conformed to this world" (Romans 12:2). They believe that the world system is controlled by the forces of evil and that true followers of Christ will be separated from the surrounding society. They dress differently because the Bible tells them to be modest, humble, and simple—not the goals of the fashion world. They eschew owning and driving cars because such fast, easy transportation keeps people scattered, separated, and away from home. They regard radio, television, and other mainstream entertainment as a pipeline for the filth of the world to come into their homes. They meet for worship in their homes because this emphasizes that the church is the people of God, not a building.

These are the ideals of the Amish, but they are the first to admit that they don't always live up to them. As in any religious group, there are devout Amish members and there are those who defame the good name of the group. In her view as a modern American woman, Rensberger doesn't put the Amish on a pedestal as she points out a number of perceived weaknesses, inconsistencies, and hypocrisies among them.

The book ends with a look at the Mennonites from whom the Amish divided in 1693. One of the most asked questions by tourists in Amish country is "what's the difference between the Amish and the Mennonites?" The answer to this question depends on which of the many groups of Mennonites one is referring to. The author explains in detail that the great majority of Mennonites have gone with the flow of the American mainstream, as far as outward matters are concerned, while emphasizing service, peace, and justice. Are these matters more important than what kind of clothes one wears or what kind of transportation one uses? The reader will have to decide who is being more faithful to their heritage and to God.

Stephen E. Scott

Stephen E. Scott is a research assistant at the Young Center for Anabaptist and Pietist Studies at Elizabethtown College. He has written six books relating to the Plain People: *Plain Buggies: Amish, Mennonite and Brethren Horse-drawn Transportation, Why Do They Dress That Way?, The Amish Wedding and Other Special Occasions of the Old Order Communities, Amish Houses and Barns, Living Without Electricity* (co-author), and *An Introduction to Old Order and Conservative Mennonite Groups.* Stephen lives in Lancaster County, Pennsylvania, and is a member of the Old Order River Brethren Church.

Introduction

You probably know the popular image of the Amish: Simple, hardworking, happy, healthy, peace-loving folk living in harmony with nature according to a cultural wisdom that the rest of society has forgotten. But look a little deeper and you'll uncover an alternative view of the Amish: A secretive people living in a tightly controlled, closed society that forbids education, questioning, and dissent.

So who *are* the people under the hats? What is the truth about the Amish?

Truth is, no single truth can describe an entire people, including the Amish. Not only is their idealized image false, it's unfair. Putting the Amish on a pedestal denies them their right to be as human as everyone else.

Of course, the Amish themselves have helped construct that pedestal by making outward appearance a standard for gauging inner purity and conviction. No wonder others assume that their inner life is as uniform as their clothing.

Like human beings of every culture, there are good Amish people and bad, happy families and those hiding dark secrets. Your perspective on the Amish depends on your experiences with them.

A Mennonite minister once repeated to me a local saying, "The broader the brim and the blacker the hat, the more there is to hide." He was expressing both the prejudice and insight gleaned from generations of Mennonite experience as close neighbors, and often relatives, of the Amish. On the other hand, sociologists who study the Amish often write with great admiration about their culture's values and ability to survive and even thrive.

What do the Amish themselves say? In both interviews and their own writing, many Amish people say they love their way of life. Yet some of those who left the Amish write of escaping an oppressive life in search of the freedom to be themselves.

So who are the true Amish? They are real human beings—complex and contradictory—and no two are exactly alike. You can dress them alike, you can teach them alike, you can even ask them to think alike—but you can't make their hearts alike.

And that's why every human society—Amish, Mennonite, or any other—encompasses both light and darkness, good and evil, tragedy and joy. That's what makes it real.

How Our Story Unfolds

This book is divided into six parts. The first five are devoted to the Amish, while Part 6 covers the Mennonites—an historically related group that is often confused with the Amish. I'll give you a quick overview:

Part 1, "Introducing the Amish: Overview and History," takes a look at who they are, their history, and some of their religious relatives, including other "Plain" groups that are easily confused with the Amish.

Part 2, "Faith of Their Fathers: Amish Beliefs and Worship," moves from religious history to religious life today. It covers beliefs, worship practices, and how Amish churches choose leaders and maintain discipline.

Part 3, "Inside Out: Religion as a Way of Life," examines how the Amish express their religious values through language, homes, transportation, clothing, and hairstyles. Then we look at life in the Amish family, from childhood through youth, marriage, parenthood, and old age.

Part 4, "In the World, but Not of the World: The Amish and Modern Society," asks how Amish society keeps its members separate from the world, what problems it hides, and what happens to those who want to leave. Finally, we look at how Amish culture adapts to changes in modern society.

Part 5, "Fruits of Their Labor: Sampling Amish Culture," celebrates the aspects of Amish culture that attract outsiders—food, quilts, and furniture. We look at how tourism affects Amish life and how you can sample Amish culture for yourself, in Amish communities or at home in your own kitchen.

Part 6, "Beyond the Old Order: Where Have All the Mennonites Gone?" picks up the story of the group most closely related to the Amish. We trace the history of schisms and modernization, ask what identifies a Mennonite today, and see how Mennonite culture approaches modern issues including women's rights, child and spouse abuse, and homosexuality.

Insider Tips

Throughout the chapters, you'll find bits of extra information designed to amaze, entertain, amuse, and enlighten:

CAUTION Make No Mistake

Not that you would, but just in case, we warn you away from the most common misconceptions and missteps.

Ironies and Oddities

Pointing out contradictions, ironies, and just plain interesting stuff about Amish or Mennonite life and culture.

Vas Es Das? _____

(Or, if you're Amish, *What is That?*) Definitions of terms, such as the name of the language (is it Pennsylvania Dutch or Pennsylvania German?) in which some of the terms are written.

The Plain Truth _____

The plain truth—or at least some version of it. Interesting info and editorial comments too good to leave out.

Acknowledgments

First, I want to thank Stephen Scott, technical editor and expert resource, for patiently answering many questions during the writing of this book and catching my errors in the final manuscript. His representations of the Amish point of view on many issues helped make this a more balanced book, though all responsibility for opinions expressed here remains mine alone.

I further wish to thank:

Miriam B. Yutzy from Menno-Hof Amish-Mennonite Visitors Center in Shipshewana, Indiana, for patiently ferreting out the answers to my questions.

Ottie Garrett, author, agent and researcher, for his help in research among those who left the Amish community.

Beth Graybill, director of Mennonite Central Committee Women's Concerns Desk, for generous research assistance of many kinds.

John E. Sharp of the Mennonite Church USA Archives at Goshen College, in Goshen, Indiana, for helping me understand the new church structure and issues of concern.

Gloria Nafziger and Amy Short of the Brethren Mennonite Council for Lesbian, Gay, Bisexual, and Transgender Interests, for generous information provided with good humor.

"Martha," for sharing her story of strength, survival, and personal triumph.

Jane Miller Leatherman, for generously sharing her experiences, perspective, wisdom, and grace.

"Paul," for sharing his story with a gentle heart, deep insight, and great compassion.

Finally, I want to thank my illustrator, Abigail Falck, for her creative contributions and patient dedication to getting every nuance of Amish and Mennonite culture just right.

Special Thanks to the Technical Reviewer

The Complete Idiot's Guide to Understanding the Amish was reviewed by an expert who double-checked the accuracy of what you'll learn here, to help us ensure that this book gives you everything you need to know about Amish history and culture. Special thanks are extended to Stephen Scott.

Trademarks

All terms mentioned in this book that are known to be or are suspected of being trademarks or service marks have been appropriately capitalized. Alpha Books and Penguin Group (USA) Inc. cannot attest to the accuracy of this information. Use of a term in this book should not be regarded as affecting the validity of any trademark or service mark.

Part 1

Introducing the Amish: Overview and History

Maybe you think you know who the Amish are, but do you really? Not all "Plain" people are Amish, not all Amish are Old Order, and the many varieties of Mennonites are related to, but not at all the same as, the Amish. So let's start at the beginning, by defining who the Amish are, where they live, and what makes them distinct from similar religious groups.

Getting to the root of Amish identity, we search out their beginnings in Europe as a group of radical Anabaptists who upset the religious and political order of their day. Soon the reformers got into squabbles of their own, and a guy named Jakob Ammann left in a huff. Next thing you know, a bunch of people called the Amish are setting sail for the New World. A century later, another dispute splits the group again, and those who refuse to budge are forever known as the Old Order Amish.

To clear up the confusion about all those other people you might have thought were Amish, we finish with a rundown on other Anabaptist groups, from Plain to mainstream.

Chapter 1

Beneath the Hat, Beyond the Buggy: Who Are the Amish?

In This Chapter

- ◆ Who are the Amish?
- ◆ How religion dictates Amish lifestyle
- ◆ What makes the Amish distinct
- ◆ Where the Amish live
- ◆ Other "Plain" people

Popular images of the *Amish* appear on postcards and in picture books for tourists. They're caricatured on restaurant placemats in rural areas that tout themselves to tourists as "Amish country." Gift shops along highways in Pennsylvania, Ohio, and Indiana sell figurines of people dressed in "plain" clothes and books about everything from their quaint speech to their quilt patterns and recipes for the food they eat.

Why are modern Americans so fascinated with the Amish? Perhaps because they're so inaccessible. They live among us, but have little contact with the rest of society. With few exceptions, they don't write or talk about themselves, and seldom invite strangers to their church services or community events. While occasionally, someone from outside the Amish community becomes friends with Amish people, most of us know little beyond the contrast between their life and ours: People driving horse-drawn buggies in a society devoted to the automobile. Women in long, dark dresses fastened with straight pins, which also hold their white prayer coverings on their heads. Men and boys with bowl-shaped haircuts whose black "barn-door" pants are held up by suspenders rather than belts.

So who are the people underneath the black hats, inside the buggies, separated from the rest of society by their religion and chosen way of life? How are they different from the rest of us, and more important, why?

Living the Faith: Religion Dictates Lifestyle

The Amish are a religious group descended from the *Anabaptists*. Unlike other Christian denominations, which have central organizations that govern church policy, the Amish are organized on a local level. Each church is independent of the others, though they may affiliate with other congregations who agree on the same standards of behavior and religious practice.

Popular images of the Amish focus on their distinctive "plain" clothing and often the horses and buggies they drive. These are the outward symbols of a religious faith with deep traditions, strong convictions, and powerful emotional ties for its members. This Amish couple probably has many older children, as well as the youngsters pictured here. Amish families average 6.5 children.

Vas Es Das?

The Amish are a Christian religious group that separated in 1693 from another early **Anabaptist** group that later became known as the Mennonites. Anabaptists were church reformers in sixteenth century Switzerland who insisted that only adults who chose to follow the biblical teachings of Jesus Christ could be baptized. Although they had been baptized as infants by the Catholic Church, they defied the Catholic Church, other Protestant reformers, and civil authorities by baptizing each other again (*ana-* means *again*). Both Mennonites and the Amish, as well as other religious groups, trace their origins to the first Anabaptist meeting on January 21, 1525.

For the purposes of this book, the term "Amish" refers to the Old Order Amish, the largest and most widely recognized group.

The largest and most conservative category of Amish are called Old Order Amish, to distinguish them from groups that have left to form more progressive groups. As a general rule, practices among the largest Amish groups are most conservative in the eastern United States, and grow more progressive as you go west across the country.

As with all generalities, there are exceptions to this rule. In the Midwest, a number of minority Amish groups are ultra-conservative. And the Amish communities in and around Lancaster County, Pennsylvania, are more progressive in technology use than many midwestern Amish.

Practices vary considerably from group to group, and the reasons for those practices are sometimes unclear even to experts in Amish culture. For example, sociologists writing about the Amish in Pennsylvania say they are prohibited from riding bicycles because, like cars, bikes have tires filled with compressed air.

Other authorities on Amish culture, though, say it's not the air in the tires that the Amish object to, it's how far you can go on one. Keeping people close to home is key to holding the group together. In Indiana, where farms are larger and farther apart, the Amish use bicycles extensively. Adults often use them to get to work, now that many men work in factories and women in stores. There are even Amish people who sell or repair bicycles from shops at their homes.

What all Amish congregations have in common is history and tradition. The Amish were founded in Alsace (a region in present-day France bordering Germany and Switzerland) in 1693 by Jakob Ammann, for whom they're named, as an offshoot of the Anabaptist group that later became the Mennonites. As Anabaptists, the Mennonites had defied both the Catholic Church and other leaders of the Protestant Reformation, started by Martin Luther in 1517.

Like the Mennonites, the Amish believed in adult baptism, nonviolence, the separation of church and state, a refusal to swear oaths, literal obedience to the scriptural teachings of Jesus, and a church leadership drawn from the community's members rather than a professional priesthood or clergy. But Jakob Ammann's followers felt the Swiss Anabaptists were becoming too "worldly" and wanted stronger church discipline. So they followed Ammann in founding a new group that would strictly regulate its members outer as well as inner lives. The Swiss Anabaptists they left later became known as Mennonites, named for a leader from the Netherlands, Menno Simons.

> **CAUTION**
>
> **Make No Mistake**
>
> There's no shame in making a mistake, but it's a shame to make an obvious one like mispronouncing the word *Amish*. The first syllable is pronounced *ah* as in llama; not *ay* as in shame.

Generally speaking, Mennonites share many of the beliefs of the Amish, but accept more aspects of modern life and grant more individual freedom to members. There are many Mennonite denominations, whose lifestyles vary from nearly as conservative as the Amish to indistinguishable from mainstream society.

What Makes the Amish Distinct?

One way to understand the Amish is to look at the rules they follow in daily life. These rules are established by tradition and enforced by the local church district and its bishop and deacons. Here are some ways that Amish life differs from that of mainstream Americans.

Their Language

The Amish speak a German dialect called Pennsylvania German or Pennsylvania Dutch, usually called "Dutch" for short. Language is one of the major ways the Amish isolate themselves from American society. Amish children grow up learning Dutch as their first language, and learn most of their English in school, though they may hear their parents speak it at home occasionally—especially when they don't want the younger children to know what they're saying! Some Amish children start school without knowing English, though this isn't as common as it used to be.

Here's another exception to the rule, though: A small ethnic group of Amish speak a Bernese Swiss dialect. These people came directly from Switzerland and neighboring France to Adams County, Indiana, in the 1850s.

The Plain Truth

The Amish speak Pennsylvania Dutch, which is not Dutch as spoken in the Netherlands. It's an oral (not written) German dialect similar to that used by rural people in the region of Germany from which the Amish originally came. The word "Dutch" in Pennsylvania Dutch is a variation of the word *Deitsch*, meaning "German."

People in communities where the Amish live are commonly referred to by their primary language. An Amish person might be called "Dutch," and anyone who isn't Amish is called "English." As a child studying geography in first or second grade, I remember wondering how I could be "English" but not from England.

How They Get Around

The Amish forbid their members to use motorized vehicles. They drive horses and buggies and farm with draft horses rather than tractors. Specific restrictions vary by region, however. Farmers in most communities are allowed to use machinery powered by motors as long as those implements are drawn by horses, rather than tractors. A few of the most conservative use no motorized machinery at all.

The Amish don't use tires with air in them on wagons or buggies; wagons have iron-rimmed wheels and buggy wheels are wooden. However, in Indiana, this doesn't stop the Amish from riding bicycles, a common mode of transportation for adults as well as young people. Solid rubber tires are also acceptable in many communities, including northern Indiana.

Though they're not allowed to own motorized vehicles, the Amish can ride in cars, buses, and on trains. They sometimes hire "English" people to drive them to work or on a trip. In Indiana, they may ask a neighbor to drive a pregnant woman to the hospital to give birth. It isn't unusual to see a van full of Amish people on their way to visit relatives or riding to factory jobs in town. You just won't see them driving.

What They Wear

One of the most visible cultural traditions of the Amish is their distinctive clothing. The "old-fashioned" shirtwaist dresses, bonnets, and head coverings worn by women and girls and the "barn-door" style pants, suspenders, and black hats worn by men are to make them stand out in contemporary society. Wearing uniform dress not only sets them apart from the world, it helps the Amish identify with their community. They can tell at a glance whether a person is of their faith, a similar but distinct religious group, or "the world."

Small distinctions in style even locate a member of the Old Order Amish by state or church district. Because of the difficulty of communication and travel between settlements, people in each state have developed slight variations on the traditional clothing over the years. A Pennsylvania head covering or *kapp* is distinctive in design from one in Indiana, for instance.

Details of dress also spell out a person's social and marital status. Unmarried girls and young women, for example, may wear black head coverings to church, while married women wear white. In some areas, ministers' wives wear black capes and aprons.

Finally, clothing styles evolve over time, even among the Amish. As with mainstream society, younger women are more likely to wear the newest styles, while older Amish women cling to the more conservative garb of their youth. See Chapter 10 for more on Amish dress.

> **Ironies and Oddities**
>
> For early Anabaptists, plain clothing was a way of maintaining humility by not calling attention to one's appearance. As the rest of the world's clothing styles have evolved, though, the styles worn by the Amish have called more attention to their appearance, rather than less. The symbolic value the Amish place on their clothing focuses the attention of their own members on appearance as well.

> **Make No Mistake** _____
>
> The small, white caps that Amish women wear on their heads are called "head coverings," "prayer coverings," or "head caps," not bonnets. These are worn at all times, because it's believed a woman needs to have her head covered when she prays, and she never knows when she might be moved to pray.
>
> Don't confuse coverings with the black bonnets that Amish women often wear in public. Women from some church districts wear bonnets whenever they go out in public, but in more progressive states, such as Indiana, most women wear bonnets only in winter.

Amish hair styles are as strictly regulated as clothing. Women and girls wear their hair uncut, but either braided and coiled at the backs of their heads for girls, or in buns.

Men's hair is cut at home in the distinctive bowl shape. After they marry, they grow beards, which they wear untrimmed. Mustaches, however, are forbidden.

They're Off the Grid!

One of the easiest ways to distinguish an Amish farmstead from its English neighbors is by looking for electrical lines running from roadside poles to the barn and house. If there are none, it's probably an Amish farm.

The Amish forbid the use of electricity and other modern inventions that threaten to bring the world into their homes. Telephones and motorized vehicles are also off-limits—sort of.

But the Amish are famous for making compromises that help them function in the modern world. They're allowed to use a telephone and electricity, as long as they don't own the building and the service isn't in their name. Thus, the Amish can run stores in leased buildings lit by electricity and work in factories with power tools. When I was growing up in Indiana, my parents owned a farm and rented the house to an Amish couple. My father wanted a telephone on the property so they could call for help in case of fire or other disaster. The Amish couple asked permission from their bishop, who allowed the phone to be installed as long as it wasn't because they wanted it for themselves.

Amish women use modern stoves and refrigerators in their kitchens, but only those powered by bottled propane or natural gas, not electricity. Why is electricity forbidden but natural gas allowed? Because electricity also can be used to power televisions and radios, which would bring the values of the outside world into Amish homes. That would be seen as a threat to the teachings and unity of their church, and is strictly forbidden.

But continually developing technology challenges Amish traditions. For decades, Indiana Amish have used telephones in homemade phone booths along county roads. Now, some of them use, and own, cell phones. In some cases, the phones may be required for work in non-Amish businesses. But one woman reports that her parents' Amish neighbors have cell phones for the whole family.

Cell phones pose a new and controversial issue for the Amish, who haven't yet formed a definitive policy on their use. It will be interesting to see how their response to wireless technology continues to evolve.

Patchwork Quilt: Where Do They Live?

The Amish live in rural communities intermingled with other *Plain* Anabaptist groups, various varieties of Mennonites (more on them in Chapter 4 and Part 6) and the worldly English. Though they don't live in closed communities, their interactions with neighbors not of their own church affiliation most frequently take place in settings that have to do with commerce: stores, feed mills, auction barns, or on their "home place" if they're selling produce or hand-crafted goods such as furniture, rugs, or quilts. In the past, public schools provided another place for Amish and English neighbors to interact, but most Amish communities now have their own private schools.

Amish communities are located throughout the Midatlantic states and the Midwest, with a few scattered settlements in southern and western states. Far and away the largest number of settlements is found in central Ohio (Holmes County and vicinity), eastern Pennsylvania (the Lancaster County area) and northern Indiana (Lagrange and Elkhart counties), in that order. Wisconsin, Michigan, Missouri, Iowa, and New York also have significant, though much smaller, Amish populations.

> **Vas Es Das?** _____
>
> **Plain** churches generally means any of a number of Anabaptist religious groups whose members follow a prescribed dress code that emphasizes modesty and simplicity. Their styles of dress generally are derived from traditional peasant clothing of northern Europe, where their ancestors lived. These groups also often regulate their members' use of modern transportation and technology as ways to enforce group identity.

According to John Hostetler, a well-known sociologist and anthropologist who writes extensively on the Amish (and was himself raised in an Amish family), Amish settlements consist of church districts, a geographic area in which all Old Order Amish families meet every two weeks for church service in members' homes.

The Amish believe the church is its members, not a building, so they don't build churches or meetinghouses for worship. This is one distinction between the Amish and some of the less conservative Anabaptist groups. Amish congregations are limited in size by the number of people who can meet in a large farm house or barn. When the population of a church district grows too large, the district is divided and a new congregation formed.

Unlike members of other Christian denominations, Amish families don't get to choose which church to attend. The church they attend is decided by where they live. They cannot stop attending one Amish church and move to another because they feel more in tune with its members, prefer its preachers, or disagree with a discipline ruling made in their home church. To leave the district, they must either move (an extreme measure for farm families, whose home is also their livelihood) or leave the Old Order and join a more liberal group. Such a move has powerful social effects, and is not made lightly.

Who's Who: The Amish and Other Plain People

Few religions are more splintered and confusing than the Mennonites, Amish, and related Anabaptist groups. For a nonviolent religion, they certainly have a surprising number of disagreements. Those disagreements have often resulted in the formation of new offshoot churches and denominations rather than compromise. This has preserved the cultural and religious traditions of the Amish and other Plain people, but often left a legacy of anger and bitterness that lasted for generations.

Ironies and Oddities

Early Anabaptists were severely persecuted for their belief that no one could be born into a church, but had to choose membership through baptism. Yet among the Amish today, choice of religion is largely dictated by birth. Though children are not church members, they are socialized into the church community from birth. The social pressure to be baptized and join the church as young adults is powerful. One cannot choose baptism without church membership: to be baptized, one must accept membership in the church. And not just any church, but the one in whose district you live.

In recent years, however, the two largest and most "worldly" Mennonite denominations have moved to reverse their history of division by reuniting, healing a split that occurred in 1860. In 1989, the General Conference Mennonite Church and its more conservative parent, the Mennonite Church, began exploring the possibility of merging. In 2000, they formed the new Mennonite Church USA. The merger process is expected to be completed in 2003—but not without a great deal of controversy. Even this newest attempt at unity seems likely to result in new church divisions as well. (For more on this subject, see Chapter 22.)

Doing the Splits: Amish Divisions in Pennsylvania

Sociologist Donald Kraybill traces three major divisions since the late nineteenth century among the Amish of Lancaster County, Pennsylvania alone.

The first, in 1877, occurred at a time when many Amish in the East and Midwest were pushing their leaders for more adaptation to modern life. Rather than accommodate the protesters, the Amish leaders held their ground and kept their rules, preferring to split the church over compromising traditions. The two groups that left the Lancaster church, according to Kraybill, became known as Meetinghouse Amish, because they built houses of worship, while the remaining church was called House Amish.

After the Lancaster split, the original group became known as the Old Order Amish, while the new groups were called Amish-Mennonites, and eventually joined the Mennonite Church.

(At that time, the Mennonite Church was popularly known as the Old Mennonites, to distinguish them from the newer and more progressive General Conference Mennonite Church.)

> **The Plain Truth** _____
>
> A common way of labeling the many Amish splinter groups is by their customs or accommodation to modern life, or after the leader at the time of the division: Car Amish, Beachy Amish, Swartzentruber Amish, and so on.
>
> One summer when we were visiting the Indiana community where I grew up, my husband (a Catholic boy from the Chicago suburbs) took note of a Plain woman using a riding mower on her front lawn. "Look," he joked, "The Lawn-Mower Amish!"

In 1910 a slightly more progressive group withdrew from the Old Order Amish in Lancaster County. This group in turn divided in 1925. The majority affiliated with the group led by Moses Beachy of Somerset County, Pennsylvania. They permitted cars and other modern technology, while keeping many outer Amish symbols, especially dress. These and similar groups are usually referred to as Beachy Amish or Beachy Amish Mennonites.

The most recent Old Order Amish split happened in 1966, when a large group of families left to form the New Order Amish. Their differences centered on the use of farm equipment, but later the splinter group split once again into several factions.

No Such Thing as Just Plain Amish

Those are just the major divisions within one settlement, Lancaster County. Many Amish groups that left eventually affiliated with or formed new factions of the Mennonites. In the century between 1866 and 1966, these splits resulted in formation of the:

- Evangelical Mennonite Church, originally called Egly Amish.

- Stuckey Mennonites, who later merged with the General Conference Mennonite Church, which has since merged with the Mennonite Church to form Mennonite Church USA.

- Indiana-Michigan, Eastern and Western Amish Mennonite Conferences, all of which eventually merged with the Mennonite Church.

- Conservative Amish Mennonite Conference, who later dropped "Amish" from their name and became more like the Mennonite Church.

- Beachy Amish Mennonite Church.

- Mennonite Christian Fellowship, which is a slightly more conservative than the Beachy Amish.

- New Order or "New Amish."

Other Plain Folks

Besides the Amish, Plain churches with Anabaptist roots include the Old Order Mennonites and Conservative Mennonites, with their many branches and independent churches, several Brethren groups, and the Hutterites. While Plain Mennonite and Brethren groups dress conservatively and may even drive horses and buggies instead of cars, most Mennonites and Brethren blend in seamlessly with mainstream society. See Chapter 4 for more on these other Anabaptist denominations.

Amish life looks simple from the outside, but the Amish lifestyle is really a complex maze of rules, traditions, and beliefs that govern their lives. Disagreements abound, leading to wide variation in what's allowed and what's not from settlement to settlement. More serious arguments have divided the church into an intriguing—and sometimes puzzling—web of related groups.

The Least You Need to Know

- ◆ The Amish are one of several Anabaptist Christian groups with common roots in the Protestant Reformation in sixteenth century Europe. Anabaptists disagreed with both the Catholic Church and Protestants on several points, including adult baptism, nonviolence, separation of church and state, and the priesthood of believers.

- ◆ Mennonites are another Anabaptist religious denomination named for Menno Simons, a Dutch Anabaptist preacher.

- ◆ The Amish, named for their leader Jakob Ammann, separated from the group that later became the Mennonites.

- ◆ Amish church rules control both personal and religious life, including language, dress, hairstyle, transportation, and use of technology.

- ◆ The Amish live in settlements primarily along the Eastern seaboard and throughout the Midwest.

- ◆ The Old Order Amish worship in homes rather than in churches or meetinghouses.

- ◆ Throughout their history, Amish and other Plain churches have divided many times over issues of how much to modernize and imitate the larger society. As a result, there are many small splinter groups, often named for the men who founded them.

Founding the Faith: Amish Roots in Europe

In This Chapter

◆ Early persecution of the Amish

◆ Reforming the Catholic Church

◆ Radical Anabaptists reform the Reformation

◆ Mennonite and Amish church founders

To understand the Amish today, we need to look to their roots in Europe nearly 500 years ago. Their identity as a group is shaped by the experiences of early Anabaptists, who for more than two centuries were persecuted for their faith. The belief that Christians had to separate themselves from the world to avoid sin was only strengthened by the need to hide from government authorities who threatened the lives of the Amish forebears. Social contact outside the group was dangerous for early Anabaptists, who fled into the countryside and lived mainly by farming.

The legacy of that experience can be seen today in the way the Amish maintain a strict separation from the world in clothing and language, and socialize within their religious community. While separation is an expression of religious belief, it has been reinforced by their history. Even their dress and hair styles originated in sixteenth century German and Swiss peasant styles. A look at Amish origins in Europe helps us understand how they came to hold so tightly to their traditions in defiance of the changing world around them.

Setting the Stage: Church and State Before 1500

The status of Christians across Europe had changed radically by the sixteenth century. Early years of brutal persecution gave way in the fourth century to official acceptance, when the Roman Emperor Constantine converted to Christianity and adopted it as the state religion of the Roman Empire.

After the fall of the Roman Empire in western Europe, the Catholic Church became even more powerful and important. At a time when kingdoms were small and local, the Pope's influence stretched across the continent. Kings sought the support of the Church, and bishops became political power brokers.

As the Church became the partner of the wealthy and politically powerful, the nature of Christianity changed as well. No longer social outcasts, Christians now dominated the social structure of their cities, towns, and villages. What had once been a movement of people committed to their religious beliefs and practices had become an institution whose members were born into its ranks. Governments required parents to have their babies baptized by the Church soon after they were born. Church baptismal and membership records were used by local governments to levy taxes and raise armies.

While reinforcing the power of the state over its citizens, the Church also had become powerful in its own right. The pope had the power to legitimize kings whose right to rule was in question. The Catholic Church owned vast tracts of land, monasteries, convents, schools, cathedrals, and churches. Its leaders lived as wealthy men at Church expense, sometimes paying the Church for the opportunity to become bishop or archbishop. Although pledged to celibacy, some clergy, bishops, and even popes were known to have mistresses and children.

One way the institutional church raised money to support itself was through selling indulgences, or the forgiveness of sin, to church members. The deceased were supposedly released from time in purgatory to ascend to heaven if their relatives made donations to Church representatives. The Catholic Church taught that people earned their way to heaven by taking the sacraments (such as communion) administered by a priest and doing good works, which included giving money to the Church.

Protest and Reform: Luther and Others

By 1517, some Christians in northern Europe were protesting corruption and misuse of power among priests and bishops. In Germany, Martin Luther nailed his 95 theses, or points of belief, to the church door in Wittenberg. Among them was, "Peace and forgiveness come to a person through faith in a gracious Christ." This was a challenge to the very beliefs taught by the Catholic Church.

Thus began the *Protestant Reformation*. The beliefs preached by these reformers threatened to take away the power of the Catholic Church over its members. They taught that God's forgiveness need not be paid for, and that God's grace alone—not Church sacraments or the declarations of priests or popes—could win salvation for a person. What need was there then for people to follow the dictates of the clergy or support the Church with their money?

Vas Es Das?

The **Protestant Reformation** is the movement led by Martin Luther and others that ended the Catholic Church's status as the state religion in many nations and the only Christian Church. Among changes demanded by protestors were the use of biblical teaching rather than church law as the foundation for church decisions, church services conducted in the language of the people rather than Latin, an end to the selling of indulgences, and allowing priests to marry. Protestant denominations today, including the Lutheran church founded by Martin Luther, trace their roots to the Protestant Reformation.

Luther also argued for "the priesthood of all believers," or equality among Christians. A pope has no more spiritual authority than any other Christian, he argued, because all receive the Holy Spirit at baptism. Luther believed that Christians could decide for themselves, using scripture and their conscience as their guide, how to follow God without the intercession or interpretations of professional clergy. These ideas would be cornerstones of the later, more radical, Anabaptist movement that spawned both the Mennonites and the Amish.

Ironies and Oddities

Early Anabaptists agreed with Luther about "the priesthood of all believers," including women. Although the Amish and early Mennonites later proclaimed this belief, they really meant "the priesthood of all men". Even today, the Amish exclude women from being ministers, deacons, and bishops. They consider women the spiritual equals of men, but subject to male authority. Some Mennonites still exclude women from ministry, too.

Reforming the Reformation: The Radical Anabaptists

One thing Martin Luther didn't protest, however, was the alliance between the Church and governments that supported his ideas. He appealed to German princes to help his cause, and eventually the Lutheran Church replaced Catholicism as the state church of Germany.

While Luther was writing and speaking in Germany, other reformers with similar beliefs arose elsewhere. In Zurich, Switzerland, Ulrich Zwingli preached church reform. He sought and received support from the Zurich City Council, whose members felt the reforms strengthened their power by weakening the authority of the pope. Zwingli only insisted on those reforms the government would embrace. This process eventually resulted in the Reformed Church, which became the state religion of Switzerland.

> **Make No Mistake**
>
> Don't confuse Anabaptists with Protestants. Although both have roots in the same historic place and time, and share more in common than they do with the Catholic Church, Anabaptists consider themselves a distinct branch of Christianity.

Some young Swiss Reformers thought Zwingli gave government officials too much say in deciding what the new, reformed doctrines should be. They argued that prayer and Bible study, not a vote of the city council, should decide matters of religious faith.

One belief Zwingli and Luther didn't share with them was that only adults could make the decision to dedicate their lives to God, represented by the sacrament of baptism. Infant baptism wasn't valid, the Radical Reformers argued, because children couldn't choose to dedicate their lives to Christ. These reformers rejected the Catholic belief that children would go to hell if they died before they were old enough to choose baptism. Instead, they believed that children remained innocent in the eyes of God until they reached the age of reason and could decide how to live their lives.

In 1525, a group of Radical Reformers met in Zurich and baptized each other as a sign of their commitment to follow Christ. Their movement was called the Anabaptists, which means those who "baptize again," because they had all been baptized first as infants in the Catholic Church. Their insistence that their infant baptism had not been valid was a challenge to the authority of both the Catholic Church and the Protestant Reformers. Both churches soon declared the Anabaptists a dangerous sect and persecuted them throughout Europe.

Crimes Against the State: Anabaptist Religious Persecution

The Swiss Anabaptists were persecuted by their government for 200 years or more. Rebaptism became a crime punishable by public execution. Governments in Switzerland and elsewhere hired "Anabaptist hunters" to ferret out members of the new religion, which they feared would undermine the social order. As a result, Anabaptists fled cities and hid in rural areas, meeting in secret in caves and barns.

Anabaptists across Europe from the sixteenth to eighteenth centuries were mutilated, drowned, burned at the stake, imprisoned, starved—the list of atrocities is truly astonishing. Others had their property confiscated and were exiled, penniless.

> **Ironies and Oddities**
>
> A book commonly found in Amish homes is *The Bloody Theatre; or Martyrs Mirror of Defenseless Christians*. The size of a large family Bible, *Martyrs Mirror* tells stories of Christians who were arrested, tortured, and killed for their faith from the time of Jesus through its first printing in Dutch in 1660. The Amish read it to strengthen their faith today.

When the martyrdom of the faithful only resulted in more converts, governments switched to oppressive laws, including heavy taxation, denial of the right to own property, requirements to seek government permission to marry, and so on.

In 1527, a group of Swiss and German Anabaptist leaders met secretly in the Swiss village of Schleitheim to discuss the principles of their new religion. They agreed to seven principles of faith and wrote a document called the "Brotherly Agreement." They referred to themselves as the Brethren and came to be known as the Swiss Brethren. Their Agreement, later called the Schleitheim Articles, included the following points:

- Only adult baptism is valid.

- Members who commit sin and refuse to confess and repent it when confronted are subject to the *ban*.

- Only baptized church members can take part in communion or the Lord's Supper.

- Christians are to be separate from the world, its religions and entertainments. They are also to separate from the use of violence for protection or vengeance, following the example of Jesus who prayed for his enemies rather than resisting evil.

- Ministers, as shepherds of the church, are vital to its members and should be replaced immediately if they are martyred or exiled, so the church can continue.

◆ Governments, although provided by God for the protection of the good and punishment of the bad, are not perfect in Christ. They rule by the sword, a violation of Christian principles. Christians, as citizens of the kingdom of God, should not take part in governing any earthly kingdom.

◆ Christians are required to be honest and truthful, so swearing oaths is unnecessary and evil. Jesus said that a person's word should be sufficient.

Vas Es Das?

Ban is the Amish term for excommunication of those who refuse to confess and repent a sin when confronted by the church. A person expelled from the church is said to be "put under the ban." A source of the split between the Amish and Mennonites, it's still practiced by the Amish today to maintain discipline.

In the century following the first rebaptism in Zurich in 1525, persecution drove many Anabaptists out of Switzerland and into hiding. They moved north along the Rhine River into Alsace (in present-day France) and beyond to an area called the Palatinate, in what is now Germany. There, a local prince eventually offered them safety for a time because they were needed to replace farmers who had been killed in the Thirty Years War.

Menno Simons Steps Up

Shortly after the Schleitheim Articles were written, a Catholic priest in Holland named Menno Simons began questioning some of the key doctrines of his church.

Make No Mistake

Although the Mennonites are named for Dutch Anabaptist Menno Simons, their church grew directly out of the Swiss Anabaptist movement. Before they were called Mennonites, those living in Switzerland were known as the Swiss Brethren. They should not be confused with the Church of the Brethren, another Anabaptist group started in Germany in 1708.

Among them was that the communion bread and wine literally turned into the body and blood of Jesus (called transubstantiation) when he blessed them.

Protestant Reformers disagreed on this point. Luther believed in consubstantiation, meaning that the priest's blessing introduced Christ's spirit into the bread and wine, but didn't literally turn it into flesh and blood. Ulrich Zwingli, who founded the Reformed Church in Switzerland, argued that the bread and wine simply represented the body and blood.

Anabaptists also believed that the bread and wine simply represented the body and blood of Christ during communion. Menno Simons also found other

Anabaptist beliefs, including adult baptism, more in line with scripture than Catholic doctrine. Inspired by their courage in the face of persecution and attempts to follow literally the teachings of Jesus, Menno Simons left the Catholic Church and joined the Anabaptists in 1536.

A prolific writer, Simons became a leading Dutch Anabaptist thinker and defender. Eventually, not only the Dutch Anabaptists but also the Swiss Brethren came to be known as Mennonites. Menno Simons' writings are still influential among the Amish and Mennonites today.

Jakob Ammann Stirs Up Trouble

Over time, differences in practice and belief developed between the Swiss Brethren still in Switzerland and the descendents of those who had emigrated. In the Alsace, where persecution was less severe, some Anabaptists feared their members were making too many compromises with the worldly society around them, threatening their identity as a religious community.

Jakob Ammann was a prominent Anabaptist elder living in Alsace. Little is known about his personal history, but some historians suggest he might have been a recent convert to Anabaptism. He was fairly young when he challenged the church elders in Switzerland over practices he considered too lax, suggesting the kind of zealous attachment to rituals and forms often seen in new religious converts. Others suggest he may simply have wanted personal power. Perhaps both were true.

In 1693, Ammann challenged the practice of holding communion only once a year to commemorate the Last Supper or Lord's Supper. In his final meal with them, which took place at the Jewish celebration of Passover, Jesus blessed bread and wine and gave them to his disciples, telling them to eat and drink in remembrance of him. He also washed his disciples' feet as a symbol of willingness to humbly serve others, and instructed them to serve one another as well.

Unlike the Catholic Church, which had made communion service a sacrament at every mass, the Anabaptists believed that an annual Lord's Supper followed the example of Jesus. But they added the caveat that to take communion, a person had to be a church member in good standing and of clear conscience. Ammann believed church members should hold communion twice a year, a move some historians suggest was a way for him to tighten control over church members.

Whatever Ammann's reasoning, the Swiss elders disagreed. Jakob Ammann then turned to other issues, including *shunning*, foot washing, and the question of whether God would save good people who were not Anabaptist church members.

Vas Es Das?

Shunning is an Amish practice dating from the early Anabaptist days. A newer term is "social avoidance." Shunning can also include "marital avoidance," meaning that even spouses are required to have no relationship with the shunned person.

Shunning is used to discipline former church members who have been excommunicated from the church for refusing to confess and repent an act that the church community has deemed sinful. The practice of shunning within families and communities has created great controversy and pain within the Amish community for centuries, and remains a key point of disagreement between the Old Order Amish and other groups.

While the Swiss Brethren at this time were still following the Schleitheim Articles, the Alsatians to the north had adopted the more recent Dordrecht Confession of 1632. According to that document, Anabaptists should not only excommunicate, or ban, unrepentant sinners, but shun them as well. It also called for practicing foot washing along with the Lord's Supper, and strict separation from the world.

The Plain Truth

Two early groups of Anabaptists meeting in different centuries and different countries wrote statements of their basic beliefs, which later became points of disagreement between the Swiss Brethren (later called Mennonites) and the group that became the Amish. A key difference was whether banned members should also be shunned.

The *Schleitheim Articles* were written in 1527 in Schleitheim, Switzerland. They included the practice of banning, but not shunning, members of the church who fell into sin.

The *Dordrecht Confession* was written more than a century later, in 1632, in Holland by several groups of Mennonites. For erring church members, it prescribed not only banning but shunning as well.

The Swiss Brethren elders believed that banning or excommunicating a person from the church was sufficient discipline, and that shunning was unnecessary and unloving. They saw no need to add the practice of foot washing (though later Mennonites in the United States did adopt this practice and hold communion twice a year, rather than once).

The Swiss elders also held an open mind about the spiritual status of people they referred to as the "True-Hearted People" or "Half-Anabaptists." These were people who had helped the Anabaptists, especially in Switzerland where government persecution was fierce. Many Anabaptists owed their lives to the True-Hearted, who sheltered, hid, and fed them. Some were relatives who had not joined the Anabaptist movement, but protected their family members from the authorities.

The Swiss Brethren were grateful for the help of the True-Hearted, prayed for their souls, and withheld judgment about whether God offered them salvation. Jakob Ammann saw this as a conflict with the belief that salvation could not be won by good works, but granted by God's grace alone. And in Ammann's view, no one who had not dedicated his or her life to following Christ, as evidenced by joining the Anabaptists, was eligible to receive God's grace.

The Swiss elder Hans Reist countered that as a human being, he could not know another person's standing with God. Therefore, he could not say for sure that a person who still belonged to the state church was not saved. He could only pray for God's mercy on that person's soul. Reist also refused to practice shunning.

1693: Jakob Ammann Draws a Line in the Sand

Jakob Ammann and a few sympathizing elders from Alsace went to Switzerland to investigate the practices of congregations there and demand that they observe both shunning and foot washing. He also grilled their ministers and elders on two other issues: whether True-Hearted were saved, and whether a liar should be excommunicated.

Ammann wanted an immediate "yes" or "no" to his questions. When he called several meetings a few weeks apart and not all the Swiss elders and ministers showed up, he excommunicated those church leaders. He then went on to excommunicate others—including people he had never met—who said they had to consult with their congregation or other ministers on matters of faith such as these.

Finally, Jakob Ammann sent a letter to all Swiss Brethren congregations in Switzerland, Alsace, and the Palatinate demanding they tell him their standing on these issues by his deadline, or be excommunicated and shunned.

Most of the Swiss congregations opposed Ammann's positions, while those in Alsace sided with him. Elders in the Palatinate tried to mediate the dispute, but Ammann refused to compromise and most Palatinate congregations sided with the Swiss. Those two factions later became known as the Mennonites, while the congregations following Ammann became the Amish.

Seven years later, in 1700, the Amish group attempted to reconcile with the Swiss Brethren. They admitted they had acted without enough consultation and been too harsh in excommunicating their brethren. As an act of contrition, Jakob Ammann and other Amish leaders excommunicated themselves!

When early Mennonite elders didn't agree with newcomer Jakob Ammann that they should shun members who didn't follow church rules, he immediately excommunicated the elders and shunned them!

The Plain Truth

Jakob Ammann was a tailor by trade and felt that the Mennonites should be dressing more modestly. Not only was jewelry too showy, but so were buttons. After the Amish split from the Mennonites, the Amish were nicknamed "hook-and-eyers," while the Mennonites were called "button people."

But the Swiss Brethren were leary of the motives of Ammann and his followers. When they met with the Amish leaders and found they weren't willing to give up the practice of shunning, the Swiss Brethren refused to reunite the two groups.

The Mennonites and Amish have been separate ever since, and sometimes still question the validity of each other's practices and beliefs.

Today, most Amish people know little about Jakob Ammann and don't consider him important to their faith. They consider themselves Anabaptists, and trace the founding of their religion to the first adult baptism in Zurich in 1525, as do Mennonites.

The Least You Need to Know

◆ In 1517, Martin Luther proposed changes in the Catholic Church that marked the beginning of the Protestant Reformation.

◆ In Switzerland, a small group of reformers felt that local Protestant reforms didn't go far enough. They wanted to separate the church from the government, baptize adults rather than infants, and renounce violence. In 1525, they performed their first adult baptism, and were dubbed the Anabaptists, or rebaptizers.

◆ The early Anabaptists were severely persecuted by the Swiss and other governments, who offered bounty for their capture.

◆ The main issues over which the Amish divided from the Swiss Brethren (forerunners of the Mennonites) were shunning, foot washing, the frequency of communion, and whether people who protected the Anabaptists from persecution could be saved by God without becoming Anabaptists.

◆ Jakob Ammann led the faction who wanted stricter separation from the world. In 1693, his followers separated and became known as the Amish.

Chapter 3

Moving Up, Moving Out: Amish in the New World

In This Chapter

- ◆ Fleeing persecution in Europe
- ◆ Perils of sea passage
- ◆ Amish settlers in the New World
- ◆ Indians, evangelists, and revolutionaries make trouble for the Amish
- ◆ Amish immigration in the 1800s
- ◆ Old Order and Amish Mennonites split

The Amish began coming to North America in the 1700s, following in the footsteps of some Mennonites who had begun emigrating even before the Amish became a separate group. They were not only fleeing persecution and oppression in Europe, but the wars, inflation, and famine that ravaged their home countries, too.

Until the late nineteenth century, the Mennonites and the Amish in North America didn't live too different from each other and their neighbors.

They were largely uneducated, lived in rural communities and were farmers or small shopkeepers, as were most Americans. Everyone drove horses and buggies in those days, and no one had electricity or telephones. All women wore long dresses, often with shawls or capes, and high laced shoes over thick stockings. Men wore hats and many had beards, though most kept theirs trimmed. There were no zippers; pants were buttoned. Farmers used horses or mules for field work, clothes and food were made at home by hand, and families were large because birth control wasn't available and children were needed to help do all the work.

In the 1800s, though, things began to change in rural America. Electricity, telephones, and gasoline engines began to become available, speeding up communication, travel, and work. To some in the Amish community, these inventions of "the world" threatened to lure people into the pursuit of wealth and status and the sin of pride.

At a deeper level, the new inventions made individuals more independent, threatening the dependence on community that had given the church so much power over its members' lives. If farmers could do more work alone, they not only could acquire more land and wealth, but it wouldn't matter as much if they were getting along with their neighbors. If people could drive farther to church, they wouldn't be as dependent on the local church district's approval. Electrical wiring connected one—physically and symbolically—to the world, making one more dependent on the wider society and less on Amish neighbors, family, and friends.

Some of the Amish felt the inventions themselves were not a threat to Christian living, but that how they were used problematic. Others believed that opening the door to the world's innovations would necessarily lead to a decline in church authority, discipline, and therefore, moral living. By the end of the century, the disagreement had split the Amish church into two factions, and only one of them remains Amish today.

A Separate Peace: Fleeing European Persecution

Throughout the seventeenth century, the Swiss government continued to hunt down Anabaptists, and to execute, imprison, brand, exile, or sell as galley slaves those they caught. The Anabaptists were forced out of the cities and onto remote farms. To survive, they developed many of the traits that later would make them economically successful, and for which they are still known today: hard work, frugality, intensive farming practices that increased the yields of small holdings, and working together as a community.

Most Amish and Mennonites in Europe were tenant farmers, living and working on the estates of large landowners. Knowing their reputation for productive farming, a duke from the Palatinate (now part of Germany) offered protection to the Mennonites (the Amish had not yet become a separate group) in return for farming his land. Several local French rulers in the Alsace region did the same. For a time, the Mennonites were able to live under the protection of these local rulers, though they were never treated the same as citizens who belonged to the state churches.

However, peace was short-lived. The War of the Palatinate, which broke out in 1688 and lasted nearly the rest of the century, prompted people of all religions to leave the area and take their chances in the American colonies over the next half-century.

> ### Ironies and Oddities
>
> The Amish who chose to stay in Europe eventually lost their distinctive identity, and their descendents joined Mennonite churches. Today there are no Amish congregations in Europe. The religion and culture has survived only in North America. Attempts to start settlements in Latin America largely failed.

Perils of the *Charming Nancy*

No one knows exactly when the first Amish person might have immigrated to the American colonies, because there was no organized Amish church keeping records. Mennonites from Holland had been coming for decades before the Amish arrived, as early as 1663. The first permanent settlement that included Mennonites was Germantown, Pennsylvania, a village near Philadelphia founded in 1683—a decade before Jakob Ammann and his followers would split from the Swiss Brethren Anabaptists. (Today, Germantown has been absorbed into metropolitan Philadelphia.)

The first known group of Amish families to immigrate to the colonies arrived at Philadelphia on October 8, 1737 aboard a ship called the *Charming Nancy*. One Amish man left a diary behind telling something of the dangers faced in the crossing. Many people died along the way, as was common for immigrants crossing the Atlantic at that time. Ships were over-crowded by captains trying to make as much money as they could on each trip. Disease spread quickly; food was scarce and often unwholesome; lice, rats, and other vermin were common; and drinking water sometimes became brackish and filled with worms.

Children were the most vulnerable to disease and pestilence. Many parents lost at least one child, or even more, on the voyage. Other parents arrived widowed, left to make a place for themselves and their children in a strange land with few resources.

The Plain Truth

One of the few remaining diaries from the time of Amish immigration was written by Hans Jacob Kauffman, a passenger on the *Charming Nancy*, which sailed from the Netherlands to Philadelphia in 1737.

The 28th of June while in Rotterdam getting ready to start my Zernbli died and was buried in Rotterdam. The 29th we got under sail and enjoyed only 1–1/2 days of favorable wind. The 7th day of July, early in the morning, died Hans Zimmerman's son-in-law.

We landed in England the 8th of July remaining 9 days in port during which 5 children died. Went under sail the 17th of July. The 21st of July my own Lisbetli died. Several days before Michael's Georgli had died.

On the 29th of July three children died. On the first of August my Hansli died and Tuesday previous 5 children died. On the 3rd of August contrary winds beset the vessel from the first to the 7th of the month three more children died. On the 8th of August Shambien's Lizzie died and on the 9th died Hans Zimmerman's Jacobi. On the 19th Christian Burgli's Child died. Passed a ship on the 21th. A favorable wind sprang up. On the 28th Hans Gasi's wife died. Passed a ship 13 of September.

Landed in Philadelphia on the 18th and my wife and I left the ship on the 19th. A child was born to us on the 20th—died—wife recovered. A voyage of 83 days.

Putting Down Roots: Early Settlers in the New World

What happened to the Amish once they arrived on American soil?

Vas Es Das?

A **redemptioner** was an immigrant who couldn't afford to pay for passage from Europe. Sea captains would take on passengers who couldn't pay, then auction their labor to colonists after they landed in America. Sometimes they even kidnapped children to profit from selling their labor. They became indentured servants, obligated to work a specified period of time to repay the employers who paid for their passage.

Most Amish immigrants arriving before 1800 sailed up the Delaware River to land in Philadelphia. From there, they moved west across southern Pennsylvania. In 1738, an Amish settlement was established along Northkill Creek in Berks County, north of Lancaster County. Few Amish families could afford land in Lancaster County; Mennonites already had settled the area. The Amish didn't move there in large numbers until later.

Some Amish colonists couldn't even pay for their passage across the Atlantic, and became *redemptioners*. Amish and Mennonites already established in this country sometimes bought the services of redemptioners, either to rescue them from harsh employers or simply to increase their own workforce. Non-Amish redemptioners—especially children—who lived and worked in Amish households sometimes joined the church themselves after their indenture.

Even those Amish who could pay their own passage faced the hard life of colonial farmers. At first, small groups of related Amish families were scattered around the countryside. The distances and small number of Amish settlers made mutual aid impractical. Families had to depend on their own members for survival, making family identity and authority stronger than that of the church. For years, all were served by one bishop who walked or rode horseback to preside over communion, baptisms, and marriages. Amish identity declined, and many Amish children left the church when they grew up.

The Plain Truth

Although they would buy redemptioners, the Amish didn't own slaves, even though slavery was legal in Pennsylvania before 1780. Perhaps they considered slave-owning a sign of worldly pride or ostentation, but it's just as likely that they found insupportable the idea of laying claim to the life of another.

Indians, Evangelists, and Revolutionaries: Dangers to Colonial Amish

The Amish had not escaped warfare by moving to the New World. The French, allied with Native Americans who saw their lands being taken over by foreigners, fought the British for control of land that included Pennsylvania. In 1756, Pennsylvania's colonial government declared war on the Delaware and Shawnee nations. Indian attacks increased in eastern Pennsylvania, and in 1757, an Amish farm was raided.

The Hochstetler Massacre

The story of the Hochstetler massacre was handed down in family lore and is told in great detail in *Descendents of Jacob Hochstetler, The Immigrant of 1736* by Rev. Harvey Hostetler, D.D.

According to the *Historical Introduction*, written by William F. Hochstetler, "Jacob Hofstedler arrived at Philadelphia September 1st, 1736 …" Over the years, the spelling of his name on documents varies, but he can be traced to a farm on the Northkill Creek in the first known Amish settlement.

> ## Ironies and Oddities
>
> Among ethnic Mennonites and Amish, descendents of the Swiss, German, French, and Dutch Anabaptists, tracing family connections is so popular it's sometimes called "the name game." Also popular are self-published genealogies such as *Descendents of Jacob Hochstetler, The Immigrant of 1736* by Rev. Harvey Hostetler, D.D. The 1191-page tome, originally published in the late nineteenth century and often called simply *The Hochstetler Book*, is well-known in the Mennonite and Amish communities for the simple fact that so many people's ancestry is included in it (including the author's). It's not uncommon for a person to find both parents' ancestors included in the book, making them distant cousins.
>
> Family genealogies can sometimes be found for sale in stores that serve Amish communities.

His wife's name doesn't survive, but apparently some in her family accused her of mistreating some needy Native Americans, who came to her door once for assistance and were turned away. Whether this is true or not, family lore credited her with bringing on an Indian massacre.

On the night of September 19, 1757, a group of young people gathered at the Hochstetler home to peel and pare apples for drying. Afterwards, they stayed to party, in the way of young people through the centuries. The family didn't get to bed until quite late that night. No sooner had they fallen asleep than one of the sons, young Jacob, heard strange noises from the family dog. He opened the door to investigate and was shot in the leg with a bullet.

Young Jacob's brothers Christian and Joseph reached for their guns to defend the family against the Indians they could see milling around outside. Jacob Hochstetler the elder, though, held to his Anabaptist belief in nonresistance and forbade his sons to shoot. For the rest of his life, according to the story, son Joseph claimed the whole family could have been saved if their father had let them shoot.

The family hid in the basement of the house, which the Indians then set on fire. The family fought off the flames with cider stored in the cellar and hoped that the Indians would retreat at dawn. Through a basement window, the family could see the Indians leaving, and thinking they were safe, came crawling out. Apparently getting mother out through the window was quite a task, because she was "a fleshy woman," and by the time the family all got out, a young warrior lingering to gather ripe peaches off the family's trees had seen them and called his comrades back.

The Amish faced the same frontier dangers as other American colonists. When Amishman Jacob Hochstetler held to his belief in nonresistance during an attack by Native Americans, several members of his family were killed.

The whole family was captured. Young Jacob and an unnamed daughter were killed with tomahawks and scalped. Mother was stabbed in the heart with a butcher knife before being scalped, giving rise to the theory that the Indians had a special grudge against her. Maybe they did, but with so many other settlers being killed and a war on, it seems unjust to hang the blame solely on Mother Hochstetler.

Whatever the cause of the massacre, Jacob senior and his sons Christian and Jacob were taken prisoner. Before they were led from the farm, Jacob filled his pockets with ripe peaches and told his sons to do the same. When they reached the Indian encampment, Jacob is said to have given the chief the ripe peaches still remaining in his pocket as a gift. The chief responded by sparing the captives from ill-treatment.

Father and sons were parted, and Jacob is said to have advised his sons in their Swiss German language, "If you are taken so far away and be kept so long that your forget your German language, do not forget the Lord's Prayer."

After about five years, Jacob managed to escape his Indian captors and make his way through the wilderness back to Harrisburg, Pennsylvania. In 1762, he petitioned the governor for help in rescuing his sons, who were returned by the Indians.

A Greater Danger: Evangelists Decimate the Ranks of Amish

A far greater danger than roving Native Americans to the identity, if not the lives, of the Amish colonists were roving evangelical preachers. Methodists, Dunkards, United

---

Make No Mistake _____

Even though religion is central to their lives, the Amish maintain that it's the way you live your life that counts in God's judgment, not spiritual experiences. For that reason, they have sometimes been accused of placing too much emphasis on following rules rather than making a direct connection with God. The Amish might respond by saying that spiritual living is more critical than "spiritual experiences."

Brethren, Baptists, and other churches were experiencing a revival movement in pre-Revolutionary America, and many Amish were swept along. This may have been especially true of young people, who lacked their parents' grounding in a community of faith such as had existed in Europe.

The revivalists preached the importance of a spiritual conversion experience—what they might describe as a powerful, emotional, mental, and sometimes even physical connection with the Holy Spirit. The Amish believed God's grace saved a person, but that it was the responsibility of the person to live out that salvation, to make it visible in daily life.

Being a responsible member of the church—the body of Christ—was key to living this changed life, in the Amish view. Baptism committed the person to follow Christ *and* to become a part of the body of believers. That belief allowed the church to set standards of Christian behavior and demand that members meet them.

Perhaps because the evangelists were drawing so many of their people, or because their children were marrying outside the faith, a number of Amish families moved together to form new settlements farther west in Pennsylvania. Even there, though, some of their members were drawn to churches that placed more emphasis on the individual relationship with God and less on living by church rules. One church that did a little of both was the Dunkards, or German Baptist Brethren. They also preached in German and espoused plain dress, making a transition to their church easier for Amish dissatisfied with their own religious life.

Traitors or Pacifists? The Amish During the Revolutionary War

When America's colonists decided to throw off the yoke of government abroad, the Amish ran smack up against their differences with their neighbors. Some of their sons decided to side with the neighbors, taking up arms and joining the war, further depleting the ranks of the Amish.

However, most Amish men stood by their principles, even though they were in conflict with the society around them. As Anabaptists, the Amish were prohibited from responding to violence with violence and they believed that taking oaths was wrong. But they also believed that Christians should obey laws and be subject to their government.

So when the revolutionaries demanded that all citizens take an oath of loyalty to their cause, the Amish faced a hard choice. In order to settle in the colonies, they had been required to sign a declaration of loyalty to the Crown of England. Now they didn't feel they should go back on their word. Neither did they believe in swearing oaths or fighting your own government.

When the Amish, as well as Mennonites and Quakers, refused to swear loyalty to the revolutionary government, they were called Tories, or English loyalists. Some were imprisoned until the war was over, and all lost important legal rights, including the right to vote, hold public office, sit on a jury, sue in court, and buy and sell land.

Unlike the Quakers, the Amish and Mennonites didn't object to paying taxes that might be used to pay for the war. When the subject of joining the colonial army was raised, the Amish and Mennonites asked if they could contribute money instead. They wanted the money to be used to help people suffering hardships from the fighting. The local supporters of the emerging revolution agreed, though they probably used the money to support the war. The Amish and Mennonite contributors never pressed the issue.

This wouldn't be the last time the Amish would be forced to choose between religion and government.

New Century, Next Wave: Amish Immigration in the 1800s

By the end of the 1700s, the Amish, as a group, barely survived in America. As a result of evangelical revivalism, war, and exposure to more liberal cultures of their neighbors, many of their members, especially young people, had joined other faiths. By 1800, fewer than 1,000 Amish people lived in the United States.

The nineteenth century, however, brought some 3,000 new Amish immigrants from Europe—around 6 times as many as in the century before. The new arrivals made contact with earlier Amish settlers, but found them more traditional than they had been in Europe. So recent immigrants moved on to settle in the newer, western territories. (Later in the

Ironies and Oddities
Even today, you can see the effects of the settlement patterns formed in the mid-1800s. Despite some exceptions, most Amish and Mennonite people in the eastern states are noticeably more conservative in dress, language, and lifestyle than those who live in the Midwest. In general, the further west you go in the United States, the more Amish and Mennonites embrace aspects of the culture around them.

century, the differences between the descendents of eighteenth century immigrants and the new arrivals would come to a head, splitting the Amish into the Old Order and Amish Mennonites.)

The Evolving Amish: Tensions and Transitions

Instead of stopping in Pennsylvania, Amish immigrants in the mid-1800s mostly settled in Ohio, Indiana, Illinois, Iowa, and Ontario, Canada. Many families moved several times before settling permanently. The "strange manners and customs" of the newcomers bothered some of the more traditional Amish, including Bishop David Beiler of Lancaster County, who complained that the church was becoming too worldly.

> **Ironies and Oddities**
>
> Jakob Ammann chose buttons as a symbol of pride and worldy fashion and outlawed them among his followers. So nineteenth century American Amish were outraged when their European cousins showed up not only wearing buttons on their coats, but playing pianos in their parlors. Amish leaders soon got together and decided such signs of worldly living had to go.

The church, now spread out across half the continent, was strengthened not only by its increased numbers and the opportunity for families to form close communities, but by stronger leadership. There were enough Amish people now for each congregation or "district" to have its own preachers, deacons, and bishop.

Church congregations remained independent, but some of their leaders began to hold regional conferences to discuss doctrine and discipline. The Pennsylvania Amish began to crack down on practices such as letting young people do as they pleased before they were old enough to join the church (though this remains a tradition, and source of controversy, today). Bishops outlawed fancy housewares and furniture, and dressing children in worldly clothes.

More serious issues arose, such as excommunication of people who left the Amish church to join another, and methods of baptism. There was a debate about whether baptism should take place in a stream, because that's how Jesus was baptized, or in the traditional Anabaptist way, by pouring water from a pitcher onto the person's head. Eventually, both were tolerated.

Sunday schools were an innovation among nineteenth century Protestants, and by the second half of the century, some midwestern Amish began sending their children to neighboring churches for Sunday school. Traditional Amish leaders objected, because instruction was based on printed materials written by who-knows-who, for interdenominational use. It might be Christian, but it wasn't Anabaptist, went the complaint. Also, Sunday schools of the day gave awards for performance, and recognizing individual achievement ran counter to the Amish ideals of cooperation and subjection of the individual to the group. Yet, eventually, some progressive Amish in Ohio started holding their own Sunday school.

They also disagreed over whether to build meetinghouses. Persecution had forced the early Anabaptists to meet in small groups, in secret, and to move their meeting place. At that time, building a house of worship was out of the question. The Amish believed that the church was its members, not a place.

Both meetinghouses and Sunday schools threatened the separate identity of the Amish church, and undermined both its uniformity and church authority. Meetinghouses didn't offer the same hospitality that host families could for Sunday meals and afternoon visits that knit the community together. In addition, meetinghouses may have seemed like an unnecessary waste of resources and a show of wealth.

The integration of work, home, family, and church, of personal and spiritual life, has always been central to Amish life. They accomplished this naturally by worshiping on the same farmsteads where they lived and worked. A meetinghouse or church would change that.

Politics and Civil War: Temptation and Resistance

The experiences of the European Amish with governments had not exactly left them or their descendents with a love of country, nationalism, or trust of government. Having experienced state churches filled with corruption, and later state persecution of those who chose a different church, Anabaptists held strong beliefs in the separation of church and state. They also believed that no one could be completely loyal to both. Government lived by the sword, Christians by love, and sooner or later, the Anabaptists believed, the two were bound to come into conflict.

Life in a democracy offered the Amish new opportunities to influence government, but history had made them skeptical. As a tiny minority, they could hardly hope to sway public policy to their way of thinking, even if they took part in elections and public debate. And politics, by its very nature, fed on competition,

---

Ironies and Oddities

Before the Civil War, Illinois was a hotbed of Amish progressivism. Most favored the Whig party, the conservatives of their time, but some backed the Republicans and the abolition of slavery. Abraham Lincoln counted several Amish men among his acquaintances, but once he was elected, they faced a big challenge. Would they follow him into war?

pride, and claims of superiority—all working against the Anabaptist values of humility and cooperation.

Yet some Amish men undertook local public service, and many others followed presidential politics and public debate with interest.

Southern states were ready to leave the union and start their own nation to protect themselves from the rule of northerners, who didn't share their economic and cultural interests. The federal government was preparing to go to war to enforce the unity of the nation under one central government and to free the slaves.

Could the Amish participate in a government that was setting out to kill others? The Amish, on the whole, hadn't been active in the abolitionist, or anti-slavery, movement like the Quakers, but they didn't support slavery. However, they did believe they should submit to the authority of their government in civil matters.

But the right to decide when a person must die wasn't a civil right, or a human right, in Amish thought; it was God's right alone. To take a life was to usurp the right of God to decide the best moment for each person's death.

The tensions in the country divided the Amish, along with other American families. Virtually no Amish lived in the South, but they divided along other lines: whether to join the Union army or refuse to fight. Most seemed to have chosen to pay a few hundred dollars to the government as an alternative to the draft. Some hired substitutes to take their place, another legal means to avoid fighting. After the Civil War, those who remained Amish generally became more conservative in their approach to public life and politics. Even those who had not served in the army had seen the death and destruction caused in their own communities and across the country. Some conservative leaders saw the suffering of the war as the judgment of God upon their own church, for letting themselves be caught up in the affairs of the world and straying from simplicity, humility, and separation from the world.

Long Division: Old Order and Amish Mennonites Split

By the end of the Civil War, divisiveness had been simmering among the Amish for some time. Since the 1840s, the northern Indiana Amish had been disagreeing on how much change to embrace.

Amish pioneers had moved into two adjoining Indiana counties, LaGrange to the east and its western neighbor, Elkhart County, starting in 1841. Those who settled LaGrange County largely came from conservative Pennsylvania settlements, while Elkhart County was settled by more progressive Ohio Amish.

The Plain Truth _____

When I was researching this book, I asked my stepmother (who was raised in Elkhart County, lived and taught school among the Amish in LaGrange County for many years, then retired back in Elkhart County) about the Amish riding bicycles. I remembered seeing both Amish adults and children riding bicycles in my youth in Elkhart County, but some of my reference books said the Amish don't ride bicycles. Perhaps they meant the Pennsylvania Amish, I thought, but I'd better check. Was my memory right?

"Oh yes," my stepmother said, "but you have to remember, you grew up in Clinton Township," in Elkhart County. "They're more conservative in Eden Township [directly east in LaGrange County], and more still in Clearspring Township." She said, "there was a time when the main street of Topeka, in LaGrange County, was the dividing line between two Amish church districts. Amish people living on one side of the street could ride bicycles; those across the road couldn't."

Even today, township by township, you can still see where the conservative, earlier immigrants from Pennsylvania drew the line between themselves and the progressives of the nineteenth century.

Well, it didn't take long for trouble to start. The Elkhart County Amish were led by some hotheads who supported public education, less plain dress, including buttons (though "fancy" is a relative term, which could only be applied to those staid-looking women in long black dresses and head coverings by their even-more-staid Amish cousins). They also let members hold public office. The LaGrange Amish elders were outraged, but both congregations hoped that the other would see the error of their ways eventually.

Meanwhile, further east, Amish in Pennsylvania and Ohio were arguing over "stream baptism," favored by the progressives, as opposed to baptism at home in the traditional way.

Church Order and Dissent

Historian Steven Nolt, in his Amish history (see Appendix B), explains why rules of dress, behavior, and church practice are so important to the Amish. These rules, collectively called the *Ordnung*, or Order, are what hold Amish congregations together in the absence of a larger institution. Unlike churches with central authorities, committees, and conferences that can set church policy and debate changes, the Amish church is a loose affiliation of independent, local congregations. What makes them identifiable as a church, as well as a culture, are their traditions, rules, and beliefs, as spelled out in the *Ordnung*. "The Amish *Ordnung* included such general principles as 'modesty' and 'simplicity,' and such specific applications as wearing certain plain clothes and avoiding costly, showy household furniture," wrote Nolt.

> **Make No Mistake**
>
> The *Ordnung*, pronounced *Ott-ning* in Pennsylvania Dutch, encompasses the rules that regulate Amish church life. It is largely oral, handed down from generation to generation, though some parts of it have been written from time to time. It can vary from settlement to settlement, but agrees on basic, biblical principles that govern Amish choices and customs.

The conservative Amish leaders emphasized the importance of enforcing the specific rules. While they didn't oppose all change, they wanted every innovation to be considered carefully and change to be accepted cautiously. Changing the method of baptism, they felt, was like opening the barn door to let out just one horse. The rest were liable to be right behind.

Progressives saw the principles, rather than the specifics, as the heart of the *Ordnung*. The way you express those principles may change as society changes, they maintained, as long as you use the principles to guide your changes. In other words, simplicity and humility are attitudes.

The Final Straw

In the end it was the conservatives, trying to bring the progressives back into line with church authority as they saw it, who inadvertently opened the door. They proposed a national meeting of ordained Amish men—bishops, ministers, and deacons—to discuss the problems and restore unity of belief and practice. Lay people could come and observe, but not debate the issues or vote on resolutions. While smaller, regional meetings had been held in the past, it would be the first national meeting of church leaders.

The progressives jumped on the idea and used it for their own purposes, making the meetings an annual event for nearly 16 years. They called the first national meeting in Wayne County, Ohio in June, 1862. Some conservatives stayed away on purpose, others later charged that not all conservative congregations were informed properly of the first meeting. Whatever the cause, the progressives outnumbered the conservatives, setting the tone for annual meetings to come.

Although they had no way to enforce any decision made, the meetings had strong effect on the congregations, unifying progressives on their positions and alienating conservatives. At first, some held out hope that the meetings would heal hurt feelings and divided opinion. But eventually it became clear that the meetings were simply accentuating the differences.

One conservative bishop who stayed away, David Beiler of Lancaster County, later complained after reading reports of the meeting that, "It seems to me that each was allowed to have his own opinion."

> **CAUTION**
>
> ## Make No Mistake
>
> The early Amish in Europe were sometimes referred to as Amish Mennonites, to identify them as a conservative branch of the parent group. Later, "Mennonite" was dropped from their name.
>
> Later still—after 1865—progressive Amish congregations that left the Amish church were considered closer in belief and lifestyle to the Mennonites than the conservative Old Order Amish. The progressives came to be called the Amish Mennonites, but this time to distinguish them as the more liberal group.

Finally, in 1865, the conservatives rallied their forces in a pre-conference meeting and wrote out a statement of their principles. They railed against practices that they believed "serve to express pomp and pride," and thereby "lead away from God." Among the possessions they thought expressed pride and wasted resources were "speckled, striped, flowered, clothing" and "unnecessary, gorgeous, household furnishings." Those who agreed with them and put their principles into practice would be welcomed back into fellowship as "brothers and sisters." In other words, the conservatives were issuing an ultimatum: do things our way, or leave the fellowship.

The conservative faction presented their statement at the national meeting, where the progressive majority basically ignored them. Few conservatives attended any more national conferences. Finally, in 1865, the Amish church officially split into two factions, although the process actually took several years. After the 1865 conference, the progressive majority became known as Amish Mennonites, while the conservatives eventually were called Old Order Amish, because they supported the traditional, or old, *Ordnung*.

The Least You Need to Know

◆ Amish immigrants began coming to the American colonies early in the eighteenth century, following in the footsteps of earlier Mennonite colonists.

◆ Throughout the 1700s, Amish families lived scattered across eastern Pennsylvania.

◆ Many of their children left the Amish church during the colonial period to join evangelizing churches or mainstream society.

◆ In the mid-1800s, many more Amish immigrants arrived and settled in the Midwest and Ontario, Canada.

◆ In 1865, the Amish church split into two groups: the more progressive Amish Mennonites, and the traditional Old Order Amish who survive today.

Chapter 4

Extended Family: Anabaptist Groups in the United States

In This Chapter

- ◆ The other Anabaptists
- ◆ Plain Mennonites: Old Order and Conservatives
- ◆ "Old" Mennonites, GC, and Mennonite Church USA
- ◆ Church of the Brethren, Old Order Brethren, and Hutterites

A seemingly simple question like "What is a Mennonite?" or "Who are the Amish?" has many answers, none of them complete. Every attempt at an answer is bound to leave out some nuance of belief or practice, because so many people lay claim to those names, which they inherited from their forebears or adopted and carried forward.

The Anabaptists grew up into a contentious lot, to judge by their history. Mennonites, Amish, Brethren, and Hutterites all are descended from the Anabaptists of sixteenth century Europe. They disagreed over issues as major as evangelism and education, and as minor as wearing buttons and using musical instruments to accompany their hymns. Sometimes the issues that led to the split later disappeared, but the division remained.

Often, a disputed change in lifestyle or church tradition symbolized a deeper disagreement over the relationship between an individual and the church community. Anabaptists prized loyalty to the community and the submission of the individual to church authority. This discipline had helped Anabaptists survive in Europe, but American society was built by people who valued their right to individual choice and freedom. The clash between the society's values and the church's often resulted in divisions.

Even their own members can't keep track of all the splinter groups, often known by local nicknames as well as their official designations. How, then, could outsiders be expected to understand the difference?

The largest group of Anabaptist churches all share the name "Mennonite"—but what a wide array of belief and lifestyle fit under that umbrella! For now, we'll look at Old Order Mennonites, because they most nearly resemble (and are most easily confused with) the Amish. (Later, in Chapter 20, we'll catch up with the rest of the clan.)

We'll also take a brief look at some other Anabaptist church groups, from Plain to "worldly," including various Brethren churches and the Hutterites.

Plain Mennonites: Old Order and Conservatives

The largest Anabaptist group that closely resembles the Amish is the collection of related conferences that call themselves Old Order Mennonites. Innovations introduced in Mennonite churches in the late-nineteenth century—Sunday schools, evening worship, singing in four-part harmony, and use of English for worship—prompted conservatives to leave and form the Old Order Mennonites. Later, when cars became common, they would disagree among themselves over whether to accept those as well.

The Plain Truth

For detailed descriptions of two Mennonite groups, see Stephen E. Scott's *An Introduction to Old Order and Conservative Mennonite Groups.* Scott's readable narrative, photographs, and tables summarize the history, beliefs, and practices, and membership of the many church groups under those two umbrellas. For other resources, see Appendix B.

When one Indiana bishop was expelled from the Mennonite Church in 1872 for refusing to accept Sunday school, a wave of churches followed him. Thirty years later, there were four distinct, regional groups known as Old Order Mennonites. Located in Ontario, Canada; Indiana; Ohio; Pennsylvania; and Virginia, they kept the plain dress of their forebears, and to the casual observer look almost identical to the Old Order Amish.

Horse-and-Buggy Old Order Mennonites

Because they formed as four different groups scattered across the country, the Old Order Mennonites aren't entirely uniform in their rules and traditions. Horse-and-buggy Old Order Mennonites in general …

- ◆ Build meetinghouses for worship.

- ◆ Conduct most worship services in Pennsylvania Dutch and German, except in Virginia, where English is used.

- ◆ Excommunicate members for disciplinary reasons, but don't practice shunning or social avoidance.

- ◆ Send their children to their own parochial schools, or those run cooperatively with Old Order Amish. Classes are taught in English, and often Old Order Mennonites and Amish groups attend and support the same schools. For many children, education ends after eighth grade.

Dress is plain, but varies from group to group. The most obvious difference between Old Order Mennonite and Old Order Amish dress is the use of small prints by the Mennonites. Dresses, aprons, and even girls' sunbonnets can be made from printed material. Men in some groups also wear suits and ties rather than the high, collarless plain-style coat without lapels, and their hat styles vary from group to group.

Old Order Mennonites dress much the same as Old Order Amish. The most noticeable difference is that dresses and girls' sunbonnets are sometimes made of printed material.

Old Order Mennonite farmers—even those who drive horses and buggies for transportation—use tractors in their fields, though some have to use steel wheels rather than rubber tires on their vehicles.

Most Old Order Mennonite homes have electricity and telephones—even those whose owners drive buggies instead of cars. To maintain their separation from the world, the buggy Old Orders simply differentiate between uses of electricity that are necessary and those they consider worldly or frivolous. Refrigerators, freezers, stoves, and washing machines are acceptable, for instance, but dishwashers and microwave ovens usually aren't. Some families choose not to use electric appliances, even though their church permits it.

As with the Old Order Amish, television, radio, movies, CD and tape players are strictly off-limits.

Car Old Order Mennonites

Though they share more characteristics than not, the major division among Old Order Mennonites is between those who drive cars and those who don't. Car-driving Old Order Mennonites, sometimes called "Car Amish" by their neighbors (a misnomer, because they have no Amish background), prevent automobiles from becoming status symbols by dictating that all must be black, and none can be fashionable. Two-door models, convertibles and generally sporty or flashy vehicles are on a list of forbidden cars. A few Old Orders even paint their bumpers black; their nickname, of course, is the "Black Bumper Mennonites."

Ironies and Oddities

The way Amish and Mennonite groups have evolved and adapted, it can be hard to tell which branch a person belongs to. Usually you can look for clues based on their home and possessions, but even those can leave a person puzzled.

Like the Indiana homestead we passed once on a family vacation with a buggy parked in front of the barn—and beside it, a trailer holding an even bigger powerboat.

The three regional church conferences of car-driving Old Order Mennonites are in Ohio, Indiana, and Michigan; Ontario; and Pennsylvania, New York, Virginia, Wisconsin, Iowa, and Missouri. They ...

- Maintain the same kind of church structure and worship order as their buggy-driving cousins.

- Conduct worship services in English.

- Dress much like buggy Old Order Mennonites.

- Forbid radio and television, but use other forms of technology.

- Allow photography, though not at weddings.

- Farm with modern equipment.

- Operate parochial schools that may go through eighth or tenth grade. A few students finish high school at a public school or through home study.

Member of a little-known sect: The Powerboat Amish.

Other Anabaptists: Brethren and Hutterites

If the various Amish and Mennonite groups might be considered brothers, sisters, and first cousins, other groups, though distant cousins, belong to the same Anabaptist family tree. Among these are the Church of the Brethren, with its various plain offshoots, and the Hutterites.

Church of the Brethren

The early Brethren were German members of the Radical Pietists, a Protestant renewal movement. They formed a new church that espoused the Anabaptist beliefs, but held that baptism needed to be by immersion rather than by pouring. Their form of baptism gave rise to the name "Dunker" or "Dunkard." This has continued to be a common nickname for plain Brethren groups, though only one branch uses it in their formal name.

The Brethren soon moved to America, where they grew and prospered. As with their Mennonite and Amish cousins, the Brethren later divided over questions of how to live out their faith. In 1908, two centuries after its founding, the main group organized the Church of the Brethren. Though originally a plain church, like the Mennonites, the Brethren majority gradually adopted modern ways of life while maintaining their Anabaptist beliefs.

Old German Baptist Brethren, Dunkard Brethren, and Smaller Groups

In 1881, a group who worried that the main Brethren body was becoming too worldly withdrew to form the Old German Baptist Brethren. Another group, calling themselves the Dunkard Brethren, withdrew in 1926. Other splinter groups later left these two. All dress in plain garb with fine distinctions such as …

> **⚠ CAUTION**
>
> **Make No Mistake**
>
> Details count in distinguishing one Plain group from another. The most obvious difference between plain Brethren women's dress and Amish women is that the Brethren dress in print fabrics, and Old German Baptist Brethren women wear distinctive triangular capes that open in front over their dresses. (Groups related to the Dunkard Brethren wear square capes closed in front, more like those worn by Amish women.)

- Whether covering strings have to be tied.

- The shape of the cape over a woman's dress (triangular or square).

- Whether women were required to wear aprons.

- The color of women's stockings (black or sheer).

- Whether beards (with or without mustaches) are required of all men, or just ministers.

- Men's hat styles.

- Whether wrist watches (with black bands only) are allowed.

River Brethren

Another Anabaptist group grew up in Pennsylvania about 1780. Called the River Brethren, because their original members lived near the Susquehanna River, they were influenced by the Brethren, as well as Mennonites, but never affiliated with either group.

Disagreements between conservative and progressive members resulted in three churches forming in the 1850s: The Brethren in Christ, which represented the original group; the plain Old Order River Brethren; and the United Zion Church.

The Brethren in Christ gradually dropped plain dress over several decades in the mid-twentieth century. The United Zion Church did the same, though they retained head coverings for church services.

The Old Order River Brethren still wear plain dress and practice nonconformity to the world in much the same ways as the Amish and other plain Anabaptist groups. Their 300 members live in Pennsylvania and Iowa.

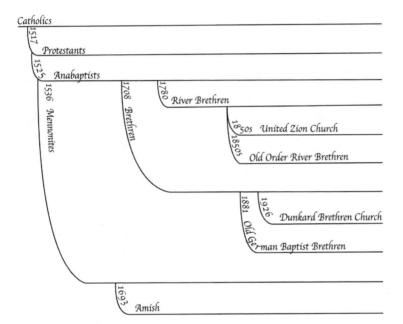

This overview of Anabaptist divisions shows the relationships between many major groups.

Hutterites

The Hutterites descend from the early Swiss Anabaptists, from whom they split in 1528. They came to the United States in 1874, settling in South Dakota. Today there are four Hutterite groups living in the United States and Canada.

Unlike other Anabaptist groups, the Hutterites live communally, sharing all property in common, working and eating together as a community. Their dress, while plain and governed by church rules, seems colorful in comparison to their more soberly garbed Old Order cousins. The distinctive triangular black scarves with white polka dots worn by Hutterite women make them stand out in any crowd. Women and men wear prints and plaids that are sometimes quite bright and colorful. The women wear a bodice over a blouse, sometimes of contrasting color, long skirts, and often aprons. Men dress in long-sleeved print or plaid shirts and have short hair and beards.

Like the Amish, the Hutterites speak a German dialect, though the Hutterite language originated in German-speaking areas of Austria and Italy and differs from Pennsylvania German.

Unlike the Amish, the Hutterites use modern technology in their farming and households. Colonies house about 100 members and divide when they get too large. They are largely self-sufficient, farming thousands of acres, raising livestock, building and maintaining their own buildings, and sometimes manufacturing products to sell to outsiders. Hutterites cook and eat meals together in a central dining hall surrounded by family apartments.

> **The Plain Truth**
>
> According to *Anabaptist World USA* by Donald B. Kraybill and C. Nelson Hostetler, nearly 13,500 Hutterites live in 119 colonies in the United States, mostly in South Dakota and Montana, with a handful each in North Dakota, Washington, and Minnesota. More than 25,000 live in 309 colonies in Canada. A similar group, the Bruderhof, have another six colonies with a population slightly over 2,000.

Hutterites renounce personal property at baptism, so aside from a few personal items, everything belongs to the colony, which meets all their physical needs. Members work together in the colony, and receive no payment for their labor.

Although they embrace technology for practical purposes, Hutterites largely reject the mass media (though some allow radios) and live more isolated from the outside world than even the Amish.

The Least You Need to Know

- Many Anabaptist groups related to the Amish are similar in beliefs and lifestyle.

- Old Order Mennonites so strongly resemble the Old Order Amish in beliefs and lifestyle that the casual observer probably couldn't tell them apart.

- Like the Mennonites, the Church of the Brethren grew from Anabaptist roots and has many branches varying from worldly to plain.

- Unlike other Anabaptist groups, the Hutterites live communally, holding all property in common, live, work, and eat together.

Part 2

Faith of Their Fathers: Amish Beliefs and Worship

Religious beliefs are the foundation of every aspect of Amish life. So if you want to understand why they drive horses and buggies or wear those hats, you need to understand what they believe and why.

Beliefs are one thing, but practice is another. What do they do all day at those church services, anyway? You can't visit an Amish church to find out, because, first of all, they don't build churches—they worship in homes. Second, the service isn't public—it's for members and invited visitors only. And finally, you wouldn't understand a word, anyway—service is conducted in Pennsylvania German.

But you can read all about it, because the details are here. Sunday services, special occasions, and who holds the reins on the congregation. We look at how the Amish organize their churches, choose their leaders, and enforce the rules. And what happens to anyone who doesn't follow along.

Keeping the Faith: Amish Religious Beliefs

In This Chapter

◆ Comparing the Amish to other Christians

◆ Putting the church before the individual

◆ Nonconformity as a tenet of faith

◆ Turning the other cheek

◆ Religious roles of men and women

What draws people to the Amish way of life? Why do they trek to Amish communities to look at these people, buy books, and watch videos about their lives?

Plain dress, horse-drawn buggies and farm equipment, farm yards full of bright flowers and children, rows of golden wheat shocks marching across a field—all these evoke a sense of peace, quiet, order, and perhaps a sense of meaning in life. All qualities too often sacrificed in modern life for more external rewards—more money, personal achievement, career, and social status.

"The world is desperate for something to satisfy its hunger, some answer to its search for meaning in life, wanting something external to base faith upon, something to see and touch and handle," observed one Amish writer in a 1989 article in the Amish magazine *Family Life*. "While they focus on our beards and buggies and bonnets, they miss entirely what our faith is all about."

To understand the Amish, it's necessary to understand what their symbols say about their beliefs. Because it's their faith, rather than the outer symbols of it, that they feel really sets them apart from the world.

Their intention in choosing to live without modern conveniences and dress in a uniform similar to what their forebears wore isn't to seek the more peaceful, less stressful life that many modern people long for. It's rather to express through their lives a silent witness to their obedience to the will of God, as they understand it.

"Clothes won't get us into heaven," wrote one contributor to *Family Life*, "but they can keep us out."

Firm Foundation: Christian Doctrines in Amish Faith

The Amish are Anabaptist Christians, and consider their church the true Christian church. Underlying their church rules are doctrines, or beliefs, shared by many other Christians. Where the Amish differ, however—and to them, this difference is all-important—is in how those doctrines are expressed through their lives.

Bucolic Amish farms give the impression of peace, order, and tranquility to those passing by. Modern society often yearns for those qualities, which it associates with the Amish lifestyle.

Divinity of Jesus Christ

The divinity of Jesus Christ is the foundation upon which Christianity—and Amish faith—is built. As Christians, the Amish believe that Jesus was the son of God, or God taking on human form without giving up any of his divine nature. They believe that Jesus died and was resurrected by God to live eternally in Heaven.

The Amish understand Jesus' ministry as an invitation and instruction to human beings to follow his example, so that God may decide to save them also. Unlike more evangelical or fundamentalist groups, the Amish don't believe that salvation is guaranteed anyone by faith in Jesus alone. In fact, they would consider it arrogant or prideful to claim certainty of salvation. That's God's decision, based on a lifetime record of faithful obedience to the church as the interpreter of God's will and the teachings of Jesus.

The Plain Truth

Though they reject telephones, televisions, and radios, the Amish enjoy writing and reading. Amish publications help them communicate with Amish people living in other states, exchange news and views, and provide wholesome entertainment.

The magazine, *Family Life*, has been published since 1968 by Pathway Publishers, an Amish-owned company, for members of Plain churches. In 1999, Herald Press, a Mennonite publisher, brought out *The Amish in Their Own Words: Amish Writings from 25 Years of Family Life Magazine*, compiled by Brad Igou. The excerpts in this book from *Family Life* are found in that book. (For more on both the book and the magazine, see Appendix B).

Word for Word: The Literal Bible

The Amish believe that God inspired the writers of the Bible, and therefore every word is true and should be taken literally. Scripture is read in church services, but interpretation is left to the ministers. Individuals are not supposed to indulge in individual Bible interpretation or show off too much biblical knowledge. The Amish discourage individuality in general, and especially in theology or biblical interpretation, because they fear individuals undermining established doctrines and practices. Unlike in many Mennonite and other Christian churches,

Ironies and Oddities

The Amish recognize the power of symbols. Baptism, for instance, symbolizes the washing away of sin by the Holy Spirit. They even believe that Jesus spoke symbolically at the Last Supper when he called the bread and wine his body and blood. Yet they reject the idea that some Bible stories, such as the creation account, might be symbolic rather than literal fact.

there are no small groups meeting to discuss and study the Bible. In fact, members can be shunned for taking part in Bible study groups with members of other churches.

Heaven and Hell

The Amish believe in the existence of heaven and hell, based on their reading of the Bible. They believe that to avoid hell, they must choose baptism and the will of God as understood by the church. The Amish believe no one can know for sure his or her destiny, nor control it. But the only way to have a shot at spending eternity in heaven rather than hell is to obey the will of God as interpreted from the Bible by the church.

The Church as the Body of Christ in the World

One of the most important Amish beliefs is that the church is the body of Christ in the world. What does that mean?

According to the Bible, after Jesus died and was resurrected, he appeared to his followers in spiritual form for a short time and then ascended into heaven. Shortly thereafter, he sent the Holy Spirit to his followers to enable them to carry on his work in the world. The believers became Christ's physical body here on Earth. The Apostle Paul wrote of the church as Christ's body, comparing individual church members to hands and feet, each with its own individual, but vital, role to play.

Where the Amish differ from other Christians is in their interpretation of how individuals and congregations function as the body of Christ. The Amish answer is that one follows the Word of God as revealed in the Old Testament, the example and teachings of Jesus, and New Testament scriptures; and submits to the counsel of the full body of Christ, the church.

CAUTION   Make No Mistake

"We wear plain clothes, but we know plain clothes do not save us," wrote an Amish commentator in the August 9, 1981 issue of *Family Life*. "We give alms, but our good works cannot earn the grace of God. We partake in communion, but know that the emblems in themselves are just bread and wine, with no power to sanctify us. We pour water at baptism, and know the water cannot wash off a single sin. We obey because God said so. Is that not, after all, the best reason, the most important reason in all the world?"

Baptism

The Amish, along with other Christians, believe in an "indwelling" Holy Spirit that church members receive through baptism. Some Christians believe the "baptism of the Spirit," an experience of feeling the Spirit overtake them, must occur first, and that water baptism merely symbolizes this experience. The Amish believe that the decision to request baptism and take its vows to serve Christ and the church will bring about *regeneration* by the Holy Spirit.

For the Amish and other Anabaptists, baptism is therefore an adult choice, and not one to be taken lightly. This is particularly true of the Amish, because in promising to live in service to Jesus and his church, newly baptized persons are also becoming church members. This implies promising to obey the *Ordnung*, the church regulations, for life.

Vas Es Das?

Regeneration is a term used by the Amish to mean a spiritual renewal or rebirth brought about by the influence of the Holy Spirit. Evangelical Christians use the term "born again" to mean a similar change, though the Amish believe regeneration occurs over time, rather than in a single, powerful conversion experience.

Most Amish church members are baptized before they're 21 years old. Before then, they're not held to the rules of the church, though their parents are expected to control them until they reach age 16, and exert a lot of influence on them after that. But the children are not themselves responsible to the church for their behavior.

Amish young people who choose not to join the church are never held to the rules, but they are likely to drift away from their community. When they leave their parents' home as young adults, they also leave behind the community of believers.

Amish church services are not public, as services in most church are. Amish church is for members and their children, and while some congregations are open to visitors, one needs an invitation. The main opportunities for nonmembers to attend services are weddings and funerals for family members and friends. Occasionally, a person seriously considering joining the church or someone living with an Amish family might be invited by a member to attend, but most services are for local and visiting Amish families only.

Baptism is perhaps the most serious vow an Amish person ever makes. Having requested baptism and membership in the church, the person is responsible to submit to the counsel of the ministers and the church for the rest of his or her life.

To keep the "body of Christ" pure, the church imposes strict consequences on those who break the rules of the *Ordnung*. If the offender refuses to confess and repent, the consequence is excommunication and shunning. The person can rejoin the Amish church by confessing his or her sin to the church body, repenting, and asking for reinstatement. But anyone who doesn't feel guilty of a sin and won't bow to the judgment of the church is banned, or shunned, for life. (As with all Amish practices, the application of the ban varies by congregation. Some churches will eventually lift the ban, especially if the person joins another Anabaptist church.)

This practice of "strict shunning" has often been a point of disagreement between the Amish and other Anabaptists. It was one of the main issues between the Swiss Mennonites and Jakob Ammann that resulted in the Amish forming their own religion (see Chapter 2).

Because the Amish take seriously the need for baptism to be a free choice, many, especially in the largest settlements, let their young people go through a period of exploring worldly ways, often called "running around" or "sewing wild oats" beginning at age 16. Some of their behavior, including drinking, driving cars, and general rowdiness, is quite contrary to Amish principles. Nevertheless, some 90 percent of Amish youth choose baptism and church membership in the end.

The Plain Truth

Family Life magazine has crusaded against "low courtship practices" by Amish youth. "Not everyone took kindly to us mentioning an Amish community with a high rate of pregnancies before marriage," the editors wrote in December 1983. "… What really disturbed us was that more than one community thought we had them in mind. Apparently, things are worse than we thought, in more places than we knew."

Sociologist Donald Kraybill suggests that their choice may be more illusion than reality. Having grown up in a closed society with a uniform worldview, clear and strict expectations, and family and social structure designed to give powerful support in exchange for conformity and obedience, young people are herded toward baptism like calves through a chute. Although the final decision is theirs, the influences of family and peers, as well as the negative examples of those who have left, make the choice to join far easier than the choice to turn away.

In addition to their family, most of their friends will belong to the Amish church. Amish young people are most likely to choose a mate from the circle of friends they grew up with, and to marry an Amish person requires that both be church members. Church members aren't allowed to marry anyone outside the church.

All these factors provide plenty of reasons besides spiritual conviction for Amish young people to choose baptism and church membership.

Not My Will But Thine: Submission to Church Authority

For the Amish, following the example of Jesus means, above all, submitting the will of the individual to the will of God. The night before his arrest and crucifixion, Jesus prayed to be spared such a painful death. Yet he ended that prayer with, "Nevertheless, not my will, but thine, be done." (Luke 22:42b)

Following the example of their Amish forebears, the Amish ideal is to voluntarily give up their own personal will to do what God would have them do. Followers of many religions share that goal, but they disagree on how to know what God is asking of each person.

For the Amish, the answer lies in their belief that the Bible is the literal, unquestionable Word of God, spelling out all his will for Christian people. They believe that God has given their church the authority to interpret for them the will of God. In other words, submission to church *is* submission to God.

Submission to higher authority as embodied by the church is a religious ideal that permeates every aspect of Amish life. Parents try to shape their children's personalities to fit a cultural ideal of the quiet, obedient child who doesn't challenge parental authority. They see it as their duty to raise children used to following, not leading, and so who will make good church members.

A good church member, in the Amish community, is one who "yields," "gives up" his will, or "gives himself under" the authority of the church. In such self-denial or yielding to the higher authority—whether it be God, church, or parents—the Amish believe one finds contentment, peace of mind, and security. The rules and roles in an Amish community are clearly defined; everyone knows what is expected of him or her. The reward for "giving under" or "giving over" is a secure identity and the approval of the community.

But woe to the person who, having joined the church, finds himself or herself unable to live the expected life. Church bishops, ministers, and deacons—all chosen by lot so as to leave

Vas Es Das?

Excommunication, also called the ban, means the same to the Amish as it does to Catholics: expelling a person from church membership. In the case of the Amish, it's accompanied by *Meidung,* or shunning, which means that church members may not associate socially with the ex-member. Spouses who remain in the church are not supposed to have sexual relations with an excommunicated spouse.

the final selection in God's hands—are the final authority in the Amish church and community. A person accused of a sin can't defend himself without perpetuating his or her sinfulness, in the eyes of the church. The only acceptable response is confession and repentance. To do otherwise brings *excommunication* and the ban.

In, But Not Of, the World: Nonconformity and Separation

One of the Bible verses most often quoted by the Amish is "And be not conformed to this world: but be ye transformed by the renewing of your mind, that ye may prove what is that good, and acceptable, and perfect will of God." (Romans 12:2)

Vas Es Das?

Nonconformity simply means to choose to be different from other people, or choose not to follow the rules of others. For the Amish, it has the particular meaning of being unlike non-Amish people in order to emphasize that they see themselves as "true Christians," and therefore unlike the rest of society.

There's that reference to the will of God again, and how to achieve it: by being "not conformed" to the ways of the world.

The Amish and other Plain people have made an art of "being not conformed." To them, *nonconformity* symbolizes their Christian identity. Their dress is a way of not conforming as is their language and their choice not to use electricity or drive cars.

But their most powerful expression of nonconformity to the world is by separating themselves from it. While they don't live communally, as the Hutterites do, Amish social interactions are almost exclusively with others of their own religion. They work and live together in socially exclusive communities. They do business with other Amish people as much as possible, run their own schools to keep their children from daily contact with "the world," discourage their young people from living and working with non-Amish people, and form friendship almost exclusively within their group. All these choices reflect their belief that too much contact with non-Christians, or those who don't live their beliefs in the same way, will tempt the true Christian to drift away from his faith.

The Amish ideal is to embody the principles embodied by Christ, including self-denial, love for one's neighbor, humility, and service. They add modesty and simplicity as ways to deny one's own self-interest in the interest of glorifying God.

The Amish *want* to appear different than the world. It's their silent witness—as well as a constant reminder to themselves—that they choose to identify themselves as children of God rather than children of the world. By emphasizing group uniformity in order to minimize individual self-absorption, the Amish demonstrate their conviction that happiness and virtue can only be found within, through "right relationship" with God and one's neighbors, not in the outer, material world.

Ironies and Oddities

"There are several reasons for wearing the kind of clothes we do. The first reason, of course, is for modesty's sake, because we want to wear the kind of clothes the Bible says we should wear rather than what the styles and fashions of the world tell us."

"Another reason is that we would rather be identified with the children of God than the children of this world."

—*The Amish in Their Own Words*

Despite the outward symbols, it would be a mistake to think that Amish people don't have their own expectations to fulfill, their own social approval to seek, and that money is unimportant in their lives. They struggle with the same temptations, needs, and pressures the modern world does—only within the context of their own society. It may look different from the outside, but inside, the feelings are the same.

Turn the Other Cheek: Nonresistance

For the Amish, the ultimate nonresister was Jesus himself, who refused to allow his disciples to fight on his behalf when he was arrested, and forgave his torturers from the cross. Jesus also preached against resisting evil. He told his followers, "If someone strikes you on one cheek, turn to him the other also." (Luke 6:29) Even sinners love those who love them, but those who really want to imitate God must also love their enemies.

The Amish try to live up to that powerful witness by refusing to participate in military service, not fighting back when attacked, and forgiving those who mistreat them. For them, nonresistance is also a way of being "in the world but not of the world," which in turn is part of the rationale for separation of church and state.

Make No Mistake

Though the Amish believe in nonresistance, they don't necessarily see themselves as pacifists. To them, pacifism means being politically active, working to promote peace in the world. Such activism would run counter to the Amish belief in living "in but not of the world." They take no part in political action, including peace activism.

The Amish are discouraged from suing people who wrong them, for instance. They see this refusal as an opportunity to practice nonresistance, by praying for their enemies rather than resisting evil. Another reason not to take disputes to court is that the court is an arm of the government. If you don't recognize the authority of the government when its edicts go against your conscience, their reasoning goes, you shouldn't try to use its authority to protect your interests, either.

Amish people with disputes among themselves are encouraged to settle them through negotiation and persuasion. When the other party in a dispute is not Amish, the Amish may choose to forfeit money or property, knowing they've been wronged, rather than fight a court battle.

Separate But Equal? Religious Roles of Men and Women

Amish families, churches, and culture are strictly patriarchal. Woman's role is considered equal in importance, but not equal in authority to man's. Whether this distinction can be made and remain true is a matter disputed by scholars and others outside the Amish community, but it's accepted as true within the culture.

The Amish base their rules governing relationships between men and women on a letter from the Apostle Paul to the early Christians at Corinth. "Now I want you to realize," Paul wrote, "that the head of every man is Christ, and the head of the woman is man, and the head of Christ is God." (I Cor. 11:3)

Believing as they do that every word of the Bible was divinely inspired—and received, transcribed, and translated without error or human influence—the Amish make no distinction between the words of Jesus and the words of Paul. These words are considered indisputable, clear, and reflecting the unchangeable will of God.

This passage is used to explain why women can't be ordained to positions of authority in the church—that would place women in a position of authority over men, against the natural order created by God. "Women vote in church business meetings and nominate men for ministerial duties," according to sociologist Donald Kraybill in *The Riddle of Amish Culture*. "They do not, however, participate in the community's formal power structure."

John Hostetler explains further in *Amish Society*, "The wife has an immortal soul and is an individual in her own right. Although she is to be obedient to her husband, her first loyalty is to God .... The wife follows her husband's leadership and example but decides as an individual whether she is ready for communion. In church council, she has an equal vote but not an equal 'voice.'" Unmarried women remain under the authority of their fathers.

Ironies and Oddities

The Amish believe in a masculine God who created the world that gives most power to those who are most like him. The Amish social order considers both gender and age in deciding who has the most power and authority. It goes like this:

◆ God

◆ Jesus

◆ Older adult men

◆ Younger adult men

◆ Older adult women

◆ Younger adult women

◆ Older boys

◆ Older girls

◆ Younger boys

◆ Younger girls

Among adults, older outranks younger, and male outranks female. The same is true among children. But even male children don't have more power than their mothers, and older sisters are given authority over their younger brothers.

Hostetler summarizes the role of women in the Amish church:

> With regard to the woman's role in religious services, the teaching of the Apostle Paul is literally obeyed: "Let the woman learn in silence with all subjection." In leadership activities, the woman is not "to usurp authority over the man." At baptismal service, boys are baptized before girls. Women never serve as church officials.

The Amish base the requirement for women's head coverings on the same chapter in Corinthians. "Every man who prays or prophesies with his head covered dishonors his head. And every woman who prays or prophesies with her head uncovered dishonors her head—it is just as though her head were shaved."

The term "head" is interpreted to mean both the physical head and whoever is in authority over the man or woman. An Amish contributor to *Family Life* writes: "[W]e can see that the veiling is more than a prayer covering. It is also a symbol of subordination. By wearing it, a woman shows her awareness and acceptance of her proper role in life—a helpmate to man."

We don't know whether the writer was a man or a woman, but either could be true. Women steeped in Amish culture their entire lives tend to see themselves as they've been taught, as subordinate but equal. When they express an interest in equal rights, it's more likely to be on issues affecting their work, such as being allowed to use power lawn mowers, than on issues of their role in church.

Kraybill quotes one Amish woman as saying, "The joke among us women is that the men make the rules so that's why more modern things are permitted in the barn than in the house."

The Least You Need to Know

◆ Basic Christian doctrines shared by the Amish include the divinity of Christ, the inspiration of the Bible, heaven and hell, and that the church is the body of Christ in the world.

◆ The Amish link baptism and church membership; to be baptized, one must vow faithful service to both Jesus and the church.

◆ Once a person joins the Amish church, he or she is held accountable by the church for keeping its rules for the rest of his or her life.

◆ Breaking the rules, and refusing to confess wrongdoing, repent, and change, results in excommunication and shunning.

◆ Amish church and society is strictly patriarchal.

Chapter 6

A Movable Church: Amish Worship

In This Chapter

◆ How the Amish spend their Sundays

◆ Where they worship

◆ The preaching service

◆ Sharing Sunday dinner

◆ After-church activities

The Amish observe two kinds of Sundays: "church-Sundays" and "off-Sundays."

People who see the Amish as extremely religious people might be surprised to know that they don't hold church service every Sunday. But Amish church services are long, intense experiences. Together with the afternoon of visiting that follows the noon meal, a church Sunday takes up three-quarters of the day. The remainder is spent driving to and from the service in a horse-drawn buggy, or walking, and doing morning and evening chores. For young people, who meet again in the evening for singing and socializing, the day extends well through the evening.

No wonder, then, that meeting every other week is enough for most Amish people. Some, especially ministers and bishops and their families, may attend church in other districts on their "off-Sunday." Ordained ministers visiting another congregation are often invited to preach.

But for most families, the off-Sunday offers a welcome rest from the week's hard work. It's still a sacred day, so activities are kept quiet. Some families teach their children German by reading their Bible together on Sunday mornings, after chores and breakfast. Visiting relatives and friends often takes up the afternoon. Parents may take the younger children to visit their friends while older children get to stay home and play with neighbors or friends their own age.

Worship Without Walls: Church in the Home

Amish people feel church buildings are extravagant wastes of money that could be better spent. Harking back to the Anabaptists who protested the expense of building and maintaining lavish cathedrals, Amish through the generations have seen church buildings or meetinghouses as the first step down the slippery slope to worldliness.

The Plain Truth _____

An article in the Amish magazine *Family Life* from August 9, 1973 tallied up how much money the Amish were saving at that time by worshipping in homes:

> If we Amish think it's expensive to build and pay for our own schools, we should just be thankful we don't have the church expenses some people do. According to a recent survey made of a large church in Winnipeg [Canada], it cost $30,000 a year to provide a one-hour service each Sunday .... That figures out to more than $500 an hour. At that rate, an Amish church service of three hours would cost $1,500!

Beneath the spoken reasons for rejecting church buildings are other reasons, unspoken and perhaps not even consciously considered, for choosing home worship. It helps weave home and church, family and congregation, into a seamless life. Once a year, every family knows its house will be on display, its adherence to the *Ordnung*, the church rules and traditions, under inspection by the entire congregation. And the long visiting period after the service strengthens community bonds.

A World Unto Itself: The Church District

Without church buildings to serve as meeting points, the church district system organizes Amish families into congregations. Districts are defined as geographic areas; all Amish families living within a district attend service together. The district is the base for all church functions, including setting local rules, disciplining members, and special services such as baptism, weddings, and funerals. Each district ordains its own leaders, who interpret the rules of the *Ordnung* for members to follow.

Home worship limits the size of church districts to the number of people who can fit into one home. Amish houses have to be large enough to accommodate church meetings, though they crowd together to an extent that most others would find uncomfortable. In the largest church districts, as many as 200 people, including babies asleep on upstairs beds, gather for a typical Sunday worship service.

The Bench Wagon: Getting Ready

Driving through a community populated by Amish people, you may see a distinctive, boxy wagon parked in a farmyard. That's the bench wagon, and it means that church was either recently held or about to be held at that home.

Every Amish church district owns a bench wagon, used to store and haul the backless benches, hymn books, and eating utensils from farm to farm for Sunday preaching services.

Preparing to host the Sunday "preaching service" is hard work, most of it is done by the women of the family. Men clean up the stables to get ready for more horses, carry carpets out of the house and bring the bench wagon from wherever it was last used.

The women clean the house from top to bottom, since all rooms will be used. Neighbor women come over on Saturday and help prepare the food for Sunday's noon meal. In some communities, they bake pies with crusts thick enough to be eaten out-of-hand, since plates aren't used for the Sunday lunch.

In most communities, the Sunday noon menu doesn't include anything as fancy as pie. But feeding 200 people or more, even on mostly bread, butter, jam, peanut butter, cheese, pickles of various sorts, and maybe bologna, takes a lot of work. And that's just the light meal of the day. Hosting church service also means welcoming the young people of courting age from several districts for their Sunday evening sing, too. The host family may invite friends and neighbors to stay for supper, then feed the young people as well.

To prepare the house for service, benches are arranged in close rows throughout the living room, a downstairs bedroom and the kitchen. In the East, Amish homes have partitions between that can be removed for church service. Midwestern homes don't have this convenience. In some communities, a large basement room might be used instead, or in warm weather, benches set up in the barn, shop, or other outbuilding. A row of chairs is set in front of the living room for the ordained men, near a wide doorway into the kitchen. The men will occupy the living room, while women occupy the kitchen and bedroom. The morning's preachers will stand near the doorway where they can see both the men's and women's sections.

Sunday Morning: Chores and Church

Like all farm families, Amish families rise early. But on church Sundays, there's extra pressure to get up early and work fast. Imagine having to feed and milk cows, feed horses, perhaps gather eggs, harness the horse, wash off the barn smell, eat breakfast, dress in Sunday clothes, hitch up the buggy, and get on the road to a neighbor's farm by 8 A.M. or earlier. And that's just the men! The women often help with milking, then cook and eat breakfast, feeding four, six, or eight children, wash their faces, dress them in their Sunday best, get themselves washed up and dressed, and very likely nurse or feed, change, and dress a baby.

Most families are on the road by 8 A.M.; some may arrive by that time. Close neighbors walk, in good weather. The men drop the women and children off near the house, then park the buggy, unhitch the horse and stop to chat with other men near the barn. Older sons of the host family often take care of stabling the horses and feeding them hay. Boys hang out in groups outside or in the barn; girls gather near the house or in the kitchen, depending on the weather. Women gather in the kitchen, and all visit quietly until the oldest ordained men start the procession into the house to begin services. Age, gender, and marital status decide when each individual enters the house for the service.

When it's time to start, the oldest ordained men enter the house first. They're followed by other adult men, roughly in order of age. Women find seats in their sections—the kitchen and main floor bedroom—while the men are being seated. Very young children enter with their parents, girls to sit with mothers and boys with fathers, except for infants. Older children come in next, girls in their groups and boys in theirs. Finally, teenaged girls and unmarried women, led by any who are baptized members of the church, find their places. Unmarried young men and boys enter last, sometimes even after the service has begun.

Ironies and Oddities
In eastern churches, men and women sometimes enter through separate doors. Men may take their hats off as they enter, piling them on the porch or hanging them on hooks. In eastern congregations, men leave their hats on until the beginning of the first hymn, then sweep them off in unison. Women leave bonnets and shawls in a designated area out of the way.

The Preaching Service

Amish "preaching services" last 3 hours, from 9 A.M. to 12 P.M., and haven't changed much over the centuries.

Preaching is done by men chosen by lot and ordained for life. On Sunday morning, Amish ministers quote scripture from memory, tell Bible stories, and exhort their fellow church members to obey the will of God, the teaching of Jesus, and the rules of the church. They emphasize obedience, humility, submission to authority, and the purity of living in the way of their forebears.

CAUTION

Make No Mistake

Amish congregations have at least one bishop and two ministers, but they aren't paid or professionally trained. The Amish consider men more likely to gain the wisdom needed to preach through life experience, devotion to the church, and God's grace, than through education. It would be considered vain for a minister to prepare a sermon in advance, or even assume he would be chosen to preach. Reading the Bible and praying is preparation enough.

First, We Sing: Order of Worship

Amish church services generally follow a traditional order, though details may vary from congregation to congregation. The typical order is as follows:

Vas Es Das?

The **Lob Lied,** meaning "Praise Song," is the second hymn sung at every Amish church service, everywhere. It begins "Oh Father God, we praise thee." After thanking God, the hymn prays for the ministers to be able to speak God's teachings, then for the congregation to be open to receiving their words, and finally for God to be present.

◆ Twenty to forty minutes of singing from the Amish hymnal, the *Ausbund*. The second hymn is always the *Lob Lied*.

◆ During the second line of the first hymn, the ministers rise and move to an upstairs bedroom for a meeting to plan the service. They choose who will preach each of the two sermons and discuss any congregational business that calls for a member meeting after the worship service.

◆ First sermon: around half an hour long.

◆ Silent, kneeling prayer. Members of the congregation turn to face the benches they had been sitting on.

◆ Scripture reading by a deacon. Congregation stands; in some congregations, men turn to face the deacon while women remain facing the benches, with their backs to the speaker. In other areas, all church members remain facing backward during scripture reading.

◆ Main sermon: an hour long, give or take 10 minutes. The main sermon ends with the preacher reading another chapter of scripture, expanding on the meaning of verses, and exhorting the congregation as he reads.

◆ "Testimonies" by other ordained men, invited by the minister to comment on his sermon, add their thoughts, or point out faults in what he said. Occasionally an unordained man might be invited to speak, if he's visiting from another district or state. Women never speak during the service.

◆ Closing words of the main preacher.

◆ Spoken, kneeling prayer. Congregation again turns to face the benches while the main preacher reads a long prayer from a prayer book.

◆ Benediction by the main minister, members standing. Near the end of the benediction, which is recited from memory, the name of Jesus Christ is spoken. At the sound, all members bend their knees slightly in a sign of deference, reverence, and obedience to Christ.

♦ Announcements, in some congregations by a deacon and others by the main preacher of the morning. Location of the next preaching service is announced, along with any member meeting that may be needed immediately after the service.

♦ Closing hymn.

♦ Congregation exits, row by row, youngest first, then older ones in order.

The Plain Truth _____

The benediction recited at the end of the Amish service can translated as follows:

Finally, dear brethren, rejoice, be perfect, be comforted, and be of one mind; be peaceful, and the God of love and peace shall be with you. Greet each other with the Holy Kiss. You are greeted by all the saints. (II Cor. 13:11-13)

So I submit myself, with you, to God and his gracious hand, that he be pleased to keep us in the saving faith, to strengthen us in it, to guide and lead us until a blessed end; and all this through Jesus Christ. Amen.

—From *Amish Society*, by John A. Hostetler

Sounds of Worship: Preaching

Amish church services are conducted in a mixture of high German, Pennsylvania German or Pennsylvania Dutch, and English. Words from all three languages may be mixed together in a sermon. Scripture readings are in German.

Preachers in some Amish districts preach in a traditional, sing-song rhythm, raising the pitch of their voice as they chant the words, then letting the pitch fall again at the end of each phrase. Some preachers also read from the prayer book in the same sing-song chant.

The rise and fall of the preacher's voice sometimes puts people to sleep. Babies can be carried upstairs by their mothers and laid on a bed, young children can lean across the laps of their parents, but adults have to nod on their benches until the sermon is over.

Amish preachers embody humility, the quality they want to instill in other church members, in their demeanor. A minister may start his

Ironies and Oddities

Being ordained a minister is viewed as a heavy burden. Men ordained as ministers are chosen by lot, and often are overcome with tears when they hear their name called. Such a humble attitude is so socially expected that it would be impossible to know if a minister developed a little pride in his heart over the authority and respect given him in his role.

sermon by declaring his unworthiness to preach, along with his willingness to give himself up in the service of his congregation despite his poor abilities, since God has willed it. In some traditional congregations, the ministers will not make eye contact with their audience as a further sign of humility.

In less traditional church districts, though, ministers speak in normal voices, without the sing-song chanting style. They use their voices to add conviction or express emotion to their words, and make eye contact with both men and women.

Sounds of Worship: Amish Singing

The sound of Amish singing is different from music in other churches. It's s-l-o-w, droning, sung in unison, and almost like a chant rather than a tune. The hymns have as many as 37 verses, though only 4 or 5 are typically sung.

The words are in German and most congregations use the *Ausbund*, the hymnal first published in 1564 in Europe. The hymns were written by Anabaptist prisoners confined to prison in the castle of Passau, Bavaria. Amish congregations know all the tunes by heart. The *Ausbund* includes only the words, which tell of persecution, suffering, faithfulness, and belief in God's redeeming love to see his people through their vale of tears.

Without written notes to follow, the Amish learn the tunes of their hymns as part of growing up in their church. Song leaders—always men—are not ordained, as other church leaders, but simply recognized for their ability with music. Several men may take turns leading hymns when asked. The song leader will sing the first few notes to the first syllable of a line, and the congregation will join in on the second syllable. Older men ask younger ones to take a turn leading a verse or two to help them learn the skill.

The pace of singing expresses the conservativeness of a congregation. The more traditional a congregation, the slower its hymn singing. More progressive groups pick up the pace a little. Singing the *Lob Lied*, the second hymn of the morning, can take a progressive congregation 11 minutes and conservative one 30 minutes. The slow, dolorous singing actually exaggerates the length of the original tunes, which were popular folk songs of sixteenth century Europe. When the Amish adopted them, they began to drag them out and embellish the notes, making them into their own art form.

Vas Es Das?

Ausbund das ist Etliche schone Christliche Lieder, or *An Excellent Selection of Some Beautiful Christian Songs,* is the full name of the Amish hymn book. It contains only words, not music, for songs written by early Anabaptist martyrs while in prison. The book also includes some of their stories of martyrdom. It's commonly called the *Ausbund.*

Musical instruments have no part in Amish worship or even home life. (The exception for recreational music is harmonicas, which are widely tolerated, perhaps because they're small and inexpensive.) For worship, instruments are considered unnecessary, ostentatious ornamentation. Singing is for the purpose of praising God or remembering our dependence on him, not for making a beautiful sound. It's the words, not the notes, that are significant. Parts singing, like solos or choirs, would simply encourage people to take pride in their talent, try to out-sing their neighbor, show off to gain attention and praise, and forget the meaning of the songs in listening to the performance.

Women and Children in the Worship Service

So far, we've focused on the men leading the worship service. What are the women doing during service, aside from kneeling, standing, singing, and listening?

They're taking care of infants and very young children, of course. The youngest children sit with them, though a young boy or even a girl may sit with the father if the mother has a baby to tend to. Amish mothers have the same problems keeping small children quiet that parents do in any church. What they don't have is a nursery to retire to, where they can hear the service broadcast to them on speakers.

Amish writers to *Family Life* magazine through the years had the same disagreements as members of other churches about the behavior of children during services. Some complain about children who make noise and can't sit still, chastising the mothers. Others disagree, feeling the importance of having children in church outweighs the inconvenience. A young mother admonished the complainers, "Please, older mothers, why not *help* a young mother with her hands full? She can't nurse the baby and at the same time give the one-year-old his need."

The Plain Truth

Women who need to nurse an infant or change diapers can get up quietly and go to an upstairs bedroom. Sleeping babies are laid down to sleep together on one of the beds, so their mothers can go back downstairs.

According to some scholars writing on Amish Sunday services, very young children may get up and walk around from time to time. Others play games with handkerchiefs, tying and folding them to make "mice" and configurations—a very old, traditional way to entertain little ones during church. In addition to fitting neatly into a pocket, handkerchiefs can double as nose-wipers and don't make noise if they fall on the floor!

Most non-Amish writers comment on how quiet and patient the young children are during the three-hour preaching services. Growing up in these Sunday services is a way of learning the qualities that Amish adults are expected to practice: patience, obedience to authority, and willingness to sacrifice individual choice in exchange for belonging to the group.

The Noon Meal

During the closing hymn, some women may get up and start preparing the noon meal. When the service is over, men carry some of the benches outside, if the weather is good, or otherwise clear space for tables to be set up in the living room area. Benches are placed on trestles to build tables for eating lunch. They build separate tables for men and women, and sometimes a table for the ministers, who always eat at the first sitting.

Women cover the tables and set them with cups, glasses, knives and forks, but no plates. They set the food on the table, and have water, coffee, and tea ready to pour. The bishop leads a silent prayer before the meal, and another after. People know that others are waiting to eat, so they finish quickly to let others take their place.

The women clear the tables as each group finishes, and set them again for the next group. Among the Amish, those with more status eat first, male and female each at their own table. Parents feed small children when they eat, but older children are expected to wait until all the adults have finished.

Visiting: The Amish Pastime

After the lunch, dishes are done, the children play, the young people gather in groups to talk or go for walks, and the adults sit down to visit.

Ironies and Oddities

Amish people have a multitude of family members—siblings, aunts, uncles, and near and distant cousins, as well as parents, grandparents, and great-grandparents, and an equal number of their spouse's relatives—to keep in touch with. If you got married and stay in the same community where you grew up, as so many Amish adults do, then most of the adults in your church have known you since you were a child. Many of them are your relatives. They also know your parents, grandparents, extended family, and likely your in-laws too—and you know theirs.

Keeping up with all those people takes a lot of time, and provides free entertainment without violating community boundaries or rules.

Visiting is one of the favorite pastimes of Amish people, and create the tight-knit communities in which everyone knows everyone else. If you're Amish, you may not be good friends with everyone, but each person in the church community is part of your life. This large social network provides many sympathetic ears, news, gossip, and entertainment, while reinforcing Amish values through peer pressure.

By 3 P.M. on Sunday afternoon, the church day winds down. Amish fathers and sons hitch up their buggies and load up the family to go home and do chores. In the evening, the parents and young children may do more visiting, either dropping in on another family or receiving visitors of their own. Amish women never know when company may arrive, but Sundays are visiting days, so they're always prepared.

For older teens, meanwhile, Sunday evenings are time to socialize. Where settlements remain small, teens often follow the traditional practice of returning to the farm where they had preaching service in the morning for an evening sing. This time, the hymns are gospel songs sung at a pace that better suits the young people than the dragging hymns of the *Ausbund*. Evening sings are courting time for Amish teens, many of whom will join the church just in time to get married, around the age of 20 or 21. When the sing ends at around 10 P.M., they linger on to visit some more before pairing off for the buggy ride home. Those who aren't dating return home with friends and cousins, brothers and sisters.

In larger settlements, though, practices have changed considerably. In Lancaster County, for instance, young people have created over two dozen social groups that cross church district boundaries. Teens join a group of like-minded peers. The more conservative stick closer to traditional, approved practice. The wilder or more rebellious sometimes hold dances in barns that include local bands, drinking, and dressing in worldly clothes. Teen behavior has been the cause of much controversy among both the Amish and their neighbors, as Amish teens have increasingly been in trouble with the law for reckless driving, underage drinking, and drug use.

The Least You Need to Know

- The Amish hold worship services in their homes, not in special buildings.
- All Amish people living within a district attend church together.
- Amish ministers are unpaid and untrained members of the congregation.
- Church services are followed by a light noon meal and afternoon visiting.
- Teenagers meet again in the evening for socializing.

Chapter 7

Seasons in the Life of the Church: Special Services

In This Chapter

◆ Importance of communion in church life

◆ Foot washing as a symbol of humility and service

◆ Choosing baptism in the church

◆ Ordaining bishops, ministers, and deacons

Church rituals serve to symbolize the relationships between human beings, and between each individual and God. In the Amish church, these rituals include some special services held as regularly as the seasons, and others that mark special times in the lives of church members.

The Body and the Blood: Communion and Foot Washing

Communion service and the special church member meeting held in preparation for communion are among the most meaningful rituals in church life. Communion is held just twice a year, but it's a long and intense experience full of significance for individuals and the group.

When the Amish take communion, they symbolically share in the suffering and death of Jesus Christ, serving as the body of Christ in the world today. But the body of Christ can't be impure if it is to fulfill its sacred function as the vessel for the Holy Spirit. Therefore, individual members and the church as a whole prepare for communion service with a period of self-examination, confession, and cleansing.

An Amish church district can only hold communion if all its members are willing to say they're in agreement with the church rules and have no unresolved disputes with each other, or unconfessed sins. In effect, members reaffirm their loyalty to the group and conformity to its standards as part of this twice-yearly ritual, strengthening the authority of the church in the lives of individual believers.

Vas Es Das?

Communion, sometimes also called The Lord's Supper, is a Christian sacrament or sacred ritual based on the words of Jesus in the biblical account of the Last Supper. Christian groups vary widely in the frequency with which they celebrate communion.

The Plain Truth

According to the account in the Gospel of Luke, on the night before his arrest and crucifixion, Jesus celebrated the Jewish holy feast of Passover with his disciples. At the meal, he took a cup of wine, gave thanks for it, and said, "Take this and divide it among yourselves; for I tell you that from now on, I will not drink of the fruit of the vine until the kingdom of God comes." Then he did the same with a loaf of bread, saying, "This is my body, which is given for you. Do this in remembrance of me." (Luke 22:17-19)

The Bishops' Meeting

The first meeting leading up to communion service in most *settlements* is the Bishops' Meeting. Held in March and September, these meetings of the bishops from church districts throughout the settlement begin the process of church cleansing.

The bishops bring up controversies brewing in the various districts. Is it all right to use computers and the Internet in an Amish-owned business? Are they really necessary to business? How about cell phones, if an Amish person's employer requires one? Can it be used from home, or for reasons other than business? If you start down that road, can you stop again?

If the bishops can agree on a policy on such issues, it becomes part of the oral rules passed on by memory, the *Ordnung*.

The bishops also agree on who will lead communion in each district. The communion service lasts all day and includes two sermons, the second up to three hours long. It's also a time of great spiritual significance, and it's customary for bishops and ministers from neighboring districts to come assist and support the congregation's ministers on that day.

> **Vas Es Das?**
>
> **Settlement** refers to an entire Amish community. Lancaster, Pennsylvania, for instance, is one settlement, while Holmes County, Ohio is another. Settlements are divided into as many church districts as necessary. Church districts are limited to the number of people who can meet in an Amish home. Most districts have their own bishop, though in Lancaster, bishops usually oversee two districts.

Counsel Meeting

Two weeks—one "church Sunday"—before the communion service is scheduled, the entire membership of a church district holds an all-day combination worship service and membership meeting to prepare themselves spiritually. This is called Counsel Meeting.

Anyone who wants to take communion has to attend the Counsel Meeting. It's important for the whole community to be in agreement with each other and the will of the church as expressed through the *Ordnung*. Every member is a vital part of the church body, which must be in complete harmony to take part in the sacred service. Lack of agreement means the congregation can't hold its communion service until the dispute is resolved.

> **Make No Mistake**
>
> Notice that the Amish "Counsel Meeting" is not called a "Council Meeting." The Amish don't have church councils, but offering counsel (or advice) to members is very important to the Amish way of maintaining church discipline.

Counsel Meeting begins the same way as a normal Sunday worship service, with hymn singing while the ministers gather in an upstairs room to plan the service. The subjects of the two sermons are already set, however, and are the same for every communion: They cover the history of the patriarchs of the Old Testament. They begin with God's call to Abraham to leave his homeland and continue through the deliverance of the children of Israel from the Egyptian pharaoh who had enslaved them. The ministers use the sermons to illustrate the need for obedience to God's commands and the consequence of disobedience.

The first sermon may be as short as half an hour; the second one stretches out another two-and-a-half to three hours. Around lunchtime, small groups of people quietly leave the room for lunch, while the preaching marathon continues. The minister delivering the main sermon usually eats early, so he's good for the afternoon. (Among the New Order Amish in Ohio, everyone takes a short lunch break together following the second sermon.)

Ironies and Oddities

During both the all-day counsel meeting and communion service, children get to stay home, or with friends or relatives who live in a different church district. Adults enjoy the break as much as children. For children, it's a chance to escape long hours of sitting still, and for parents, an opportunity to spend a few hours without children to supervise.

But there's a deeper symbolism to leaving the children at home. Not only are the services too long for young children to sit through, but they're also for church members only. No one not baptized into the Amish church can take communion with the group. Visitors and children are not invited, so for Amish young people, taking part in Communion is a rite of passage to adulthood.

After the second sermon, they start the business of the day: getting right with the church and God. The bishop recites the *Ordnung*, the oral tradition of practices required and forbidden by the church. He restates such traditions as the dress code, and reports on any new additions to the rules agreed upon at the recent Bishops Meeting. Thus the bishop counsels the congregation on how to lead Christian lives.

Counsel Meeting is also a time for public confession of sins. Unlike the Catholic Church, which also places great importance on confession, the Amish church requires a public confession, or at least acknowledgement, of sin.

According John Hostetler's *Amish Society*, "Each member is asked whether he is in agreement with the *Ordnung*, whether he is at peace with the brotherhood, and whether anything 'stands in the way' of his entering into the communion service. Faults must be confessed and adjustments made between members who have differences to settle."

A person who breaks a rule or harbors ill feeling toward another may choose instead to go to an ordained person in private and confess his or her wrong prior to the

Counsel Meeting. If the offense is significant, the bishop summarizes the offense before the entire church at this point in the Counsel Meeting. The bishop recommends a punishment such as a kneeling or seated confession, which the offender then performs before the full congregation. By making the confession public, the church makes use of humiliation as a powerful tool in enforcing the social order and maintaining discipline.

Among the Amish, confession isn't always voluntary. A person caught breaking church rules or a biblical commandment can be confronted in private by the ordained leaders, then before the entire church. If the offender confesses the sin and asks forgiveness before the church, he or she is permitted to take communion. Anyone who refuses to confess, however, but is known to be guilty as accused may be "set back" from communion, or not allowed to partake.

The Plain Truth

People who have been excommunicated may regain their status as members and enjoy full fellowship again by confessing their wrong at Counsel Meeting and asking forgiveness of the body.

Finally, every member of the church is asked whether he or she agrees with the *Ordnung* and whether anything stands in the way of his or her participation in communion. This is called "taking the voice of the church." Two ministers walk down the aisles, one for the women and one for the men, pointing at each member in turn and asking, "Are you agreed?" Each is expected to respond, "I'm agreed." If not, he or she must come to the front of the church and give sound reasons for their disagreement. The social pressure to go along with the group will and tradition is strong, and usually prevails. Then the church is said to be "at peace" and can proceed with communion in two weeks.

Imagine how strongly an individual would have to feel to publicly disagree with the *Ordnung* and prevent the body from being at peace and taking communion! More often, those who disagree quietly leave the church. Disagreements have occurred, however, and prevented some congregations from taking communion for years until agreement could be reached or the disagreeing party was excommunicated.

Fasting: Cleansing the Body and Soul

The next step in preparing the congregation for communion is a morning of fasting and prayer or reflection. Held between Counsel Meeting and communion, either on the "off-Sunday" when no church is held or another significant day such as Good Friday, the fast consists of skipping breakfast and spending the morning reflecting on the state of their hearts and souls and their readiness to share the suffering of Jesus.

Communion: A Day-Long Ritual

Communion service is both a solemn time and a celebration of love and unity in the Amish congregation and with Christ. It's a long day devoted to the service of God and each other, and also a day when parents get to focus on their own spiritual needs rather than the more urgent needs of bored, hungry, and tired children.

Freshly cleansed of wrongdoing, feeling at one with each other and the will of God, church members welcome the day-long ritual of communion. The day begins with hymn singing and a ministers meeting, as usual, at 8 or 8:30 A.M., and concludes around 4 P.M. Again, the service with its long sermons continues nonstop, with small groups of people taking short breaks for lunch and returning so others can take their place at the tables in another room.

The first of the day's two sermons again begins with Genesis and recounts the stories of the Old Testament through Noah and the flood, repeating much of the ground covered by the Counsel Meeting sermons two weeks before. This time, though, the speaker chooses stories that foretell the coming of the Messiah. The second sermon, again about three hours long, begins with the birth of Christ and ends with his suffering on the cross. Some ministers time their retelling of the crucifixion and death of Jesus to occur at three in the afternoon, the time of his death according to biblical accounts.

The suffering of Christ is the emotional high-point of the sermon, and as the preacher tells the story, two ministers or deacons bring a loaf of homemade bread and a cup of homemade wine into the room. They set them on a table by the bishop's side, and while he finishes his sermon, cut the bread and hand a piece to the bishop.

Ironies and Oddities

Occasionally, Old Order Amish rules and practices seem less conservative than those of their more worldly Mennonite cousins. For example, the Amish are less uniformly strict in forbidding the use of tobacco and alcohol than Mennonites.

Historically, the Amish didn't take a strong stand against alcohol use, though they condemned drunkenness, nor did they forbid smoking. In recent decades, the Amish have moved closer to the historic position of the Mennonites in forbidding both alcohol and tobacco use, though their position varies by congregation.

Mennonites (except for Old Order Mennonites) traditionally were forbidden from using alcohol, and always use grape juice instead of wine for communion service. Some of the more progressive Mennonite congregations no longer prohibit social drinking, but even they don't bring wine into their church services.

The congregation stands for a prayer and remains standing while the bishop breaks off a bite-size piece of the bread for himself, then gives one to each of the ordained men. When they have eaten, the bishop (sometimes assisted by one of the ministers) walks among them breaking off pieces of the bread and handing it first to the men, then to the women. Each person holds the bread a moment, bends his or her knees as a form of genuflection or reverence, eats, and sits down.

A prayer is read, and a similar procedure is followed with the cup of wine, which all members share.

Foot Washing as a Sign of Humility

Foot washing follows communion as part of the same service, but is a separate ritual. Unlike the Lord's Supper or Last Supper, which is found in all four gospels, the story of foot washing is found only in the Gospel of John. According to that scripture, after the Passover feast, Jesus washed the feet of his disciples as an example of the humility and service with which they should treat each other after he was gone.

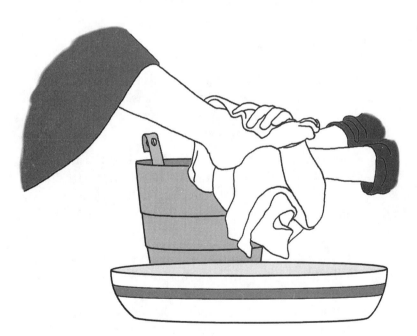

Jakob Ammann disagreed with the Swiss Brethren (later Mennonites) in part over whether to practice foot washing and hold communion twice annually. Eventually, even though Ammann left to form the Amish, the Mennonites adopted both practices. Today, only more traditional Mennonites still practice foot washing.

Vas Es Das?

The Holy Kiss is an old custom based on the Apostle Paul's instructions to the early Christian church at Corinth, "Greet one another with a holy kiss." (I Cor. 16:20) The Holy Kiss, which is on the lips, is only exchanged between people of the same gender. In more conservative Amish congregations, people may still greet each other with a Holy Kiss on Sundays before church.

The foot washing service begins with a minister reading this story from the Bible, while others bring in pails of water, wash basins, and towels, and set them around the rooms. The congregations sing hymns while members pair off with the person sitting next to them, men with men and women with women, and take turns sitting before the basins. They remove their shoes and stockings, and take turns stooping to dip the seated partner's feet in the water and drying them. When each has washed the other's feet, they shake hands and exchange *the Holy Kiss*.

Finally, communion service is over. As the congregation files out the door, a deacon stands nearby to collect contributions to help members with special financial needs. This is the only time a collection is taken during Amish church services.

Baptism: The Most Holy of Vows

Amish baptism is a lifelong vow, not only to follow Jesus, but also to remain Amish and live by the rules of the church both in life and death. It means accepting the absolute values of the church, the black-and-white judgment of the community that is symbolized by the formal clothing they wear to church.

By the time they request baptism, Amish youth know intimately what Amish life requires of them. Most request baptism between the ages of 16 and their early 20s. Girls tend to get baptized younger than boys, but the majority of both genders choose baptism before they reach 21. Ninety percent of children raised in Amish families join the church.

Most baptism services are scheduled for September, so new members can take part in the fall communion service. In the Midwest, many baptisms are scheduled for March, before spring communion. Most church districts have one baptism service a year, a few have two, and Lancaster settlement districts schedule only one every two years. Young people there who want to be baptized before the next scheduled service simply take part in the baptism class of another church district.

At the next Sunday service after a communion service, the bishop in each district will ask young people to consider their readiness for baptism. Those who decide they're ready speak privately to one of the congregation's ordained men, either after a service or at his home during the week.

All through the season preceding the baptism—summer for a fall baptism and winter for one held in spring—baptismal candidates meet individually with the ministers at the beginning of each church service, while the congregation is singing hymns. The ministers meet with each candidate between 6 and 9 times, reviewing the 18 articles of the Dordrecht Confession of Faith and expectations of church membership. During the third instruction session, the ministers review the rules of the *Ordnung*. At this point, those who want to join the church are expected to start demonstrating their earnestness and ability to live by the rules.

The congregation keeps an eye on the young baptismal candidates to make sure they're leaving behind any worldly ways they enjoyed during adolescence. On the Sunday two weeks before baptism is scheduled, a meeting is held to ask church members whether they are willing to accept the candidates for baptism into the church.

The baptism service is scheduled for a Sunday morning at the end of a regular preaching service. The day before, the candidates meet with the ministers and again are given an opportunity to change their minds without formal consequence.

Boys have to make another pledge, to accept the responsibility of the ministry if their name is ever chosen by lot, as all Amish ministers are selected. To be baptized and join the church, every young man must promise to accept this responsibility if it ever falls to him.

Make No Mistake

Baptismal candidates are told it's better not to make a baptismal vow than to make it if they can't keep it. There is no penalty for not joining the church, but to join and leave later results in excommunication and shunning.

On Sunday morning, baptismal candidates meet with the ministers one last time while the congregation begins its usual hymn singing. Afterward, they file into the church service together, first the boys and then girls, and sit on benches reserved for them near the ministers' bench, divided by gender as their elders are. The candidates sit with bowed heads, symbolizing their readiness to submit to God and the church.

After the morning's two sermons, the bishop speaks to the candidates about the seriousness of the vow they are about to take, while the deacon leaves the room and returns with a pail of water and a cup. The bishop then asks the candidates to kneel if they still believe it's the way to "obtain salvation."

All kneel, and the bishop asks a few questions, which vary by district and settlement. All ask essentially the same thing, however. According to Donald Kraybill in *The Riddle of Amish Culture*, one bishop asks these three questions:

◆ "Can you renounce the devil, the world, and your own flesh and blood?"

◆ "Can you commit yourself to Christ and his church, and to abide by it and therein to live and die?"

◆ "And in all the *Ordnung* of the church, according to the word of the Lord, be obedient and submissive to it and to help therein?"

One by one, the candidates answer *"Ja"* to each question. Then the bishop asks the congregation to stand, while the candidates remain on their knees, and reads a prayer from the traditional Swiss Anabaptist prayer book.

An Amish boy kneels before the bishop, who baptizes him with water.

The congregation sits again and the bishop stands before the first baptismal candidate. The deacon with the pail of water stands beside him, and if the candidate is a girl, the deacon's wife unties her prayer cover or *kapp* and lifts it off her head.

The bishop holds his hands on the head of the applicant and says, "Upon your faith, which you have confessed before God and these many witnesses, you are baptized in the name of the Father, the Son, and the Holy Spirit, Amen." The deacon fills the bishop's hand with water, which drips between the bishop's fingers onto the head of the candidate.

Ordination: Making Ministers of Men

When a church district needs to replace a deacon or preacher, the bishop asks the church members to confirm, after a period of reflection and prayer, that they are in harmony and ready to ordain a new man. This usually takes place one service (two weeks) before the Counsel Meeting prior to communion. At the end of the Counsel Meeting, the bishop will take the "voice of the church," and if all members agree, the ordination is set to follow communion service.

During the two weeks before communion, all members are asked to consider and pray about who would make a good preacher or deacon, as appropriate. Husbands and wives each have a vote, and this is one case in which the husband is not supposed to dictate a decision. Each person is to search his or her heart and ask God's guidance to decide on the best nominee.

The Plain Truth

Each church district has one bishop, two "ministers of the book," also called preachers or ministers, and one deacon. All are chosen by lot, to let God make the final selection.

Men who might want the job wouldn't dare say so. To say you felt called by God to ministry would automatically disqualify you, because the Amish hear ego in such a claim.

The Plain Truth

The Amish ministry is considered a burden to be accepted with humility, a heavy responsibility rather than an honor. It's a lifelong commitment, and one that no man in the Amish church is allowed to refuse. Instead of congratulating the newly ordained, they are more likely to console him, as well as his wife. For the spouse and children of an ordained man must also embody the highest standards in the community, submitting to the authority of the church as an example to others. Ministry is a burden felt by the entire family.

After communion service, the bishop will announce the ordination and say a few words about the qualities the person must have. The ordained men go to an adjoining room, or the congregation moves out of the house to gather on the lawn outside. All church members file past a door or window opened into the ministers' room, and each whispers the name of a nominee to a deacon or minister inside. In some congregations, men file past a door on one side of the house and women to a door on the other side of the house.

Make No Mistake

The ordination of a bishop is slightly different, as the lot includes only the previously ordained ministers of the district. After being chosen by lot, a man being ordained bishop kneels, and two presiding bishops from other districts lay their hands on his head as the charge to the bishop is spoken. No one ever is brought into a district to serve in leadership.

The deacon or minister who receives the nominations passes each name on to the bishop, who writes down the name and tallies the votes for each. Only men nominated by at least two, and in some districts three, church members are entered into the log.

The bishop writes a scripture verse on a slip of paper and places it in a copy of the *Ausbund* hymnal. He chooses enough additional copies of the hymnal to equal the number of men in the lot, then fastens a rubber band around each. He shuffles the books, then asks the ministers if any of them want to rearrange the books as well. When they are shuffled to the satisfaction of all, the men carry the hymnals to a table in front of the room where the congregation waits.

The bishop calls the name of the men who were included in the lot, and they come forward and sit on an empty bench at the front of the room. The entire congregation kneels for silent prayer, and then sits down. The bishop instructs the men in the lot to come choose a book from the row standing on the table whenever they feel led by the prompting of the Holy Spirit. One by one, they go forward, take a book, and sit down.

When all have selected a hymnal, the bishop walks down the line and opens them one by one. When he opens the book with the slip of paper, the bishop calls out the name of the man upon whom the lot is said to have "fallen." The man and his wife may both react with tears and sobs.

According to author Stephen Scott, the bishop then says, "If you can accept this service, you may rise to your feet. I give you my hand; stand up." The chosen man rises, and the bishop pronounces the *charge* "laid upon" him for his service.

Vas Es Das?

The **charge** "laid upon" an ordained man is a statement of what duties he is expected to perform. For a bishop it includes performing baptisms, communion, weddings, ordinations, and excommunications. Ministers or preachers are charged with preaching, reading, and praying with the church. Deacons assist ministers at services, collect and distribute alms for the poor, are sent by the bishop to speak with those suspected of breaking church rules, and act as intermediaries between prospective bridegrooms, and the bride's parents.

The bishop greets the newly ordained man with the Holy Kiss and words of comfort and support, as do the rest of those in the lot, the other ordained men, and finally the rest of the male church members. The women of the church greet the man's wife in the same way, and the ordination is finished.

The Least You Need to Know

- Amish congregations hold communion twice a year, at an all-day service attended only by church members.

- The congregation can only hold communion if all members are in agreement with the church rules (*Ordnung*) and at peace with each other. Communion is followed by foot washing.

- Amish baptism is a lifelong vow of loyalty to Jesus and the Amish church and its rules.

- Men are nominated for ordination by a secret vote of all church members. Candidates draw lots for the office, so that God makes the final selection.

- Amish men must agree to accept ordination if it falls to them, and remain ordained for life.

Chapter 8

Patriarchy and Hierarchy: How the Amish Church Is Run

In This Chapter

- Power and authority in the Amish church
- Leadership positions
- How tradition is passed on through the *Ordnung*
- The dreaded excommunication and shunning
- Silence as social control

As far as the Amish church has separated itself from the Roman Catholic Church, which the early Anabaptists wanted to reform, they have kept one common characteristic: both are run by a hierarchy of men. Women hold no positions of leadership or authority in Amish churches.

Though scholars of the Amish church note its all-male leadership, they tend to interpret it as less important than the fact that Amish leaders are chosen by lot.

John Hostetler, a leading scholar and popular writer on the Amish of the twentieth century, wrote in his book *Amish Society*, "The Amish method of using nominations for election and selection by lot helps to prevent manipulative power and personal ambition. Authority is widely distributed among all members so that no single leader or subgroup will have all the power."

Except, of course, men. The power to nominate, which women share, offers far less opportunity to shape a culture than the power to lead and the authority to discipline others—a power that Amish ministers hold for life.

Though much has been made of the *way* the Amish choose their leaders (by drawing lots), the question of *who* is eligible to enter the drawing does much more to shape Amish lives and culture.

How can we tell? Two other Plain church groups, the Old Order River Brethren and the Old German Baptists hold similar nomination processes, but elect their leaders by vote rather than by lot. Though the selection process is different, presumably opening the door for ego and human preference to play a role, the resulting churches and cultures are very similar.

Drawing Boundaries

The Amish church is organized by district, which like a parish includes all Amish within its geographic boundaries. Amish people don't choose where to go to church; they're expected to get along with their local congregation and its leaders. Districts that are in "full fellowship" with each other, meaning they agree on the basic rules laid down by the church, respect each other's disciplinary actions. One district won't receive into its fellowship anyone excommunicated from another district, even if he or she moves into its territory, unless the person first confesses and is restored to good standing in his former district.

All districts in close proximity, such as in the same or adjoining counties, make up a settlement. Leaders from throughout the settlement may gather to schedule services such as communion, when leadership is shared between districts. But while leaders sometimes confer on issues facing them all, and may share "counsel" or opinions and advice, none can remove another with whom he disagrees.

Powers That Be: Deacon, Minister, and Bishop

Amish church leaders are never trained or paid for their church duties, no matter how much time their office requires. They continue to earn their living through farming, owing a business, or working for others. The Amish believe that church leadership is a call from God, not a profession to be chosen or sought by individuals.

All ordained leaders of the Amish church share the following characteristics:

- ◆ They're always men.

- ◆ They are married.

- ◆ They display humility in daily life.

- ◆ The success of their farm or business and the harmony and obedience of their family demonstrate their sound judgment, hard work, and ability to exert authority.

- ◆ They never, ever seek a leadership position.

Make No Mistake

Even though the Amish church ordains bishops, ministers, and deacons, these are just the closest English words to describe the offices they fill. Amish church organization is very distinct from other churches, and its bishops, ministers, and deacons have different roles and responsibilities than leaders in other churches who have the same titles.

Church leaders hold their office for life. (In some settlements, a man ordained as a deacon remains eligible to be nominated as a minister. In other settlements, a deacon cannot abandon the responsibilities he accepted for life at his ordination in order to take another position.) Even if they move to a different church district, they take along their office and authority to perform its duties.

If a congregation is extremely unhappy with the way a minister or bishop is performing his duties, or the beliefs he is preaching, he can be "silenced," or prevented from continuing to preach—a rare occurrence. A minister or deacon might be able to move to another church district if his congregation is dissatisfied with his performance, but a bishop generally isn't allowed to.

A bishop can, however, move to a new area and start a separate group that is not "in fellowship" with the original community. That's often how church splits occur; leaders who disagree with the congregation as a whole or other ministers or bishops go off and start their own group.

Role of the Bishop

In German, an Amish bishop is called a *Voelliger-Diener*, or "minister with full powers." The bishop is head honcho, the ultimate authority in a church district. The bishop decides, for example, whether a telephone can be installed in a rented house if the landlord insists. Together with other bishops of the district, he decides how to handle new technology, such as cell phones or the Internet used for work. He decides when a violation of the rules is severe enough to send the deacon to ask the person to change the offending behavior.

The bishop also decides when counsel has been unsuccessful, and when discipline, such as excommunication or shunning, is required. Nevertheless, he is still required to seek the counsel of the full membership before taking such extreme action. The bishop also may restore an excommunicated member to full fellowship if the person relents and confesses the sin of which he or she is accused.

On a happier note, the bishop also performs what in other churches are called sacraments: baptism, communion, marriage, and ordinations. He takes a turn preaching the main sermon at Sunday services. When he is too "old and weak" to continue in his role, the bishop is required to ordain the man chosen to succeed him.

Role of the Minister

The German term for an Amish minister or preacher is *Diener zum Buch* or "minister of the book." His role is primarily to preach the lessons of the Bible, without notes or a copy of the Bible in front of him. He is to teach people what God wants of them, and warn them against sin. Ministers also assist the bishop during communion and other services, and frequently visit districts other than their own on "off-Sundays," where they may be invited to preach.

Role of the Deacon

In German, the Amish deacon is called the *Armen-Diener* or "minister of the poor." It's his responsibility to collect and distribute money to members in need, with the approval of the congregation.

He also serves as a go-between or mediator in several situations. Before the bishop gets involved in a dispute between members or a case involving a member breaking the rules of the *Ordnung*, he sends the deacon to investigate, mediate, and counsel the parties concerned. When a couple decides to marry, the man speaks to the deacon about it in private, and the deacon then calls on the parents of the prospective bride to ask if they approve. If so, he then tells the bishop so the couple's intentions can be announced and the wedding arranged.

Finally, the deacon assists the bishop and ministers during church services. He reads a chapter from the Bible at each Sunday service. When a ceremony requires special props and equipment, whether it's a pail of water for baptism or a loaf of bread for communion, the deacon acts as stage manager, supplying the right tool at the right time.

Rules of Order: The *Ordnung*

As noted previously, the *Ordnung* orders every aspect of Amish life, from personal appearance to occupation to whether to stand or kneel during prayer.

Every congregation has its own version of the *Ordnung*, seldom written down, but known by heart by every church member. Though each district interprets the code of behavior in its own way, differences are minor. They reflect different ways of interpreting the principles embraced centuries ago by the early Anabaptists and their Amish descendents. The *Ordnung* reflects an understanding reached by all members of a congregation on how to apply those principles in their own lives.

Basic Christian rules of behavior also don't have to be stated explicitly in the *Ordnung*. The Ten Commandments are one example; murder and adultery are understood to be wrong. The *Ordnung* also doesn't bother mentioning behavior rejected by the larger society regardless of faith, such as incest.

The Plain Truth

The *Ordnung* spells out ways in which the Amish separate themselves from the rest of the world. Some rules, though, are so obvious that they don't have to be spelled out. One woman told sociologist Donald Kraybill, for instance, that though Amish women aren't allowed to wear makeup, "It's something the bishops don't need to mention." If you're Amish, you just don't go there.

The purpose of the *Ordnung* is to clarify ways in which Amish people are to be different from the world, rather than simply reinforce every commonly agreed upon rule of human behavior. Some of the most basic traditions of Amish life and worship might be considered part of the informal understanding of the community (which is the definition of *Ordnung*), but not part of the formal *Ordnung* recited at church meetings. Such items include …

- Probition of divorce.
- Prohibition of military service.
- Requirement to drive buggies.
- Speaking Pennsylvania German at home.
- Preaching in high German.
- Order of the worship service.
- Kneeling for prayer.

The formal *Ordnung* spells out both what is required and what is forbidden. Aspects of life the *Ordnung* oversees include the following:

◆ Men and women's clothing styles and colors

◆ Acceptable buggy accessories, such as lights

◆ Courtship rules

◆ Marriage within the church

◆ Use of horses for farm work

◆ Steel wheels on machinery

Practices forbidden by the *Ordnung* include:

◆ Flying on airplanes

◆ Central heating in homes

◆ Wall-to-wall carpeting

◆ Electricity from public power lines

◆ Owning television, radio, and CD or tape players

◆ Telephones installed in the home, though cell phones are starting to be used in some districts

◆ Filing a law suit

◆ Owning cars and trucks

◆ Using tractors for farm work, though power machinery may be used if pulled by horses

The *Ordnung* does change over time, though only slowly and with great deliberation. While the Amish want to maintain separation from the world, that doesn't mean they reject all changes in lifestyle. They just want to evaluate each one carefully, making sure that it doesn't conflict with their larger goals. Any technology which …

◆ Encourages individual desires, goals, or pride

◆ Exposes church members to worldly ideas and values

◆ Encourages individual decision making over submission to the group will

◆ Might lead to questioning the wisdom of the leaders or tradition

◆ Undermines patriarchal authority either in the church or at home

… is forbidden because they threaten the unity and obedience of the community and spiritual health of its individuals. The Amish believe that obedience to the church symbolizes obedience to God and is essential for spiritual salvation. Therefore, they believe that anyone who leaves the church or is excommunicated for refusing to follow the Ordnung gives up his or her chance of reaching heaven.

You Can't Go Home Again: Excommunication and Shunning

The Amish believe that the Bible instructs church leaders to keep the church pure by excommunicating those who willfully embrace sin and refuse to change. The early Anabaptists also practiced excommunication, including those who would later become Mennonites.

Today, only the most conservative Mennonites practice excommunication and still fewer practice shunning to the degree practiced by the Amish. For the Amish, excommunication and shunning are the last step in a process meant to maintain the purity of the church and its authority over every aspect its members' lives. They are the fences around the faithful, disciplines severe enough to keep the vast majority of members from straying.

Of course, the Amish don't want to lose anyone from their fellowship. They hope that by shunning someone, the offender will realize the seriousness of his or her transgression, confess, and repent so he or she can be welcomed back into full fellowship. Faced with the loss of family and friends, this is often the result. Banned and shunned members are often deluged with pleas from family and church members begging them to submit to the judgment of the church, allowing them back into full fellowship.

Ironies and Oddities
Jakob Ammann split with the Swiss Brethren over the issue of shunning. Ammann called for strict shunning by all church members, including the spouse of the shunned person. Ironically, Menno Simons largely agreed with Ammann, though he felt spouses shouldn't be forced to shun their mate. Though the Swiss Brethren later became known as Mennonites, they never adopted Menno's position on shunning.

First Step: Confession

When an Amish person either breaks a rule of the *Ordnung* or commits an act defined as sin by the Bible, the first step in rectifying the situation is confession.

Amish confessions differ from confession as practiced in other churches. Amish confession may be made first in private, but if the offense is serious enough, the offender will be required to confess again in front of the entire church membership. As a way of shaming the offender, public confession serves not just to clear the conscience and unburden the soul, but as a punishment in itself. It's the first step in a process designed to bring more and more peer pressure to bear on anyone who puts individual preference ahead of group identity.

Voluntary confession begins with an Amish person going privately to a deacon or minister to admit a feeling of guilt over a transgression. The matter could be minor, such as buying or using forbidden technology or having a forbidden interaction with an excommunicated relative. Or it could be more serious, such as sexual relations outside marriage, or cheating at business, joining a forbidden organization, or attending Bible study run by another church.

The Plain Truth

Private confessions take place at Members Meeting following a worship service, and can take the form of sitting, kneeling, or kneeling followed by a six-week excommunication.

A private confession may be enough to resolve the less serious matters. More serious transgressions are taken to the bishop for resolution by one of the forms of public confession.

Many confessions, though, aren't voluntary. They're based on reports from other church members who notice a person going astray, indulging in marginal behavior or something strictly forbidden by the *Ordnung*. Sometimes, these reports are based on jealousy and gossip, or vague accusations such as showing too much pride or aggressive business practices, rather than on an actual infraction.

As with all Amish practices, what happens when a person is accused of wrongdoing depends heavily on the local bishop or other ordained man who confronts the offender. Some ask the accused for information and take what he or she says into consideration; others don't. Once the case is presented in a formal church meeting, though, the offender is pretty much limited to answering, "yes" or "no" when questioned. Attempts to deny the accusations may be counterproductive, and if the fault is not confessed and results in excommunication, any attempt to maintain that the church is wrong would most likely result in shunning.

Sociologist John Hostetler writes in *Amish Society*, "There is normally no problem when the transgression is clearly defined, as in the case of moral lapses, and the accused accepts the severity of the offense." However, he says, when people feel wrongly accused, excommunication can "turn sour":

A person is such circumstances has no recourse, no court of appeal, and no alternative, for only the church has the power "to bind or to loose" .... [A]n excommunicated person must show submission, even if no wrongs have been committed. Should such a person seek justice for himself or engage in arguments, he would certainly bring shunning on himself.

If the case is controversial in the church and some members side with the accused, it can result in splitting the congregation.

Such instances have occurred throughout Amish history, but they're rare. More commonly, the bishop sends the district's deacon and a minister to ask the accused about the reported behavior. Sometimes it's obvious; a tractor with rubber tires, for instance, or an automobile are hard to hide. If the case involves personal behavior, though, truth can be hard to determine.

In the Amish church, though, maintaining individual submission to group authority is the highest priority. Culture is the public witness of the church, a testimony to the righteousness of its member, and submission to the church represents submission to God. A distinct and separate culture can only be maintained by keeping strict control over life choices of members. Conformity is necessary to uniformity. So arguing, defending oneself or attempting to justify or deny behavior only brings on the wrath of the church and its leaders.

If the confronted person confesses to breaking the rules, expresses regret, and agrees to stop, the matter is easily resolved. It can be ended in private, if most members are unaware of the issue and it's considered minor.

On the other hand, a more serious offense or one that's been noticed and discussed in the congregation has to be publicly resolved so other members aren't tempted to follow suit, and know that their leaders are making sure everyone else has to follow the same strict regulations. The ordained leaders will discuss the matter and agree on a suggested punishment during their next regular meeting before a Sunday service. At the end of the service, a Members Meeting will be announced and all nonmembers leave the room. Matters of discipline are for church members only, a privilege of membership and an opportunity to reinforce the suffering in store for anyone who tests the limits of accepted behavior. A sitting confession can be made right away. From his or her seat, the person simply says, "I want to confess that I have failed. I want to make peace and continue in patience with God and the church and in the future to take better care."

Serious offenses require a kneeling confession. The person is asked to come forward and kneel near the ministers' bench, where the bishop will question the offender about the offense. Then the person leaves the area, going to an upstairs room perhaps, while the bishop tells the congregation what has been reported about the accused. The whole congregation has to agree to any punishment, and members who have more information on the accused's behavior are supposed to speak up at this point. If nothing comes to light that would change their minds, the bishop recommends whatever punishment the ministers agreed to at their morning meeting. The congregation votes, stating one by one whether they agree with the bishop. Not surprisingly, most people agree most of the time.

A person accused of a serious offense, such as breaking a major rule of the Ordnung *or committing a sin condemned in the Bible, must confess whiling kneeling before the entire congregation.*

Once everyone has agreed, the accused is brought back into the meeting. The bishop asks the accused whether he or she is willing to accept the discipline of the church, and if so, the person is either forgiven on the spot or put under a temporary, six-week ban.

During the six weeks, the excommunicated person must attend preaching services and meet privately with the ministers for "admonition" during the hymn singing. The banned person sits near the ministers bench, bent over, with one hand covering his or her face to show humility and submission. After church, the person leaves without the usual lunch or visiting with other church members.

When six weeks is over, the person makes another kneeling confession in a Members Meeting, is asked whether he or she accepts the punishment and believes he or she is forgiven. The bishop then takes the person by the hand and helps him or her stand, welcoming the repentant sinner back into full fellowship. If the forgiven is a man, the bishop greets him with a Holy Kiss; the bishop's wife performs this office for women.

A Last Resort: Excommunication

Excommunication, or being "put under the ban," is used as a last resort by Amish churches. Only those who refuse to repent after six weeks of temporary excommunication, or who simply refused to come to church and cooperate with the process of confession at all, face permanent excommunication. Even then, they can always return by confessing their errors, repenting, and forsaking the offending behavior. The goal of excommunication and the shunning associated with it is to bring offenders back into the church, in conformity with Amish regulations of behavior.

One of the hardest duties of the deacon is said to be his role in communicating between the church and errant members. He's the person sent to confront the accused, and when attempts to counsel the person back into compliance with the church fail, it falls to the deacon, along with a minister, to deliver the news of excommunication to the banned.

When a person refuses to confess a sin before the church, the membership votes to ban or excommunicate and shun the individual. Shunning, which requires a spouse to refuse to have sexual relations with the banned person, or eat at the same table, or receive anything from him or her, wreaks havoc with the marriage relationship. Often a spouse will ask to be banned along with the offender rather than shun his or her partner. The church places more value on the vow of baptism than on the marriage vow, and anyone caught not shunning a banned spouse faces excommunication unless he or she is willing to confess it as a sin and repent.

> ### Ironies and Oddities
>
> When the deacon and minister go to deliver the excommunication decision, they engage in a bit of ecumenical ritual by using the formula followed by the (Catholic) Benedictines. They recite a Bible verse translated into German by Martin Luther: "To deliver such an one unto Satan for the destruction of the flesh, that the spirit may be saved in the day of the Lord Jesus." (I Cor. 5:5)

Social Avoidance: Shunning

The practice of shunning has always set the Amish apart, and often throughout their history been the cause of divisions within those who left to form other groups. Shunning, or *Meidung* in German, is a powerful form of social control. The threat of isolation, until one confesses and returns to accepted Amish behavior, or for life if one refuses, prevents most people from coloring outside the lines of Amish boundaries.

Shunning is especially painful in a society made up of small communities and large, interrelated families. Amish children aren't taught independence and self-reliance;

quite the opposite. They're taught to submit to authority, to do as they're told, to work in groups, and gain approval through obedience. Amish people spend very little time alone; social interaction is almost constant.

So for an Amish person, excommunication and shunning means losing the companionship and support of an entire social network. No wonder few withstand the pressure to come back into the fold.

The Plain Truth

Some Amish families bend the rules of shunning at home. At family gatherings, the mother may spread a large tablecloth over two tables only inches apart, rather than seat banned relatives at a separate table. This way, church members can follow the rules without ostracizing relatives. But in public, all church members have to strictly observe the rules of shunning.

By requiring family members to shun their own spouse, brother, sister, parent, child, aunts, uncles, or cousins, the church also demonstrates and enforces its authority over the family. The church is the highest authority in Amish society, then the family, and last and least, the individual.

Members can talk with shunned members, but can't accept anything from them or even shake hands. They can't do business, eat at the same table, or accept a car ride from a shunned person, and as mentioned earlier, spouses can't have sexual relations with a shunned spouse.

The practice of shunning casts a pall over the shunned for the rest of their lives. A few have even committed suicide following their banishment from their Amish family and friends.

While stricter Amish church districts continue to shun the person unless he or she returns to the Amish church, others take a slightly less severe course. If the person later joins a Mennonite, Brethren, or other pacifist Anabaptist church, the shunning edict may be dropped.

Words Unspoken: Silence in Amish Culture

The Amish (as well as their cousins, the Mennonites) are known for their refusal to take up arms against others. Nor do they often engage in verbal confrontations.

Silence, on the other hand (both literal refusal to speak and simply ignoring another as though he or she doesn't exist) are used by the Amish to express anger and disapproval, or pressure a person to change behavior. Silence can also be imposed on the other person by depriving him or her of the right to speak or refusing to listen.

In his book *Amish Society*, John Hostetler makes a powerful point about the destructive use of silence in Amish culture to control and hide behavior in the church, home, and community.

> Of the many uses made of silence among the Amish, some bring pain and misery to human relationships. Silence following excommunication is a punishment wrought with finality, as is the silence of shunning at the table. Silence is turned into aggression when an offended father does not speak to his family at the table. He expects his wife to know from the context and the series of past events what the trouble is. The silenced preacher, bereft of his audience, suffers the punishment of his calling, for there is much he would say but he is "benched." No one will ever know how many crimes are smothered in silence. When a bishop's house burned to the ground well after midnight, two persons lost their lives. Although the police found evidence of arson, the investigation was met with silence.

The Least You Need to Know

- Only married men can be ordained in the Amish church. Each church district has one bishop, two ministers or preachers, and one deacon.

- Amish leaders are nominated by the congregation but chosen by lot.

- Those accused of an offense who refuse to confess, either privately or before the whole church, are excommunicated or banned.

- Banned persons are shunned until they repent and ask to rejoin the church.

Part  3

Inside Out: Religion as a Way of Life

How does their language help preserve Amish culture, and why can they ride in cars, but not own them? Take the bus, but not a plane? Use electricity, but not inside their houses? And how are the rules changing? Religious beliefs shape Amish family life as well. We'll take a look at how children are raised and educated, the relationship between husbands and wives, and what happens when people get old or sick.

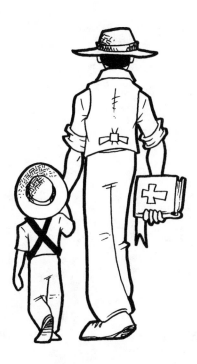

Chapter 9

A Living Faith: Separation in Daily Life

In This Chapter

- How language forms Amish identity
- Amish homes and farms
- Compromises with telephones and electricity
- How horses fit into Amish life

The Amish seek separation from the world as a way to maintain religious purity. Their values are radically different from mainstream American society. They value group identity over individual identity; obedience over individual initiative; humility over pride; and cooperation over independence. In all things, their culture requires conformity to the group as a sign of giving up individuality for obedience to God.

The Amish fear too much interaction with the world would lead many of their people to adopt the easier life promoted by mainstream values. The greatest concern of the Amish is to perpetuate their faith among their own people. Their culture is designed to do that by applying religious principles to every aspect of life, making life and faith one.

Mother Tongue: Language Defines a People

The language we speak defines us in many ways. It identifies us as belonging to a certain culture or region. Our accent and slang help pinpoint the place we live and the people we grew up with. Language also affects our definition of ourselves. It shapes our ideas about the world and where we belong in it.

Language helps bind us to our native culture. The tongue we learn as children remains the one in which we speak most freely, express our thoughts and feelings most accurately.

The Amish use three languages: one for daily conversation, another for religious or sacred purposes, and a third for commerce with the world around them.

Pennsylvania German: The Language of Home

The native tongue of the Amish is a dialect, or branch, of German called *Pennsylvania German* or, more popularly, *Pennsylvania Dutch*. Their sixteenth century Swiss German forebears spoke the dominant language of their culture. But when the Amish came to America, keeping their native language became a symbol of holding to the traditional ways, as well as a means of defining themselves as separate from the rest of society.

> **Vas Es Das?**
>
> **Pennsylvania Dutch** is a popular term for the German dialect spoken by the Amish, more accurately called Pennsylvania German. "Pennsylvania" refers, of course, to the colony where most early Amish (and Mennonite) settlers lived and where the language was most frequently heard. *Deutsch*, the German word for "German," sounded like "Dutch" to English speakers, so they started referring to the language by that name.

Amish children learn Pennsylvania German from their parents, and it remains the language of home, family, and friends throughout their lives. Most don't learn English until they go to school, and few become as comfortable in that language as in their own. Pennsylvania German is primarily an oral language; though its words have been recorded in writing, the Amish read and write in German and English.

Though their dialect continues to be the language of daily life for the Amish, it's becoming diluted by the English words and phrases they sprinkle in. However, they consider speaking too much English among themselves as a sign of pride, showing off one's knowledge. English is associated with education and the world. Too much knowledge or education remains a sign of "high" culture, promoting individualism and pride. Amish culture values just the opposite, and sometimes discourages its members from learning too much.

Old German: The Language of God

For the Amish, German is a sacred language. They read from Bibles written in an old version of German, translated from Latin by Martin Luther, and consider it the "original language." Prayer books and the *Ausbund* hymnal, the *Martyrs Mirror* and other religious books are all written in this old version of German. But a few recent editions of religious books printed in German with English translations can be found on the shelves of Amish stores, and even a translation of key scriptures from the old high German into Pennsylvania German.

Though German is the preferred language for religious services, Amish leaders have little education and most are not fluent in high German. In worship services, they read aloud from the old German language scriptures and prayer books, and sing the old hymns. But they preach mostly in the Pennsylvania German dialect, with smatterings of German and even a few English words now and then.

> **Ironies and Oddities**
>
> Although the Amish speak in dialect, not all speak Pennsylvania German. A group of Amish from Switzerland and France settled in Adams County, Indiana in the 1850s and brought language with them. Today their descendents, perhaps 10 percent of the Old Order Amish, speak a Swiss German dialect that Pennsylvania German speakers can't understand. When they get together, they often have to communicate in English.

English: The Language of Commerce

English is the second language of the Amish, the language they use to interact with the larger society around them.

The Amish learn English mostly to conduct business with the English-speaking world, and to a lesser extent to be able to read its publications and know in general what it's up to. When almost all Amish men worked as farmers, they needed little English beyond the words for measurements and money, the language of buying and selling, of the feed mill and auction barn. Women needed to know enough to buy at English-run stores whatever they didn't produce at home, and perhaps to sell hand made goods and home grown foods to English customers from their home.

Since the Amish economy has widened considerably in the last quarter century, today's Amish workers may need to know considerably more English. The more they work around English speakers, the more technical and business language they require.

Ironies and Oddities

Until the 1960s, when small, rural schools were combined into larger schools to offer better education, Amish children frequently attended local public schools, especially in the Midwest. (The move to parochial schools started in the 1930s in Pennsylvania.) Public school teachers were always "English," college graduates from the mainstream culture. Most Amish children attending public school learned English at home as preschoolers, but every year, a few would come to school knowing only their native language. This put them at a disadvantage with teachers who didn't know Pennsylvania Dutch, and made it hard to keep up with their class.

Since then, however, the Amish in most communities have pretty well taken over their own education and now most Amish children attend Amish schools. Students study English in school and teachers use it for instruction, but teachers as well as students are Amish and speak Pennsylvania Dutch for everyday use.

Yet it all remains the language of business. The Amish church discourages friendships between the Amish and their more worldly neighbors, even Mennonites. Some Amish people are naturally outgoing and do enjoy friendships beyond their culture, of course, even inviting English friends into their homes. Yet on the whole, language helps define the Amish community and encourages socializing within the group, because they always feel most comfortable speaking in their native tongue.

House and Home: The Amish Homestead

The *Ordnung* forbids Amish homes from having many of the modern conveniences that are standard in other homes. Doing things by hand requires more hands, builds cooperation and camaraderie among family members, and prevents appliances from becoming status symbols or sources of pride. Because they conform to the community style, Amish homesteads remain recognizable, even as they evolve to meet new economic needs.

The old farmhouses were built over generations, often with one gable facing the road and a long addition stretched out to the side, fronted by a long porch. Some are huge, rambling structures linked by a walkway to a second house as big as the first, the *grossdaadi haus* where the grandparents move to make room for the younger generation's family. The farmyards look pretty much like other farms, with a big

The Plain Truth

Though Amish and "English" children in public schools were often friends on the playground, they didn't invite each other home as they would friends of their own culture. When Amish children felt uncomfortable with the differences of their English classmates, they would retreat into their own language, sharing secrets and jokes with their peers.

red or white bank barn and a number of outbuildings: a chicken house, maybe a pig barn, a wood shed, an outhouse.

Amish farmhouse with attached grossdaadi haus.

Newer Amish homesteads often feature a large, square white house built near the road on a few acres carved out from the home place or a neighbor's farm. These have a smaller white barn, big enough for a horse or two, a buggy, hay, and feed. But they're not farms; they're the homes of adult Amish children who can't afford a farm and have to seek work elsewhere.

In northern Indiana, the trend in new Amish homesteads returns to the old style of building the homestead at the end of a long lane, distancing it from the roadside. The new homesteads, though include a cluster of buildings around a central gravel yard at the end of the lane. One is the primary home, and often a second, smaller home stands nearby, apparently replacing the large, attached *grossdaudi haus* of earlier years. A medium-sized barn may accommodate horses and buggies for both families, and several small outbuildings serve various functions. Often an extra building houses as a shop for an Amish business.

Yet all these styles of homestead and house look distinctly Amish. The houses are white, the barns red or white. Window treatments vary by settlement—white window shades in some communities, green in others, or blue or white curtains—but are always simple and uniform within the community. A large, weed-free vegetable garden grows in tidy rows at one side of the house, and a brilliant display of flowers grows in neat rows in the front or side yard. On a Monday morning, line after line of clothing hangs drying in the breeze beside the house.

Amish homesteads change gradually, though, as surely as the rest of society. It just takes them longer, and the changes are subtler. Indoor plumbing is now the norm.

On a recent visit to Indiana, the bright yellow and red flowers gardens seemed fewer and smaller. More and more Amish homes had curtains at the windows, where once only white pull-down shades were allowed. A few of the newer houses, covered in modern, manufactured siding, were pale gray or another subtle color, rather than the white that has been standard for centuries. I even saw an Amish farmer standing at the edge of his field along a back road, talking on a cell phone!

> ### CAUTION Make No Mistake
>
> Though the Amish forego many modern conveniences, they don't live like pioneers. They often have stoves, refrigerators, washers and dryers, water heaters, and even overhead lights, all of which can be powered by bottled gas. Kerosene space heaters replace wood stoves in many homes. Indoor plumbing was once forbidden, but now is accepted in all but the most conservative districts. Dishwashers, small electrical appliances, and electric sewing machines still are not used.

Opening the Door to Telephones and Electricity

One of the most obvious signs of an Amish homestead is the lack of electrical or telephone lines and poles running from the road to the house and barn. Nevertheless, using telephones and electricity has become common in Amish life.

Though telephone ownership was banned by Amish bishops early in the twentieth century as too worldly, using phones, like riding in cars, was never banned. A few decades later, the Amish started building homemade phone booths—white-sided buildings that matched their houses—at convenient roadside locations. These would be shared as "community phones" and used for emergencies. Gradually, the Amish moved these phone booths to the ends of their lanes, near the road. The rationale was that keeping it outdoors prevented the telephone from dividing families, tempting women to gossip rather than work, and interrupting family life with incoming calls.

Similarly, the Amish forged a compromise with electrical power. By 1920, the bishops had banned electricity from public lines or private generators, as well as electric light bulbs. But they accepted 12-volt battery power, so gasoline or diesel motors could be used to power stationery farm equipment (though not tractors for field use) and flashlights. Some feared electricity itself, not understanding what it was and how it worked, while others simply feared that it would break down the boundaries between the Amish and the world.

Over the years, the Amish bishops have adapted the rule to accommodate economic necessity. The first change occurred when farm equipment manufacturers quit producing the machinery Amish farmers needed and old equipment wore out. To make their own, or adapt tractor-drawn equipment, the Amish needed electric welders run by generators. So the bishops allowed one rule to change so another, more significant one could be preserved.

> **CAUTION**
>
> **Make No Mistake**
>
> Despite all the compromises with modernism made by the Amish in recent decades, most Amish homes are still quite unlike those of most Americans. Old Order Amish homes don't have electricity, wall-to-wall carpeting, telephones, central heating, television, radio, tape or CD players, computers, toasters, microwaves, or other small appliances.

A similar compromise happened in milk production, allowing bulk tanks required by processing plants to be run by generators like the ones that run welders. Later, power tools were allowed to run off the same kind of generators, allowing Amish men to move into the construction business. The generators can also be used to charge 12-volt batteries for a variety of uses.

Finally, the invention of inverters, which can take power from a 12-volt battery and convert it into the same kind of 110-volt power available from power lines, made it possible for the Amish to use diesel generators to make homemade electricity. This is used in Amish businesses to run cash registers, copy machines, fax machines, calculators, and other office machinery. Yet by requiring electricity to be run through the battery instead of using it directly from the generator, the bishops limit the number and power of electronics that can be used.

And always, they have allowed Amish people to use electricity and telephones owned by non-Amish people. Rented homes and businesses can have electricity and telephones, and the Amish can use them. But if they buy the building, the Amish have a year to tear out the electrical wiring. Phones have to be removed immediately.

Cell phones are a whole new ball of wax, presenting a challenge that's hard to meet. Initially used by men working in non-Amish businesses, they're finding wider acceptance. Because they get around the rule against connecting to the world's grid of wires, they so far have slipped through the *Ordnung*, in some communities and the Amish, who have used telephones and even voice mail for years, are quick to embrace the practicalities of cell phones.

Real Horse Power: Enduring Symbol of Amish Life

The horse and *buggy* is the mostly widely recognized Amish symbol. Amish people in different areas of the country drive various horse-drawn vehicles besides buggies, including spring wagons, open carriages, and farm wagons.

Buggy design varies by settlement. The most common Pennsylvania version has gray sides and top, while from Ohio westward, the buggy is black. Midwestern buggies lack the rounded top edges of Pennsylvania buggies, giving them a boxier look. Local variations include yellow and white tops in parts of Pennsylvania.

Vas Es Das?

Though the term **buggy** technically means an open carriage such as those sometimes seen in Pennsylvania, in many Amish settlements the word is used to refer to any covered Amish carriage. In Lancaster County, Pennsylvania, "carriage" means an enclosed, two-seated vehicle. In Holmes County, Ohio, a two-seater is a "surrey" while a one-seat carriage, with or without a top, is called a "buggy."

Make No Mistake

The burden of safety falls on motorists when sharing the road with Amish buggies, because cars pose a far greater danger. When I learned to drive, my father taught me to take my foot off the gas near the top of a rise in the road and get ready to brake, in case there was a buggy on the other side. It's still a good precaution.

Buggies can have one or two seats, but while the single seat model is uncovered in Pennsylvania, most midwestern Amish enclose both the single and double seat models. The Swiss Amish in Indiana and elsewhere have never covered their vehicles.

On the outside, the buggies look quite standard. They roll on wooden wheels, drawn by a single horse. Most states with substantial Amish populations require buggies to have battery-operated headlights and turn signals. Another state requirement, a red and orange reflective triangle on the back—called a slow-moving vehicle sign—to help motorists see the dark buggies at night. This requirement has sometimes met with Amish resistance. In most groups, however, these safety measures are accepted.

What you can see from the outside looks quite uniform, much as it has for the past century, making the buggy an enduring symbol of Amish culture. But today's buggy owners can order a variety of carpeting, upholstery, and accessories built into their vehicles, such as a four-wheel brakes, clocks, and speedometers. (Why would a buggy need a speedometer? Good question.)

Construction and comfort has improved over the last quarter century as well, from basic wooden wagons covered with painted canvas tops and sides to fiberglass bodies and shafts with vinyl tops and sides. The side doors used to be rolled up curtains made of the same material as the sides, but the newer style has sliding doors with glass windows. Glass windshields are now standard in most communities.

Horses haven't changed, though, and remain an undiluted symbol of Amish identity for both themselves and outsiders. Used for transportation, horses limit the distance traveled and the pace of life. In practical terms, this means more time for reflection or conversation in the buggy, and limits the size of Amish settlements.

> **Ironies and Oddities**
>
> A driving horse is a common six-teenth birthday present for Amish boys, a sign that they're old enough to attend the Sunday night gatherings of young people without their parents. Those who really want to "sow their wild oats," though, don't stop at buggies—they go right for cars.

On the farm, machinery—even if it's powered by a diesel engine—still must be pulled by draft horses or mules. Horse power limits the pace of work, the size of farms, and the hours in the day that work can be done. At the same time, horses and mules are cheaper to buy and maintain than today's expensive tractors, combines, and other farm equipment. And farming with horses requires more workers in the field and barn, insuring family and community cooperation.

Horses tie the Amish to the land, keep them from migrating to cities, and reinforce their agricultural roots even for families that work in factories instead of on farms.

Above all, the horse is a symbol of tradition and identity that can't be modified. Teenage boys may decorate their buggies, but they can't blend into the world traveling at 10 to 20 miles an hour behind a horse.

The Least You Need to Know

- "Pennsylvania Dutch" is actually "Pennsylvania German," because it's a dialect of German. It has nothing to do with the Dutch language of the Netherlands.

- Amish homes have evolved over the years, but they're still not allowed to have electricity or telephones, central heating, wall-to-wall carpeting, radio, TV or electronic entertainment, small electrical appliances, or computers in the house. Phones can be installed outside, and cell phone use is growing.

- Major appliances are run on bottled gas, giving Amish women in some communities the convenience of refrigerators, stoves, water heaters, and even bright overhead lighting, while other Amish women still cook on woodstoves and a few use iceboxes.

◆ Buggy designs vary only slightly by settlement and have changed little over the years, but their construction, inside appearance, and comfort has improved greatly in recent decades.

◆ Horses remain the most unchanged symbol of Amish identity, both for transportation and farm work.

Chapter 10

Flags of Faith: Amish Dress and Appearance

In This Chapter

- ◆ How Amish fashion symbolizes faith
- ◆ What women and girls wear
- ◆ What men and boys wear
- ◆ Hair styles and grooming standards

Americans find the Amish way of dressing quaint and peculiar. Yet Amish clothing isn't so different from the long, dark habits worn by traditional Catholic nuns, or the broad-brimmed black hats of Hasidic Jewish men.

Stephen Scott points out in his excellent book on the dress of Plain people, *Why Do They Dress That Way?*, that Amish clothing is a type of religious garb intended to set its wearer apart from the world. The difference is that the Amish have no separate religious orders; as Anabaptists, they believe every Christian is called to devote his or her life to God. Plain dress proclaims this commitment to a higher order, the belief in a purpose greater than individual expression. It's a badge of religious faith.

Amish clothing also serves as a kind of ethnic flag, recognizable to both insiders and outsiders. For the Amish are both an ethnic and religious group. A person born to Amish parents becomes automatically part of that culture—speaking, dressing, working, and cooking in the ways of their ancestors.

Plain clothing is important in forming and reinforcing group identity, giving those who choose it a sense of security and belonging. It serves as a constant reminder to the wearer, as well as others, of his or her religious commitment. Plain clothing also erects a visible barrier between the Amish and those outside the group. By preventing its wearer from identifying too much with "worldly" people, and vice versa, it reinforces the Amish "us and them" view of the world.

Fashion Statement: Symbolic Meaning of Amish Clothing

Amish clothing embodies the personal qualities that they value most and believe Christians are required to exhibit. These include humility, modesty, nonconformity to the non-Christian world, and commitment to the church.

While other types of clothing could meet these particular requirements, the Amish pattern of dress has evolved over centuries into a powerfully symbolic language that they read with ease. Outsiders see a person in plain dress and simply think, "Amish." But subtle details of dress and grooming tell another Amish person much more, such as …

- Whether he or she is Old Order Amish, Beachy Amish, Old Order Mennonite, and so on.

- The person's home settlement or even church district.

- The person's marital status.

- Whether a man is ordained.

- Whether a woman is married to an ordained man.

- Whether he or she is dressed for work, a trip away from home, or going to church.

Amish clothing follows certain general guidelines. Garments are supposed to be practical, durable, relatively inexpensive, and conceal rather than reveal the body. They should help the wearer blend in (at least with others in plain dress!) rather than stand out in a crowd. Plain clothing is deliberately old-fashioned, declaring its owner's allegiance to tradition rather than fad or contemporary society.

The Amish reject adornment of any kind because it expresses pride and the desire of the individual to be admired by others. They follow the instructions to early Christians found in I Timothy 2:9 and I Peter 3:3, which forbid wearing "gold and pearls" and "gold jewelry," respectively. Decorative clothing, hair ornaments, and jewelry—including wedding bands—are out. Even wristwatches are considered jewelry, though they're one of the first things to be accepted among more liberal groups. Eyeglasses, being functional, are accepted, though they should have metal or plain black plastic frames.

> **Make No Mistake** _____
>
> Don't assume everyone wearing plain dress in an Amish settlement is Old Order Amish. It can be hard to distinguish one group from another, especially in areas like eastern Pennsylvania, where so many live intermingled. Old Order Mennonites, for example, dress very much like the Old Order Amish, but in most groups, married women wear black strings on their head coverings instead of white.

Why the Uniform?

Requiring uniform clothing accomplishes several Amish goals. The Amish believe that every Christian is equal, and express that by requiring everyone to wear the same simple style of dress. Even among the Amish, wealth varies by family and can cause jealousy. Dressing everyone alike makes it harder to tell the "haves" from the "have-nots." (Private and even some urban public schools require student uniforms for the same reason.) The dress code also reminds the "haves" that wealth doesn't make them better than others, and helps prevent money from being a source of social status. (Requiring identical vehicles serves the same purpose.)

Uniform, modest clothing also helps direct attention away from personal appearance so that virtues can shine through. Though Amish people certainly notice beauty, they don't place as high a value on it as contemporary society. And when everyone dresses the same and wears the same hairstyle, it's amazing how much more interesting personality and character seem, even to adolescent boys! Amish girls can be beautiful or plain, but the difference between the two doesn't seem as great as in contemporary society. A ready laugh, lively personality, and sparkling eyes seem to count for more than a perfect face.

Basics of Amish Clothing

The Amish wear only solid color fabrics, but specific color combinations may vary from one community to another.

The composition of fabric depends on what's available from manufacturers; synthetic blends are most common. Older women often wear darker colors than younger women, and little girls' dresses and boy's shirts may be pastels. Dark blue, slate blue, forest green, burgundy, gray, brown, and black are colors often worn by older women, while younger women might branch out into royal blue, purple, peach, or teal, for instance.

Black is the color of formality and mourning. Women wear black dresses to communion and funerals, and when in mourning. Brides can't be married in white, but they can be buried in it, if they belong to the Lancaster Amish. Elsewhere, though, they may be buried in black. White is also the color of innocence; babies are buried in white.

Most men's work pants and jackets are made of dark blue denim, though black denim is preferred by the Lancaster Amish. Sunday pants, vests, and coats are usually black. In summer, men and boys wear natural straw hats for work and, in some areas, to church. In the Midwest, black dyed straw hats are worn for church, but in winter, black hats of fur (usually rabbit) felt are the rule in all areas.

Amish men's coats and pants, both for work and dress, are usually made by Amish seamstresses or small manufacturers. Hats are manufactured especially for the Amish market, in all the required styles. Amish country stores carry men's and boys' clothing, infants and standard children's clothing, and women's nightwear and underwear from standard manufacturers. Even women's head coverings (*kapps*) and bonnets are now available ready-made by Amish women for sale in local stores, another way for them to earn money from home. Only women's dresses, capes, and aprons seem to still be universally homemade.

Make No Mistake

Age has the same effect on Amish people as it does on the world; as they get older, they tend to dress more conservatively. Along with wearing darker colors, older Amish women wear their skirts longer and are slower to adopt changes than younger women.

Plain or Fancy?

Plain and fancy are sometimes in the eye of the beholder, or the symbolism assigned by tradition. In hat brims, for instance, wider is plainer. Pennsylvania Amish men wear wider hat brims than those in the Midwest, and ministers' hat brims are wider than those of nonordained men.

Brims are one thing, but bands are another. In hat bands, wider is showier, and therefore narrow is plainer. The same applies to the waistbands on women's aprons.

The general rule about the Amish being more conservative in the eastern United States and getting more liberal as you move west holds in clothing—with the exception of small, ultra-conservative groups here and there.

Dressing Women and Girls

Old Order Amish women wear solid-color, shirtwaist dresses with high, round, collarless necks. The bodice opens in front, and is held shut with either straight pins or snaps; buttons are considered too showy. Skirts are pleated or gathered at the waist, depending on local custom.

Sleeve and skirt length vary, and provide a little room for self-expression—or else an opportunity to challenge tradition a little. Younger women usually wear their skirts somewhere from just below the knee to mid-calf. Middle-aged women usually are seen in mid-calf length skirts, and elderly women wear them ankle length.

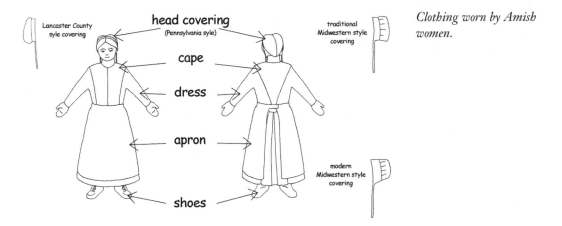

Clothing worn by Amish women.

Sleeve length and style show interesting variations by age and settlement. It used to be that women wore long sleeves without cuffs, the style that still prevails on dresses worn for church or other dress-up occasions, and on older women. But in summer, it's also common to see middle-aged women wearing sleeves just below the elbow. Young women and teenaged girls in some settlements get away with short sleeves gathered into cuffs or with elastic, just above the elbow or even shorter.

From infancy until adolescence, girls in many settlements wear dresses with bodices that button in the back, with pinafore style aprons over them. The aprons also button in back, just below the neck, but are open below. Aprons may match the dresses, or be made of contrasting black or white fabric, depending on the local custom. In some settlements, girls wear aprons only to church, not to school or at home.

Capes and Aprons

Amish women wear a cape over their dress bodice, and an apron over the skirt. Customs vary somewhat from settlement to settlement; some women don't wear a cape for working at home, while others always wear theirs.

In the Midwest, particularly, the cape and apron are usually made of the same fabric as the dress and is virtually indistinguishable from it. Lancaster Amish women make their capes of black fabric; capes may be either black or match the dress. Aprons worn away from home have waistbands that are pinned at the side (except in Lancaster, where they're pinned in the back), while work aprons have longer strings so they can be tied in back. In a few Amish groups, women wear old-fashioned aprons with very long strings that cross at the back of the waist and tie in front.

> **Ironies and Oddities**
>
> Sometimes you can see a trend coming by observing young Amish people who quietly challenge traditional clothing styles. A young Amish woman waitress in Indiana recently was seen wearing sleeves that were not only short, but that flared widely around her arms—clearly a more "showy" style than is traditional! Old Order people say that such gradual changes in style, if left unchecked, lead to "drift."

Amish capes are triangular pieces of fabric worn with the wide point tucked into the back of the apron waist band or strings, and the two narrow points draped over the shoulder and tucked in the front waistband. Some groups cross the narrow front ends, while others bring them straight down and tuck the ends in at the waist. Others cut the points off and sew the ends of the cape directly onto the dress itself.

> **The Plain Truth**
>
> The colors of capes, aprons, and head caps are highly symbolic, but the exact symbolism varies by settlement. Sunday capes and aprons are usually made of white organdy, but married women in some groups wear black, or ones that match their dresses. From their teens until they marry, girls in most settlements wear a black *kapp* to church, denoting their single status. Middle-aged single women sometimes change to white *kapps* when they become resigned to not marrying.

In some settlements, girls are dressed in capes and aprons, rather than pinafore style aprons, beginning around age eight.

Head Coverings

Whether they're called *kapps, prayer coverings, prayer veilings, head caps,* or simply *coverings,* Amish women's head coverings are among the most symbolic items of clothing they wear.

As one Amish man told sociologist Donald Kraybill, "The head covering is a symbol of the woman's subjection to the man and to God. It is worn at all times, especially in the presence of men and while praying."

The Plain Truth

Because it's so powerfully symbolic of submission, the size and use of head coverings diminished among women in the twentieth century who wanted a more equal role in the church and at home. Until the last quarter century, women still wore small prayer coverings in the Mennonite Church, and older women wore them at home. Members of the more conservative churches wore larger coverings both at home and at church. But as you moved from Old Order groups up the ladder of "higher" churches, the covering shrank in size with relative liberalness of the group. Finally, it disappeared altogether from all but the most conservative Mennonite churches.

One sign of "drift" among Amish women is the diminishment of the size of their head coverings and wearing them with the strings untied. This causes strong feelings among the traditional Amish. One writer to *Family Life* magazine quoted an old proverb: "Cap strings flying loose on the down road to hell." Amish coverings are worn on the back of the head. Tying strings under the chin is a sign of conservatism, and women always tie their cap strings for church. At other times, many women and girls leave them hanging down and pin the caps to their hair with straight pins, though older and more conservative women tie them. Many women even wear specially made coverings to bed, since they never know when they might want to pray.

Kapp style varies by settlement, with the most conservative having a wider front band that covers the ears. The back or crown of the covering may be heart-shaped with one pleat down through the middle of the crown (as in the Lancaster, Pennsylvania settlement) or round with many pleats along the sides of the crown. In some areas, a small bow is sewn at the bottom of the crown, at the nape of the neck, while others have a drawstring in back.

Vas Es Das?

Kapp, prayer covering, head cap, covering, and prayer veiling are all terms used for the small, white cap with long ribbon strings that Amish women wear on the back of their heads to cover their hair and show submission to God and men.

Little girls wear prayer coverings for church from about four years of age or even earlier, depending on the community, though in many areas they don't start wearing a covering full-time until they reach adolescence. Girls wear white coverings at home and black ones to church, until they marry; then they wear white ones all the time.

Outwear, Shoes, and Stockings

In cold weather, Amish women wrap themselves in black wool shawls and wear large black bonnets over their prayer coverings when they leave home. They wear short, dark coats for working, and many younger women also wear them for going to town or other informal occasions. Some conservative groups won't permit coats unless they're covered with a shawl.

Summer bonnets are made of lightweight material, and among less traditional groups are often dispensed with altogether. Bonnet styles vary not only by season, but by settlement and group affiliation.

An older style outer garment, less often seen, is the mantle—a cape with a collar that buttons in the front or is closed with hooks and eyes or snaps. (Some Amish do use buttons on garments too heavy for hooks and eyes to hold shut, and in other cases when they're simply more practical.) Young girls wear mantles in many settlements, as do women in a few very conservative Amish groups in Pennsylvania.

> **Ironies and Oddities**
>
> In Indiana, covering styles have changed in the last decade. Ready-made coverings sewn by single Amish women are made of stiff white material that's more washable than organdy. They have a deeper back section (hinnerdale) and wider front band (fedderdale) than the homemade pattern, which might make them seem more conservative. But older women often still wear their traditional, softer coverings handmade of organdy.

Older Amish women wear black stockings for going away from home, and Amish women of all ages wear them to church. But younger Amish women in progressive settlements often wear flesh-colored hose for working or shopping.

Shoe styles have changed, as the preferred, high black laced shoes preferred by the Old Order Amish became harder to find. Black tie shoes are still required for church and dress-up events, but tennis shoes have become common among some groups for children and even adults. And, of course, the Amish have always saved money by going barefoot in summer when possible. Children go barefoot at home, and even sometimes to school and church. Women and girls often work barefooted in summer around the home.

Dressing Men and Boys

While Amish women use straight pins or snaps to fasten their dresses, most Amish men wear buttons on their shirts, but they observe other restrictions. Most now wear standard, open-fronted shirts that open down the front and have turnover collars, but without pockets. For a number of groups, this represents a change from the traditional pullover style shirt that opens only part way down the front and fastens with a few buttons. The most conservative groups, though, retain the pullover shirt with either a standing or turnover collar. Among the conservative Amish of Swiss descent, men wear hooks and eyes on their shirts.

For everyday work, shirts are worn with only suspenders over them, weather permitting. But on Sundays, men cover their shirt with at least a vest in warm weather, or a coat in cold weather.

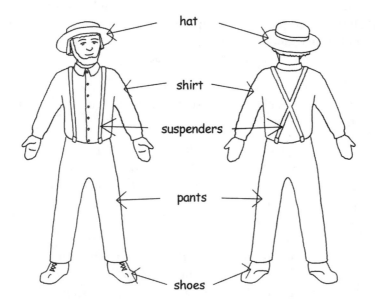

hat

shirt

suspenders

pants

shoes

Clothing worn by Amish men.

Coats for Every Occasion

Men's coats are a symbolic fashion, changing with age, role, and occasion as do women's capes and aprons. Both coats and vests fasten with hooks and eyes. Coats come in two styles: the straight cut, loose sack coat styled like a standard suit coat, but with a standing collar and no pockets, and the old-fashioned frock coat. The frock coat reaches to mid-thigh and features a kind of tailored skirt and a center back panel that is split below the waist.

Frock coats are the formal church wear of baptized members. Adult men wear frock coats (with or without vests, depending on local custom) to church in cool weather, vests alone in warm weather, and sack coats for other dress occasions. Ministers are required to wear frock coats to church in all weather. Until baptism, boys wear sack coats to church and for all dress-up occasions.

For work, men wear navy denim jackets fastened with hooks and eyes or, in Lancaster, buttons. Increasingly, though, Amish men buy the navy or black nylon-covered insulated work jackets with zippers available from mainstream manufacturers.

Broadfall Pants and Suspenders

Amish men's pants have popularly been called "barn door" pants for their wide front flap, but their proper name is broadfall pants. They originated as an alternative to the eighteenth century narrow fall style, whose front flap didn't extend all the way across the front. The broadfall was easier to make, and perhaps more convenient to wear as well. It became the popular style, and the Amish and other plain people carried it forward. Four buttons across the top fasten the fall at the waist.

To hold those pants up, Old Order Amish men wear suspenders rather than belts. Different groups make various rules about the suspenders, including how they fasten to the pants and what the back looks like.

Make No Mistake

Never underestimate the ability of the Amish to attach significance to the smallest detail of their clothing. Those tiny differences that you might mistake for signs of personal preference often have important symbolic meaning.

One group permits only one strap, worn diagonally across the chest and back over the right shoulder. Some permit elastic suspenders, while others forbid elastic as too new and worldly. Some wear only suspenders that cross in the back, forming an X, while others require those that meet in back, forming a Y, and some prefer either the X type or those with a small cross-piece between the back straps, forming an H. The great majority wear suspenders that fasten to their pants with buttons, but a few communities permit the more modern snap fasteners.

One small, ultra-conservative group, the "Nebraska Amish" of Mifflin County, Pennsylvania (so named because their founder came from Nebraska) reject suspenders all together as too new or worldly (having not been introduced until the late eighteenth century). They still lace their pants up the back as men did before the introduction of suspenders.

Hats and Shoes

Amish men cover their heads almost as often as women, and men's hats have their own symbolism. The width of a hat brim, shape of its crown, and width of its black ribbon band identifies the wearer as conservative or progressive. The wider the brim, lower the crown, and narrower the hat band, the more conservative the man, and his church, because hat styles are strictly regulated.

Black Sunday hats are made of fur felt, and worn for all dress occasions in cooler weather. The most conservative group, the Nebraska Amish mentioned previously, require a four-and-a-half inch brim on their hats, while comparatively liberal, mid-western groups allow brims as narrow as two-and-a-quarter inches. Most are around three inches to three-and-a-quarter.

Crowns can be plain (slightly rounded), creased, or depressed. Some Pennsylvania groups even regulate the crown of straw hats, requiring that they be flat, not creased. Natural straw hats have very narrow, black ribbon bands, while the bands on felt hats are slightly wider.

In summer, Amish men wear straw hats for work and to church. Some groups wear the same natural colored straw hats for both, but in the Midwest, black straw hats are common for Sunday wear.

Midwestern Amish boys and men often wear knitted navy blue *zippelkapps* for working in cold weather, but never to church. Boys wear hats like their fathers' for church, but often either go bareheaded to school or wear stocking caps in cold weather.

Vas Es Das?

Zippelkapp is the Pennsylvania German term for a knitted stocking cap.

Most Amish men and boys wear black laced oxford shoes for church and dress occasions. Older and more conservative men wear high-cut black dress shoes. For everyday, men and boys wear standard brown or black work boots.

Hair Styles for Women and Men

Amish women don't cut their hair, but always wear it up, parted in the middle and pulled back tightly into a bun at the back of the head. (Plain dressing but less conservative Mennonite women also wear their hair in a bun, but they pull it back less severely, allowing the hair to frame their faces more softly.)

Girls' hair is either braided and wound around the back of their heads or also gathered into a bun. I recently asked a young Amish woman working in an Indiana store whether adult women ever braided their hair, too, since their coverings always hide it. She said, "Hardly anybody even braids the little girls' hair anymore. It takes too much time." So buns are becoming more common for children, too.

Men and boys comb their hair in all directions from the crown. In the Midwest, the hair is cut (at home) in the shape of an inverted bowl. Eastern Pennsylvania groups, including those in Lancaster County, cut the sides longer than the bangs, a style often called "Dutch boy." In both styles, the back is blunt cut, rather than shaped to the back of the head.

Most Old Order Amish men grow beards when they marry, though some more conservative groups use the beard to signify baptism and church membership rather than marriage. What gives Amish men their distinctive look is that while they don't trim their beards, they do shave their mustaches, unlike worldly men who wear both a beard and mustache.

The Least You Need to Know

- ◆ To the Amish, the most minute details of dress signal important differences in church affiliation and home location.

- ◆ Women wear capes and aprons over the dresses to disguise their figures, but skirt and sleeve length vary by age.

- ◆ Women's prayer coverings are their most symbolic attire, symbolizing submission to God and men.

- ◆ Amish men's hats signal whether they belong to conservative or progressive groups.

- ◆ Amish men wear beards without mustaches as a sign of adulthood, growing them either when they marry or when baptized into the church.

11

Go Forth and Multiply: The Amish Family

In This Chapter

◆ Families fuel church growth

◆ Life, work, and faith all depend on families

◆ Men's and women's roles in the family

◆ Amish children at home

◆ Coming of age in the Amish culture

What makes Amish life *feel* different from your life or mine? If you were Amish, how would you think differently about yourself?

While most Americans think of themselves as individuals first, Amish people think of themselves first as members of a family, of an extended family, and of a community of families related by blood, marriage, beliefs, and shared activities. Every aspect of life, from birth to death, encompassing work, worship, and social activities, takes place within the family. Almost everything happens at home—either your own home or a neighbor's or relative's.

Amish life is lived as a group. The non-Amish farmer has plenty of time alone to contemplate while driving his tractor or combine. Amish farmers work their fields with sons, fathers, brothers, sometimes sisters and wives. Their horses are slower, but even when they're pulling mechanized implements, most often more than one person is needed to both drive the horses and accomplish the work. These same principles are carried over into Amish businesses, which involve as many family members as possible and employ other church members when necessary.

When family members aren't needed to lend a hand, they're often taken along to learn the skills involved, or just for company. The Amish farmer will take a son along when he plows a field or drives a wagon of grain to the feed mill. The youngster may help by hopping down from the plow to move a large stone out of the way, or helping to shovel grain and load bags of feed. But he's also learning his life's work and his role as an Amish man. The same is true in Amish shops, where teenage boys learn a trade from their father.

The Amish saying, "Many hands make light work" expresses their approach to work. Groups make even big jobs go faster and easier, and talking, joking, and playing games while you work makes it fun.

Growth Through Increase: The Amish Secret to Survival

Amish people don't try to convert others to their faith. How, then, do their groups keep growing, moving to new areas, and forming new settlements?

The answer is simple: They're very good at keeping their children at home in the faith. The large Amish family is the key to maintaining their culture and faith in a world whose values often conflict with their own.

Over 90 percent of Amish children decide to join the church when they grow up. Why? Because, as John Hostetler wrote in his book *Amish Society*, "Amish children are raised so carefully within the Amish family and community that they never feel secure outside it."

The main job of Amish adults, both women and men, is to raise Amish children. Sex is strictly prohibited before marriage, as is birth control after marriage (though some couples now reportedly do take steps to limit family size). While women do the majority of child care, the fact that most men work at home as farmers or, increasingly, in cottage industries, means their children spend many hours under their supervision as well. As soon as a child is old enough to do even minor chores like feeding chickens or helping pick up stones in a field, he or she helps out *Dat* as well as *Mam*.

The church teaches parents that their biggest responsibility is the spiritual welfare of their children. To them, protecting their children's souls requires training them in the "true religion," the "right way," which is the Amish way. Even as adults, Amish people who choose a different way are considered disobedient to their parents.

The subject of proper child rearing has garnered plenty of discussion in *Family Life* magazine over the years. One person wrote, "Probably no theme comes up in our sermons more frequently than the great responsibility that parents have to bring up their children in 'the fear of the Lord.' We have all heard again and again the saying that 'Children are the only treasures on earth we can take with us to heaven.'"

Vas Es Das?

A few Pennyslvania German words sound so much like their English counterpart that they hardly need defining. **Mam** is the word for Mom or mother; **Dat** means Dad or father.

Mam and *Dat*: The Amish Marriage

Like the Amish church, Amish families are patriarchal. The church and culture emphasize the biblical teachings of the Apostle Paul about the roles of men and women—that men are the head of women, as Christ is the head of the church, and that women are to "reverence" their husbands, and men to love and protect their wives. Amish couples believe that their relationship, to be approved by God and the church, must follow this teaching.

Authority in Amish families follows gender and age, so husbands have more authority than wives, grandfathers than fathers, grandmothers than mothers, older children more than younger. Boys don't begin to have greater authority than girls until late adolescence. Since the Amish consider authority God-given in both the church and family, and obedience a Christian duty, it's important for family members to know who has the most authority in any given relationship.

Women's Work Is Never Done

The old saying, "Men work from dawn to set of sun, but women's work is never done," could have been written about the Amish family. Amish men and women carry out traditional roles, sharing the work of farm and family—though as one Amish woman told sociologist Donald Kraybill, "Even my Dad says that he thinks the Amish women get the brunt of it all around."

That's because women not only wash, clean, cook, sew clothing, quilts and comforters, garden, and can food for the family, but also are responsible for yard work and sometimes helping with barn chores and field work. Men may help with some childcare, but never with cooking or dishwashing. And while Amish men have adapted modern sources of power to run the machinery they need to make a living, whether in the barn, field, or shop, the men who run the church haven't seen fit to make the same allowances for easing women's work.

Amish women are responsible for lawn care—without the help of power tools.

More recently, though, some of the laborsaving hydraulic and air pressure power used to run power tools and farm equipment has been adapted to household appliances. Washing machines, sewing machines, even mixers and blenders are available to many Amish kitchens. Propane gas ranges and refrigerators have long been available, though freezers require too much power to run without electricity, and were outlawed in some districts years ago. And of course microwaves, dishwashers, and other appliances that seem more luxury than necessity continue to be out of bounds.

Some Amish women do notice the difference between expectations for men and women, and feel that they carry more than their share of the burden. But even these women would probably not expect to have equal roles in the home and church. They've been raised to believe their highest calling is in serving, assisting, and supporting. They find satisfaction of having a clearly defined role in which they are well prepared to succeed.

> ### Ironies and Oddities
>
> I heard an Amish woman from Pennsylvania a few years ago talking about an argument in her church about using power lawn mowers. The bishops were refusing to allow them, though they allowed mechanized hay mowers and balers. The difference? Lawn mowing was women's work. One man reportedly stood up to the bishops, saying, "I won't use my wife like a mule."

Unlike women in contemporary society, who are often torn between expectations of success on the job and the needs of their family at home, married Amish women can concentrate on the demands of managing a household and rearing a large family. Demanding as that is, it doesn't divide their attention the way a job away from home would. And Amish women, and their husbands, firmly believe that children need lots of time and attention from their own parents to learn what they need to know.

The Plain Truth

Raised to expect fulfillment in marriage and motherhood, unmarried Amish women may struggle to feel valued by their culture and make a life for themselves. Those who work as "hired girls" for Amish couples are paid too little to support themselves, forcing them to live with their parents or seek work elsewhere.

One woman wrote to *Family Life*:

I often feel that the single Amish girl is discriminated against .... I'm single and on the shady side of twenty-nine. I skimped and saved for over 12 years before I was able to obtain a home of my own. Sad to say, I did not earn my money working for the Amish .... Most older girls had to sacrifice their biggest dream of all, that of having a family of their own. So why should they be asked to sacrifice a home as well?

Children assist both their parents with their work. Younger children help first around the house and in the yard and garden—the woman's realm. Older boys help with barn chores, as may girls, if they're needed. Older girls also help their mothers take care of younger children and with other woman's work.

While women are considered "boss" of the house and yard, and men are "boss" of the barn, fields, and any other areas used for supporting the family, final decisions rest with the man as head of the household. A woman's authority is whatever her husband grants her; it's not God-given, like his. In most households, the wife has authority to buy food, clothing, and household necessities, but the money to do so is handed out by her husband. He may trust her judgment on larger purchases that fall under her authority, such as furniture, but that's his choice. He certainly won't consult her on buying cattle or machinery. On the biggest decisions, though, such as where to live, whether to move, what real estate to buy, most husbands and wives try to reach a mutual decision.

Partnership, Not Romance

Amish couples not only live together, in many instances they work together. Even when they're performing different tasks, the work of each supports the other. They are not only mates, they're partners. The most important thing in an Amish marriage is not romance, but a feeling of harmony in sharing life's work.

Expressions of affection, in either gesture or word, are rare between married Amish couples. Their culture values deeds over words. Anger is more often expressed through silence than through shouting, leaving others to guess what's wrong. Just as they believe in living out their faith rather than speaking or writing about it, the Amish believe that living with their spouse, treating him or her with consideration and respect, is proof enough of love without having to declare it.

Nevertheless, Amish couples work as hard or as little at their relationships as worldly couples. In letters to *Family Life*, both men and women agonize over the loss of love in their marriage, advise that both partners need to work at making a happy union by making each other happy, and report both sadness and joy in their marriages.

Amish men and women consider themselves dependent on each other. The man recognizes the economic value of his wife's contributions. She bears the children, whose help is essential on their farm. Her gardening, preserving, and cooking feeds the family, and much of the family clothing is still made by her. She, in turn, knows she would be hard-pressed to support herself, let alone the children, without her husband to do the heavy work and supervise the boys. Healthy Amish marriages, like marriages in any culture, are based on mutual respect. The power balance is agreeable to both parties, because it's what they were raised with and consider both natural and ordained by God.

The Goal of Successful Parenthood

All parents want their children to grow up healthy and happy. But to Amish parents, that means something radically different than it means to parents in mainstream America. Ours is a society of individualism, where each person is responsible for his or her own life. We raise our children to become independent adults, to succeed on their own, self-supporting and self-sufficient. We expect young people to leave their parents' home in late adolescence and live with friends or in college dorms, to make a life for themselves with their peers. We pride ourselves on their willingness to strike out on their own, to survive without us, seeing it as a sign of our success as parents. If they eventually marry, we expect them to start a family of their own, whether across the street or the country.

Amish parents have a very different definition of success. They raise their children to become integral parts of their immediate family and community. Their goal is a seamless transition from childhood to adulthood, one stage of interdependence to another. Amish young adults are expected to live at home with their parents until they marry. They're not expected to rent apartments together, move out of the community or work outside the family. If they do take jobs "in town" or at a factory, as many Amish people have to today, they continue to live at home. Amish parents want their children to marry Amish spouses and move nearby, where the parents can visit regularly and help raise their grandchildren.

The Plain Truth _____

This 1978 excerpt from *Family Life* magazine spells out the Amish view of child-rearing:

> Our people have certainly been right to resist consistently any government demands to send our children to high school. It is already bad enough that they are away from their parents for eight school terms .... A family needs to do more than pray together. It needs to work together, visit friends together, read together, plan things together, eat together, share their joy and sorrows, hopes and disappointments. In short, the family needs to *live together.*

Not all young people are content to stay at home, of course, even if they are content to stay Amish. Those who want to meet new people and experience other communities may go work for Amish people in another settlement, but they remain part of the larger Amish community. Their parents can trust that someone in the church will hold their young adult accountable for his or her behavior.

When young adults choose not to join the church, they often move away from the family home as well. Letters to *Family Life* magazine from anguished parents talk about children who have left their Amish faith "leaving home," with everything home encompasses for them—family, faith, community. Amish parents aren't just pained by losing the companionship of their child; they fear for the life of his immortal soul if he doesn't come home and join the church.

Growing Up Amish: Amish Children

Much as parents in mainstream society love their children, each birth represents another mouth to feed, another education to fund, the cost of clothing, toys, transportation, food, lessons, and activities. Amish children, on the other hand, in addition to being loved represent an asset to their parents and community. Every birth boosts the social status of the parents, because children help insure both cultural and economic survival.

Children not only help insure the survival of the Amish church, but of their parents as well. On the farm, their value in labor outweighs the cost of raising them to adulthood. Children begin learning to work at age four. By six they have chores to do after school and during summers until they quit after eighth grade.

> **CAUTION**
>
> ### Make No Mistake
>
> Just because the Amish family sounds ideal, don't assume all Amish families are. Just as mainstream families aren't all like those in *Leave It to Beaver* or *Father Knows Best,* there are happy and unhappy Amish families, loving and abusive parents and spouses. In any culture, those who grow up loved are prepared to raise loving families in turn, and nurture happy and secure children.

By age 13, or when they finish eighth grade, children begin working full-time for their parents, either by farming, helping in the house and with childrearing, or working in the family business. They're expected to continue until they reach the age of 21. Young men who continue working on the farm after that age receive wages. Girls sent to "work out" among the non-Amish for wages turn their paychecks over to their fathers, though they usually get to keep a small percentage for themselves, which they may be required to bank until they reach 21.

Stages of Childhood

John Hostetler names four stages of childhood recognized by the Amish:

- **Babies**   from birth until the child walks
- **Young Children**   from walking until the child enters school
- **Scholars**   children of school age
- **Young People**   from adolescence until they marry

Amish children only go to school through eighth grade, so they make the transition from scholar to young person earlier than someone outside their culture would.

Amish culture loves and values babies, and their needs are attended to by all the older children and adults of their extended families. Amish children don't need godparents—the entire church community and extended family is supposed to help parents as needed. All children belong, not just to their immediate families, but to the community as well.

At around age two, when the child starts to exert a will of his own separate from his or her basic needs, the parents start to discipline the young child. Amish parents use physical punishment to correct any unwanted behavior, spanking with a hand, a switch, a buggy whip, or a strap. Most try not to hurt the child too much, but their culture expects them to use physical punishment to teach the child to give up his own will and obey those in authority. If a parent uses excessive force, it's unlikely other adults will notice or challenge him or her on it.

According to one Amish parent, most of the spankings are over by age six. By the time the child goes to school, he or she has learned to respect elders and follow orders.

Amish children spend most of their time with their parents, learning Amish values such as humility, obedience, respect for authority, admission of fault, and forgiveness. They also learn to work, starting around age four, and to carry out their respective gender roles.

The Plain Truth

My stepmother considers herself fortunate to have taught for more than 20 years at a public school where most students were Amish. "They were so easy to teach," she said. "Whatever the teacher said, they did. And the parents were behind us." She said Amish parents took a very active interest in their children's education, and both usually attended school conferences.

When children finish their formal schooling, they start to take on the adult roles of their society. They work full-time for their parents at home on the farm or in the family business. Or if the family needs more money, they may "work out" away from home. The Amish prefer for their children to work for other Amish people, so they're not exposed too much to the mainstream culture. Young people who "work out" for English people, whether in a business or home, are more likely to leave their Amish culture by choosing not to join the church.

Coming of Age

Coming of age in Amish society, taking on the full role of adults, is marked by two great events: Joining the church and getting married.

As Amish young people approach the age when they have to decide whether to join the church, the society suddenly relaxes a little of its control on them. They still work and live at home, but at age 16 they choose a "gang", "crowd", or "buddy group" to run around with on Sundays after church and at evening sings and other activities. In Pennsylvania, the groups are named and cross church district lines. Some groups follow the example of their parents, while others are made up of rebellious young people who buy themselves cars, get together on Saturday nights to drink, play cards, or dance. Occasionally, an Amish youth gets arrested for drunk driving or the police raid an underage drinking party, much to the embarrassment of the church leaders.

Nevertheless, Amish culture tolerates a degree of rebellious behavior that many non-Amish parents would be unwilling to accept. Until the young people join the church, however, they're not subject to its rules. And by the time they reach late adolescence, those who have lived under the strict control of their parents for so long are often unwilling to tolerate it anymore. Parents are torn between not wanting to send their older child away from home, and the fear that the younger ones might be harmed by the bad example of their older brother or sister.

Many Amish parents believe that the young person who longs to try the forbidden fruit has to at least taste it before he can voluntarily give it up to choose the church instead. Yet finding the mixture of discipline and forgiving love that will bring the wayward young person home and back to the church remains a challenge for Amish parents and elders.

The practice of letting young people "run around" gives them and the community the illusion of free choice, which is critical to the Anabaptist belief that baptism has to be an adult choice. Yet in reality, the child reared to be Amish, to think and feel Amish, is not likely to feel secure and comfortable choosing anything else as an adult.

Courtship

There is no Pennsylvania German word for "dating," but the Amish use the English word when they need it. Amish young people enjoy complete freedom in choosing their mate, though if they're to remain Amish, they have to marry within the faith or their intended has to become Amish before they marry. Amish people can marry others from outside their own church district and settlement, as long as the two congregations are in "full fellowship," meaning they agree on basic issues. Marriage to a member of a more liberal group is sanctioned only if the less conservative person joins the more conservative church. Very rarely, a non-Amish person might join the Amish church to be able to marry an Amish person.

The Amish consider romantic relationships and sexual attraction to be strictly private, so courtship is practiced secretly while parents look the other way until the couple comes to them for permission to marry. Only then does the relationship become public knowledge, after the couple's intention to marry is "published" or announced at preaching service. Young people socialize with others from districts throughout their settlement at Sunday evening sings, and through activities sponsored by their "gangs" of friends.

Ironies and Oddities

The Amish dating system seems out of sync with their strict prohibitions against premarital sex and immodest behavior, yet it's less so today than in earlier years. In earlier times, the Amish practiced "bundling," a custom carried over from European peasant culture in which the young man and woman lay, fully clothed, on a bed together during the night. What they did during that time remains a matter of speculation, but the practice seemed to arise partly from the need to keep warm in houses with no central heating. What was wrong with the fireplace or the woodstove remains a mystery as well. Bundling fell into disfavor with the Amish bishops some time ago.

A dating relationship is likely to begin when a boy offers to take a girl home after a Sunday evening sing. Of course, since he's driving a buggy and the girl may live in a different church district, it can take until morning to get home again. When a couple is more serious, the young man will come calling on a Saturday night—when no church service is scheduled for the next morning. He waits to arrive until her parents are in bed, and the girl lets him in the house. They sit in the living room, sometimes in the dark, though some parents require a light to be on in the room, and visit through the night. Sometimes other couples join them. Young men of courting age drive home in the early morning to sleep during their "off" Sunday.

Marriage: Founding a New Family

When a young couple agrees to marry, the young man must obtain the permission of his fiancé's parents. In the Lancaster and Mifflin County, Pennsylvania settlements, the next step is for the prospective groom to visit his district's deacon or minister to inform him of his intentions. That official becomes the go-between, paying a secret call on the intended bride, to ask if she has remained "pure." If not, then a confession in church would be required before the wedding could take place. The deacon also makes sure the bride's parents agree to the wedding—by now, merely a formality. Once he hears the agreement of the parents, he informs the bishop, who announces, or "publishes," the couple's plans at the next preaching service.

Couples in other settlements don't use the traditional go-between. In the Midwest, the couple usually visits a minister in the bride's church district to discuss wedding plans.

A wedding is a serious affair in Amish culture, because it signals a lifelong commitment and founds a new family. The wedding service, noontime wedding dinner, and evening wedding supper take all day, and the preparation of the food and house takes a full day. For that reason, weddings are held on midweek days—Tuesdays,

The Plain Truth

The bride and groom wear new clothes for the occasion, but they're the same kind of clothes worn for every church service. The bride chooses matching fabric for her and her attendant's dresses, often in shades of blue or, in Lancaster and related settlements, purple. Swiss Amish brides wear black wedding dresses. After the service, the bride switches from her black cap to a white one, symbolizing her new status as a married woman.

The Plain Truth

For a much more detailed description of Amish wedding practices, see Stephen Scott's *The Amish Wedding and Other Special Occasions of the Old Order Communities.*

Wednesdays, Thursdays, or Fridays, depending on the settlement—after harvest season. In Lancaster, November is the favored month, but Midwestern Amish weddings are held most anytime.

The bride and groom choose two couples as attendants, who sit beside them in the front row at the service.

The service is usually held at the house of a neighbor of the bride, except in Lancaster where it takes place at the bride's home. The wedding is a standard three-hour Amish church service, except that the sermons focus on biblical accounts of marriage and are followed by a few questions for the couple, the answers to which constitute their vows.

After the wedding, everyone moves to the bride's house (if they're not already there) for a reception that lasts all afternoon and evenings. It takes a lot of help to put on an Amish wedding. Friends, aunts, and uncles and other relatives of the couple are asked to serve as ushers, cooks, and waiters. Both men and women serve in these roles.

The parents of the bride oversee the food and table preparation, which takes a dozen or more couples the entire day before the wedding, and fill the role of hosts at the reception. The parents, though, have no special role in the wedding service.

Two long tables are set in an L-shape in the living room. The bridal party sits at corner where the tables meet, the place of honor visible to most people. Other tables are also set up in the kitchen and downstairs bedroom to accommodate as many guests as possible. Even so, people must eat in shifts.

The couple receives gifts of household items and hand tools, which are displayed on an upstairs bed and may remain in the bride's living room for some time.

Midwestern couples set up housekeeping right away, but in the Lancaster and Mifflin County, Pennsylvania settlements, where weddings take place at the beginning of winter, they take their time getting used to married life. Young couples live with their parents until they have a house ready to move to, often the following spring. During that time, friends and relatives continue to bring gifts. On weekends, the newlywed couple makes overnight visits to close relatives and daytime visits to other friends and more distant family members. They sometimes go along with other newlyweds, since so many are visiting at the same time. This brief period of freedom without the responsibilities of maintaining a home or farm takes the place of a honeymoon.

The Least You Need to Know

◆ Family life is central to Amish culture, since almost everything happens at home.

◆ The Amish church grows through the increase of its ethnic population, rather than by seeking converts.

◆ Amish families are strongly patriarchal and traditional, with men in charge of making a living and women in charge of the household, yard, and garden.

◆ Amish children are loved and valued, and raised under strict discipline to obey the authority of their parents and the church.

◆ Young people choose their own mates, and weddings are all-day affairs celebrating the founding of a new family.

The Least of These: Amish Care of the Young, Old, Sick, and Handicapped

In This Chapter

- ◆ Amish education
- ◆ Health care, wellness, and traditional healing
- ◆ Old age among the Amish
- ◆ Support for the handicapped

It's been said that a society can be measured by the way it treats its most vulnerable members—the young, the old, the ill, and the handicapped. By that measure, Amish culture is a compassionate one.

Amish families embrace those on the margins of life as fully as those in the middle. One benefit of large, extended families is that there are usually more healthy than unhealthy members. Children can be trained early to help care for each other, and each set of parents has many adult children to care for them by the time most of them need it.

Another way of looking at society is how its members express unhappiness or stress. By this measure, Amish society may come out less favorably. Physicians reported on one survey that their Amish patients have more stress-related disorders, such as bedwetting and digestive disturbances, than non-Amish patients. John Hostetler, reporting this result, notes that illness is an accepted way for the Amish to express emotional needs for attention, affirmation, and sympathy, which would be considered self-centered if expressed verbally.

Close to Home: Amish Education

As discussed in the last chapter, Amish parents have very different goals for their children than most of their mainstream counterparts. The Amish want their children to become farmers and homemakers, or when that's not possible for financial reasons or lack of affordable farm land, to work at home in some trade.

> **Make No Mistake**
>
> Amish men who work in businesses that grow sometimes do become executives of manufacturers with large budgets and many employees. But that's not the ideal, nor is it the norm, and Amish children aren't educated with that goal.

They don't want their children to receive higher education, or to become doctors, lawyers, accountants, or business executives in large corporations. They want their children to stay close to home, work with others of their faith, and not be exposed to more of the larger culture than necessary so they won't be tempted to leave the faith.

The Amish View of Education

The concerns the Amish have about education include ...

- Distance of schools from home
- Size of schools
- Length of school year
- Years of required schooling
- Curriculum
- Control over hiring teachers

All these factors affect how strongly parents are able to control the socialization of their children and shape their futures.

The Amish need their children to help with farm work starting at planting time in early spring, and they want their children to experience the Amish way of life when they're young enough to become attached to the rhythm of seasonal work and fellowship within the family and community. In particular, they don't want children taken away from their parents' influence during their teen years, when they're most likely to be swayed by the behavior and values of their peers. Particularly then, the Amish find it important to limit their children's peers to family and Amish friends.

The Amish family keeps its children down on the farm in part by letting them know how valuable their labor is to the family. Children who help raise, preserve, and prepare the family's food feel like important members of their society.

When children are in their mid-teens and finally capable of performing adult labor, they get to begin to taste the adult rewards of Amish life, such as satisfaction in a job well done and the appreciation of their families. To send them to high school deprives parents not only of their assistance at home, but of this chance to ground them more firmly in Amish life just as those teenagers are starting to decide for themselves who they want to be.

Public "Amish" Schools

For most of their history, the Amish sent their children to public elementary schools. In many rural elementary schools, the Amish were even in the majority. As long as rural schools were largely under local control, with teachers who were known to the community often teaching in one-room schools, the Amish felt comfortable that their children weren't being led astray.

In the twentieth century, state governments gradually exerted more control over schools, dictating how long they should be in session and pressuring local school districts to consolidate the one-room schools into larger, regional schools. The Amish of Pennsylvania resisted state control almost from the beginning, while the Midwestern Amish continued to send their children to the larger schools for many years.

These still remained local schools, gathering children from an entire township rather than the square-mile area served by one-room schools. Amish parents could reach them easily by horse-and-buggy for meeting with parents and school activities; they didn't mind sending their children on public buses as long as they weren't leaving the community.

As a child growing up in the northern Indiana Mennonite community, I attended a typical rural, consolidated elementary school like many formed in the early twentieth century to replace one-room schools. Called Clinton Community School, the brick building housed four classrooms for eight grades, a small gymnasium in the center with a stage at one end, a music room, a tiny office for the principal, a small library, and a kitchen used initially for community pot-lucks and occasional fish fries, since a school lunch program wasn't started until the 1960s. As the student population grew, it became harder to teach two grades in each classroom, and classes spilled over into the music room and even the stage.

Amish students were in the majority, and their parents took part in running parent-teacher activities. Students who weren't Amish were either some variant of Mennonite or Brethren; though public, it was an Anabaptist school environment.

Though children were bussed to school instead of being able to walk, and had a different teacher for most grades, local Amish parents still felt comfortable because they knew the teachers and had sufficient control over these consolidated schools. The public school allowed Amish children to learn about the world beyond their family and ethnic boundaries—but not too much more. For example, when I was in the early elementary grades, a Mennonite minister came to school once a week to teach Bible studies. Though most likely this was not legal even then, no one wished to challenge the practice, so the dominant local religion was allowed to permeate the school environment.

The Breaking Point

What changed was the increasing push by state government for ever-larger schools, which could be more efficiently funded to provide better educational resources. Small rural high and junior-high schools were consolidated into even larger, more distant schools, and the same was true of elementary schools. Consolidated schools included students from outside the Amish-Mennonites settlements, and were sometimes too distant for parents to reach them conveniently by horse and buggy. Teachers weren't as familiar with and sympathetic to Amish beliefs as they had been when most of their students were Amish, and parents had less influence on the school.

High school became more of an issue at that time. In Indiana, state law required students to attend school until the age of 16. Amish students would start high school, but drop out the day they turned 16.

In Pennsylvania, how long children had to be schooled had been an issue for some time. As early as the 1920s, the state began the process of making education compulsory, requiring schools to be in session more days each year, requiring more years of education, and consolidating schools to make them more efficient. As noted previously, the Pennsylvania Amish began resisting almost from the start, and by 1938 opened their first school. Through the years, they withdrew more and more into their own private schools. A number of Amish parents went to jail rather than send their children to high school.

In all the Amish settlements, the trend toward building and running their own schools grew in proportion to the influence of state administrators over public education. The issue of how much education a child was required to have grew more intense as high schools grew larger, farther from Amish influence, and the curriculum, student body, and facilities more worldly.

The issue of state control over Amish education took different forms in different states, but one of the key battlegrounds was the issue of whether the state could dictate how long Amish children had to remain in school. Various proponents of religious freedom took up the cause of the Amish, and finally, in 1972, the Supreme Court settled the issue. The Court ruled, in a case from Wisconsin, where a new Amish settlement had been started a few years before, that the state's right to educate its citizens didn't outweigh the right of the citizens to choose their religious practices.

Private Amish Schools

Since winning their legal battle, most Amish children have been educated in the local Amish schools, which now dot the landscape of their settlements. The schools are small, usually with one or two classrooms and teachers. They are built by Amish labor, according to Amish designs that make best use of natural lighting, since the buildings don't have electricity. Some have indoor plumbing, but most don't. All have large grounds for playing baseball or softball and other games, plus room for parents to hitch their horses and buggies.

The teachers are usually young Amish women with no special education or training, hired by the school's board for their interest in teaching

Ironies and Oddities

As states consolidated public schools, they needed larger school buildings. At the same time, the Amish were starting their own schools and some of Mennonite denominations also expanded their parochial schools. They often bought school buildings that had once housed public schools. This was the fate of my elementary school, which was bought by a nearby school run by Conservative Mennonites.

and good character. Teachers have to exemplify the kind of Amish church member and good citizen that the community wants its scholars to become, and have enough knowledge of the curriculum to teach it. They are trained by more experienced teachers the same way that other Amish occupations are taught, by apprenticeship. Three years of teaching under the guidance of an experienced teacher qualifies an Amish educator to teach on her own.

School boards consist of three to six members. The church may appoint board members, or parents may elect them; in either case, they are accountable to both. Parents pay tuition, and church district members also contribute to the running of their local school. In addition, of course, the Amish pay property taxes that support the public schools, as do other parents of parochial school students.

In the Classroom

The classroom is run much like the Amish family. Children are taught to obey the teacher, as the authority entrusted with their education. They are to respect each other, and cooperate rather than compete with one another. As at home, older children help younger ones with their lessons when the teacher, who is responsible for around 30 students in eight grades, is busy with others. Teaching is of the old-fashioned variety, and children are asked to memorize facts rather than take part in classroom discussions or learn critical thinking. Students are said to be neither praised for being quick learners or disparaged for being slow, since each person's gifts are up to God, not the individual.

> ### The Plain Truth
>
> The Amish children I attended public school with in the 1960s were cooperative with the teacher, but to non-Amish kids, they were anything but gentle or non-competitive. Boys, especially, were very critical of others and quick to tease anyone they thought was "different" or weaker.
>
> When you teach children that they belong to a special people apart from the world, they may consider anyone outside their group less worthy. Or perhaps the Amish kids were reacting against being immersed in the dominant culture, where they didn't feel at home. We non-Amish kids, though outnumbered, were studying in our native tongue, dressed like the teachers, and knew more of "the world" than our Amish classmates.

Because Amish schools comply with state curriculum requirements, the exact subjects taught vary somewhat from state to state. Classes are conducted in English, and all students study English grammar and spelling, and learn some writing skills, in addition to the math needed in daily life and work. History, geography, and health are also common subjects. Science is rarely taught, and sometimes agriculture replaces history and geography.

Amish schools are modeled after the one-room schools of the nineteenth century.

Religion isn't taught as a subject, though students sing religious songs and memorize German Bible verses. Among the Amish, only ordained men have the authority to interpret scriptures or give religious guidance. Amish parents are responsible for the religious instruction of their children at home. Amish schoolteachers are only entrusted with the teaching of academic subjects.

Pathway Publishers, an Amish-owned publisher, produces a series of readers used by many Amish schools. Another alternative is the secular school text books reissued by the Old Order Book Society in Lancaster County for use in Amish schools. Statewide meetings held every year for Amish teachers and school boards help communicate ideas for more effective teaching. Amish teachers even have their own professional journal, called *Blackboard Bulletin*, published monthly by Pathway Publishers.

Health Care: Medicine, Magic, and Folk Remedies

Health care among the Amish is a mixed bag integrating modern western medicine, complementary or alternative medicine, herbal remedies, nutritional supplements, and folk cures. Like other aspects of Amish life, health care is influenced heavily by tradition and the recommendations of elders and other Amish people. Because health and science are subjects little studied among the Amish, they tend to give more weight to remedies that seem holistic and natural, rather than based on intrusive medical practices. In the shadows remain traditional folk healing practices based on magic rooted in Switzerland and Alsace, and passed down by Amish practitioners.

The Amish value health highly and will go to great lengths to get relief from illness. They tend to first try home remedies, perhaps using herbal remedies, changes in diet, or nutritional supplements recommended by a family member or passed down by tradition. If the condition persists or worsens, the next step would be to seek help from outside the community from someone with specialized knowledge, such as a physician, homeopath, chiropractor, massage therapist, or reflexologist, depending on the condition and the beliefs and experiences of the patient and his family. Sometimes a patient diagnosed by a physician with an illness requiring surgery or another highly invasive treatment may seek a more "natural" treatment before resorting to standard medical treatment. The Amish hesitate to subject themselves to what they consider "strong medicine."

Home Remedies and Nutrition

Many herbal remedies, such as teas and poultices, were handed down from grandmother to mother to daughter and are used for treating common illnesses and discomforts. Amish also are big consumers of modern herbal remedies, nutritional supplements, and natural foods, which they often buy in Amish stores. These stores may sell a number of lines of supplements, vitamins, toiletries, and skin care products based on natural ingredients, bulk herbs, homeopathic remedies, and organic foods.

Visiting the Doctor

They go to doctors and hospitals for many of the same ailments as other Americans, though perhaps less often. They also rely more heavily on alternative practitioners, such as chiropractors, reflexologists, and homeopaths. The Amish, after all, don't buy commercial health insurance (or any other kind of private insurance; they practice mutual aid instead). They pay for doctor appointments from their own pockets.

Time is another factor. To visit a doctor, an Amish person has to make the trip by horse and buggy. When you add in the time spent at the appointment and the return trip, it can take all or most of the day, depending on how many miles the patient lives from the physician's office. For this reason alone, it's impractical to go to the doctor for minor ailments or those the person could be expected to recover from with time, such as colds or flu.

Then, too, Amish people are suspicious of worldly knowledge, and doctors embody the kind of highly educated, specialized professional that the world honors and the Amish distrust. Their limited education doesn't prepare Amish adults to evaluate a doctor's credentials or what a physician tells them about their health. While the rest of us might look for a doctor with the best credentials or expertise in an area of health care we need, the Amish assume a physician will be competent. What they look for is someone who understands them, listens to their concerns with respect, and takes time to communicate with them.

The Amish also aren't as familiar as other Americans with how diseases are prevented and transmitted. Far fewer Amish children get the kind of vaccinations against severe diseases that children in the wider society do, in part because their schools don't require vaccinations for attendance, as public schools do. Amish religious beliefs don't forbid vaccinations, but they simply don't see the point in taking precautions against every disease that could occur, no matter how small the chance. When an outbreak of disease occurs, though, the Amish will vaccinate themselves and their children.

Pregnancy is considered a natural condition among the Amish, and with women having so many babies, it's not surprising that they don't see another pregnancy as reason to seek medical care. Most wait until around the sixth month to start prenatal care. While hospital births were once the norm and are still common, more Amish babies are born at home today than 20 years ago. Midwives often attend home births. In northern Indiana, a new, free-standing birthing clinic in the midst of the rural Amish settlement gives women another alternative—closer to home and more home-like than a hospital delivery, which would require traveling some distance, probably by hired car, yet with more medical facilities and personnel than a home birth.

Alternative and Complementary Care

Chiropractic care is very popular among the Amish, perhaps because it's based on restoring the natural alignment of the body, which a patient can feel and understand, rather than taking medicines based on modern scientific knowledge the Amish know nothing about.

Homeopathic remedies, made from plants and without side effects, are popular as well. Many Amish see homeopathic physicians, and over-the-counter homeopathic remedies are sold in local health food stores.

Reflexology, the manipulation of the feet to affect the health of various parts of the body, is another form of alternative health care used by the Amish.

Powwow Medicine

Less often practiced, especially by younger Amish generations, is the folk medicine called "powwow medicine," "powwowing," or "conjuring." Amish people may turn to traditional healers who practice this blend of incantations, spells, and rituals for cures to conditions for which medicine has no answers.

Many Amish, from the most progressive to those who work to preserve traditional Amish values, are strongly against the use of "powwow medicine." Other say it's no longer practiced or that sometimes traditional healing was more like faith healing than an occult practice.

A clinical social worker conducting research on traditional healing interviewed members of one Illinois Amish community in 1993. He found that "powwowing" (also sometimes called "brauche," a word their German ancestors used for folk medicine) was still practiced in the community.

Some practitioners combined secret prayers with rituals involving such ordinary objects as string, eggs, or butter knives. One said that the methods could only be taught to a younger person of the opposite gender who promised to keep the prayer secret. The practitioner then taught such a prayer to the researcher, who found its content to be orthodox Christian. The researcher observed that the ritual symbolism aimed to externalize symptoms and relieve anxiety in patients.

Other healers (including one said to have "the gift of electricity") used prayer, sometimes combined with touch, to relieve headaches, earaches, and even bleeding. Practitioners tended to specialize in only one or two types of ailments, and none took money for their services.

Some Amish people interviewed saw powwowing as a gift of God, while others expressed suspicion that some of the practices might be witchcraft. "I'm slow to call it good," said one ordained minister. "Good and evil are mixed and it is difficult to divide them. Seek a spirit of understanding," he advised, "and forgive those who do not understand."

Among the Amish today are some healers who see patients regularly in their homes and act pretty much like health care professionals. They may combine various methods of healing, which may or may not include the spells and rituals associated with powwow medicine. Other healers are older members of the community who help those who come to them in time of need, but not on a regular basis. These "powwow doctors" repeat spells and sometimes use objects in rituals intended to free the person from affliction by driving out the illness. The cure can sometimes be performed without the afflicted person present, but faith is required to make it effective.

Make No Mistake _____

Though often referred to by the term "powwow," Amish traditional healing has nothing to do with Native American healing practices. It stems instead from the practices of their forebears in the Rhineland and Switzerland, who were known for their success in healing both animals and humans. Originally known as doctors and using herbal remedies, eventually some healers started using magic spells or charms to augment their practices. According to John Hostetler in *Amish Society*, "The practice is not unique to the Amish, for at one time it was a common healing art among Pennsylvania Germans." (Some of the same Pennsylvania Germans, perhaps, who painted hex signs on their barns to ward off evil.) Hostetler says some of the spells used have been published and can be traced back to thirteenth century Cologne. The Amish who use powwowing, however, have learned the formulas from oral traditions.

The Amish visit, support, and pray for the sick, and anoint the seriously ill with oil, following biblical practice, but don't engage in the laying on of hands or other spiritual healing practices used by some fundamentalist Christian groups.

Mental Health

One study of mental health among the Amish of Lancaster County more than 20 years ago showed that the Amish suffered mental illness at roughly half the rate of the rest of the population, and another study reported Amish suicide rates less than half that of the rest the county's population.

Yet, as John Hostetler points out in his book *Amish Society*, suicide rates vary by settlement. Two Amish people told him of 15 suicides in their community. Hostetler says suicide is more common among younger people and men, and especially among those who feel caught between "contradictory expectations." Younger ministers who have to live up to the stricter standards of their older bishops are especially stressed, Hostetler says. He also points out that writings by the Amish, such as letters to Amish publications, reveal that Amish women who have no legitimate way of complaining about frustrations or mistreatment in their marriage often become depressed. Their culture gives them no way to voice their complaints; their role is to submit to their husbands. Being depressed or sick is more acceptable in Amish

The Plain Truth _____

Many Amish people believe powwowing is a form of sorcery, invoking evil spiritual powers rather than God to free a person from illness. Some believe it has ceased to be practiced at all, while others simply disapprove of those who resort to it.

Ironies and Oddities

The Amish define psychological problems differently from mainstream society. To the Amish, signs of mental illness include "frequent visits to doctors, failure to find full satisfaction in a day's work, preoccupation with problems of religious orthodoxy, rigidity of attitude, and among males, the failure to marry," according to John Hostetler in *Amish Society*.

society than to be angry or defiant. Those who are sick or depressed get sympathy and care, whereas those who defy the traditional order and authority get excommunicated and shunned.

Mental illness among the Amish may be underreported, since like those with other illnesses, they mainly try to care for the person at home. They encourage the patient to stay busy working, and include them in family activities.

The family physician is more likely to recognize the need of an Amish person for psychiatric care than the person himself or his family. Some Amish patients prefer to go to Mennonite-affiliated psychiatric hospitals in Pennsylvania, Maryland, and Indiana rather than other facilities.

The Elderly

As Amish people reach retirement, most of them can move seamlessly into a new niche without leaving the family home. One or another of their grown children will take over operating the farm, while the grandparents move into their own wing of the house or a smaller home on the property.

Since the growth of Amish settlements can result in a shortage of farmland, more and more Amish men are supporting their families with a home industry or by working in a factory instead of farming. Even so, when they build a new home on a few acres of rural land, they plan for the older generation to live with them.

Amish in-laws are no more guaranteed to get along than in-laws in any other culture. Letters written to the Amish magazine *Family Life* attest to this. Yet respecting and caring for elders is an Amish ideal, and many families happily integrate three or more generations.

Most Amish people retire sometime between 60 and 70 years of age. For men, this means they're no longer expected to contribute to the heavy fieldwork, but may offer to help out with lighter chores. Women still have a house to keep, though a smaller one, and may offer to help their daughter or daughter-in-law in the main house or with childcare.

Amish grandparents do have to support and feed themselves. They may rent the larger home, attached or detached, and the farm to their adult children for income.

Or they may live on some combination of savings and income from part-time work or handicrafts. The Amish don't draw social security or other government subsidies, including Medicare. They rely instead on their family and church community to support them when they can no longer support themselves.

Even though they may have had large families, Amish widows and widowers are subject to loneliness and feeling unneeded, just like their mainstream counterparts. This may be especially painful to them, however, after a lifetime of being surrounded and needed by family members.

Just as the Amish don't send their elderly to retirement homes, neither do they send the very old and sick to nursing facilities when they no longer can care for themselves. If a family can't care for its grandparents when they get ill or incapacitated, the church will pitch in to care for the person at home. Church contributions help pay the medical bills of the elderly, too, when they are more than the family can afford.

> ### Ironies and Oddities
>
> Some Amish couples like to travel in retirement, and there is even an Amish retirement community in Florida where the elderly like to spend the winter.

The Plain Truth

When a family member dies, the most conservative Amish still keep the body cool with ice and alcohol until burial rather than embalming. Most groups, however, send the body to a funeral home for embalming, then have it returned home for visitation and the funeral. Members of the same sex as the deceased dress the body, either in white (in some Pennsylvania settlements) or in Sunday attire.

Church members take care of funeral preparations, cook meals, and do both farm chores and housework for the bereaved family. Visitation takes place for two days, with people coming to view the body in its plain wooden coffin, comfort the family ,and visit with each other for several hours.

Hundreds of people may crowd into the family house or barn for the funeral, usually on the third morning after the death. If the number is too great, two services may be held simultaneously in the barn and house to accommodate the entire crowd. After the service, the coffin is carried by horse-drawn hearse to a family or neighborhood cemetery. Following the burial, mourners may return to the family home for a meal prepared by members of the local church district.

The Handicapped

Whether a person is handicapped mentally or physically, through disease, genetic disorder, or accident, the Amish try to treat the person as an integral part of the family. Nevertheless, from reading letters to *Family Life*, it's evident that just as in other families, Amish siblings may treat a handicapped brother or sister like a bother or a burden. In a society that values a person's work so highly, what may hurt most is if a family can't find a way to make the handicapped member feel needed.

The Plain Truth

One Amish man from my childhood community was born with a hip disorder. Though he couldn't walk without crutches, the man owned a very successful shoe repair business. He earned respect as well as money, making a valued contribution to a community where nearly everyone wore leather shoes and few replaced them if they could be repaired instead.

Amish families attempt to embrace their handicapped members, caring for them at home rather than sending them to institutions, and integrating them into the family. Their condition is considered part of God's will, not a sign of inferiority. Mentally retarded children are sent to school so they can experience life with other children. They're included in community and family events, and accepted as part of both.

Since the early 1960s Amish people with physical handicaps have met in national meetings held around the country to share fellowship, information, and encouragement. The physically handicapped often support themselves with handcrafts.

The Least You Need to Know

◆ Though the Amish used to attend public schools, today almost all Amish children attend Amish schools.

◆ In Amish schools, one or two teachers teach first through eighth grade in one or two classrooms.

◆ The Amish blend a preference for traditional herbal remedies and alternative or complementary medicine with use of modern medicine.

◆ The Amish care for all family members, whether sick, handicapped, or ill, at home unless the patient needs hospitalization.

◆ The elderly live in homes adjacent to an adult child and his or her family.

Part 4

In the World, but Not of the World: The Amish and Modern Society

If no man is an island, no group of people can be, either. Like it or not, the Amish can't completely ignore the world around them. And the more that world changes, the more their own people are tempted to change, too. The Amish keep their flock from changing too much or too quickly by fencing them in with rules of behavior, group solidarity, and peer pressure.

For all their ideals and squeaky-clean image, life inside the Amish fold isn't perfect. Under pressure to conform, families sometimes suffer. As in all societies, those who have the least power are most vulnerable, and among the Amish, that means women and children.

Furthermore, not everyone born Amish wants to stay, of course, but leaving is never easy. The Amish view leaving the faith—especially after baptism—as a spiritual death sentence. Those left behind have to cut off relationships with family members who leave the Amish. Yet for some, there's no other way.

Chapter 3

Fencing in the Faithful: What's In and What's Out

In This Chapter

◆ Conforming to a standard of nonconformity

◆ Forbidden behavior

◆ Sanctioned entertainment

◆ The role of Amish publications

Why is it that you can identify an Amish person as Amish without exchanging a word, yet you can't identify a Methodist, a Baptist, Catholic, or even necessarily a Mennonite? Or for that matter, a person of Czech, German, or Irish descent? What makes the Amish stand out as a separate culture within modern American society?

It's not only because their dress, transportation, and language are all different from the rest of the world's—*nonconformed*, in the words of the Amish. It's also because the Amish are highly *conformed* within their own culture.

Nonconformed Conformity?

Amish women voluntarily sew their dresses to conform to a traditional pattern that's almost precisely like that worn by every other Amish woman. The same goes for men's clothing, hair styles, language, transportation, home styles, and even occupations. The Amish are much more conformist within their culture than people in the culture around them.

Vas Es Das?

Nonconformed is the word the Amish use to describe the relationship of their culture to the world around them, based on the Apostle Paul's command to early Christians at Rome: "… Be ye not conformed to this world: but be ye transformed by the renewing of your mind, that ye may prove what is that good, and acceptable, and perfect, will of God." (Romans 12:2)

How does a Methodist dress? What does a Baptist drive, or a Catholic do for a living? The variation is endless, because on the whole, modern American culture values individual freedom of expression over group identity.

What are exceptions to that rule? Young people in every culture often dress like their peers—and unlike their parents. Those who really want to stand out as individuals adopt a personal style distinct from both. In certain occupations, such as business administration, modern Americans follow a dress code and judge how serious others are about their career by how closely they conform.

In language, more than in most cultural traits, Americans conform. Immigrants learn to function in English, just as the Amish learn English so they can do business with those around them. Yet even in language, the United States is becoming more pluralist. In large cities, particularly on the coasts, Spanish and a variety of Asian languages are commonly heard on the streets, along with the occasional conversation in French or Russian.

The difference that makes the Amish stand out is that modern Americans decide *individually* which standards they will conform to, and in what situations. The buttoned-down business executive can dress in black leather and ride a Harley on weekends; no one cares. Young people who dress down for college can dress up for job interviews.

The Amish, by contrast, don't get to pick and choose. The standards are set for them, and their only choice is to conform or leave their culture. How does Amish culture persuade so many of its own to conform?

God First, Others Next, Yourself Last: Formula for Conformity

Soon after they learn to walk and talk, Amish children begin to learn that conformity is expected of them. Everyone they come in contact with, all those who love and care for them, dress alike, work together, follow the rules. As they grow, Amish children learn a separate language from mainstream culture and learn by example how to think and act like an Amish person.

Amish children aren't taught to think for themselves, question assumptions, or challenge authority. They're taught that God has placed church leaders in positions of authority over church members, men in authority over women, and adults over children—and it's their God-given duty to obey those in authority.

Rebellion is punished early, before the age of six, to prevent it arising again—until adolescence, that is. By that time, parents hope, the child will be so accustomed to being Amish that any rebellion will be short-lived and end with the young person choosing to follow his elders' example by voluntarily joining the church and Amish society.

Don't Dare to Be Different

To be different in Amish society—to call attention to yourself or stand out in any way—is considered a sign of pride, one of the most dreaded sins. Their clothing, homes, and manners are intended to be outer signs of inner humility, so the Amish—consciously or unconsciously—compare themselves and judge others by their degree of conformity.

> **CAUTION**
>
> **Make No Mistake**
>
> The Amish are aware that pride can grow insidiously, and without realizing it one can fall into pride in one's plainness or humility.

Don't Think Too Well of Yourself

While many non-Amish adults are concerned about instilling self-esteem in their children and recovering their own, the Amish have the opposite goal. To avoid the sin of pride, they believe it's necessary to "not think too well of yourself." They believe that all people are unworthy of the love and life that God has bestowed on them, and that all their effort over a lifetime won't make them worthy. Even so, it's their duty to spend their life striving to overcome their inherently inadequate and faulty nature.

Because they know their neighbors and relatives are watching, the Amish also strive to avoid even the *appearance* of self-satisfaction. The Amish don't distinguish between pride and self-esteem, or between humility and feelings of unworthiness or shame. In fact, the Amish use shame as a tool for social control, through public confession of sins and shunning those who persistently break the rules.

The Amish formula for humility is God first, others next, yourself last. It's also a recipe for conformity, because it undermines the individual's feeling that his or her personal feelings matter. Amish people are urged to put aside their own feelings when those feelings conflict with the group's standards. On the other hand, in personal relationships, Amish people are urged to show love for each other by working out conflicts.

As pointed out earlier, authority in Amish relationships is clearly defined: group over individual, male over female, older over younger. The person with less authority is supposed to submit to the will of the person in authority, who in turn is responsible for showing love, compassion, and understanding to the less powerful. Authority carries with it responsibility to treat those under one's authority with love.

The Plain Truth

One reason people disagree about whether Amish life is peaceful, harmonious, and happy, or whether it is repressive and miserable is that the Amish give so much power to individuals with authority. The system works when the individuals are responsible, loving, kind, and respect the feelings of others. Problems arise when someone in power abuses that power. It's hard to challenge a person in authority under Amish social and church rules.

Forbidden Fruit: Off-Limits Activities

In addition to the obvious behavior forbidden in the Ten Commandments, such as murder, theft, and adultery, the Amish prohibit many specific activities, including the following:

◆ Working, shopping, or doing business on Sundays

◆ Gambling

◆ Playing musical instruments (except harmonicas, in most settlements)

◆ Dancing (In some communities, however, young people play group games involving singing, holding hands, and swinging partners. This type of folk dancing also takes place at wedding receptions.)

◆ Drinking

No Smoking ... Well, Maybe

Rules on smoking vary by district, and over the years has been a subject of debate among Amish church districts and members. Smoking used to be common among the Amish in Pennsylvania, where tobacco was an important cash crop. In the 1960s, when the government started educating the public on the health risks of smoking, many Amish people began to argue for its ban. Of course, raising a crop they forbid members to consume also would have created a dilemma for the Amish conscience.

"Though many of our church people both raise and use tobacco, there are also many with growing convictions against it," one Amish couple wrote to *Family Life* magazine in 1977.

Today, smoking is largely discouraged by the church, even in Pennsylvania, though as in mainstream culture, the rebellious young are likely to smoke in secret.

> **Ironies and Oddities**
>
> Interestingly, Mennonites strictly forbid smoking. According to John Hostetler in *Amish Society*, among Amish groups that allow smoking, "quitting may be seen as a sign of 'changing one's thinking' by identifying with the Mennonites." For some then, smoking is a sign of identifying with Amish culture, while giving up smoking can foretell giving up the Amish church to join the Mennonites.

A Dry Religion

Drinking alcohol is banned by the Amish church. Yet drinking by Amish young people during their "running around" years has become an open social problem in the largest settlements, where the police have sometimes broken up Sunday night parties.

Reading the book *The Amish in Their Own Words* by Brad Igou, one gets the impression that some Amish adults tolerate beer and wine, though not "strong drink" such as whiskey and other hard liquors.

Mennonites were traditionally much less tolerant of alcohol, although in recent decades drinking in moderation has become acceptable among the most liberal groups.

Can-Do Entertainment: Social Gatherings

In a culture that forbids so much, does anybody have any fun? Of course, but they find different ways to have fun.

The favorite activity among the Amish is socializing. They love to talk, to play word games and number games, joke and laugh together. "Visiting" is the number one Amish entertainment.

Formal visiting takes place at home and after church, when adults take some or all of their children to another family's home. In traditional Amish homes, no one phones ahead, though perhaps in more progressive homes where cell phones exist, this convenience may be growing. Since an "off-Sunday" afternoon is a traditional visiting time, the family being visited may be off paying a visit of their own. In that case, the visitors just drive to the home of another friend or relative, who always lives close by.

Informal visiting permeates every aspect of Amish group life. The Amish, especially women, create occasions to get together, either solely for socializing or for working together.

Work Frolics

The Amish find fun in pitching in together to meet a common goal. They gather for many kinds of all-day work *frolics*, including barn raisings, quilting bees, apple butter frolics, and even husking bees in the most conservative Amish communities, where corn is still husked by hand rather than by a corn harvester.

At frolics like this barn raising, the Amish enjoy talking, laughing, and working together to accomplish big projects.

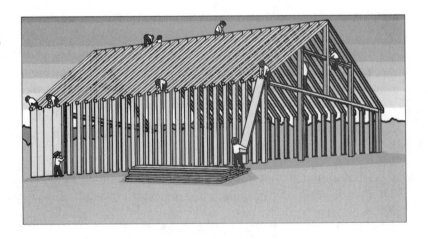

When fire destroys a barn, the church may pay for some or all of the materials to replace it. A crew of a hundred or more men come not only from adjacent church districts, but sometimes from far-flung settlements as well. As they put up the barn, the men visit with friends and relatives, some of whom they may not have seen for a long time. New friendships are formed as well. Meanwhile, women gather in the house to prepare a huge noon meal and snacks for coffee breaks that keep the men going. All labor is donated—for the volunteers know that the same help will be available to them if they ever need it. When a new farmstead is built, the farmer buys the materials, but the free labor cuts the cost of new buildings considerably. Houses are usually built with much less volunteer labor than barns, and take more time to finish.

Vas Es Das?

Day-long work parties are called **frolics** because they combine fun with the labor-intensive tasks that need to be done.

With more people working in nonfarm businesses or milking larger dairy herds, work frolics are getting harder to organize than they were in the old days, when farmers could put in a long day helping others between the morning and evening chores.

Sisters Days

In some families, grown sisters hold regular "Sisters Days" in each other's homes. They get together to visit, and while they talk, they might sew, quilt, put up fruit or vegetables, clean house, or do whatever else needs to be done.

Reunions

Many Amish people in the same occupation hold a national reunion every year to form and renew friendships and share information. Annual reunions are held by Amish woodworkers, "harness makers, machine shop operators, wooden shed builders, and quilters," according to Donald Kraybill in *The Riddle of Amish Culture*. Support groups formed around handicaps, mental illness, or other special interests also meet annually.

Auction Barns and Farm Auctions

Auction barns are a fixture of rural life, a popular place to gather, meet neighbors, socialize, and check out the going rate for cattle, hogs, sheep, and other livestock. Amish men enjoy attending sales, as do their non-Amish neighbors. Women sometimes accompany their husbands to the sale, but in general, it's a crowd of farmers who can take an afternoon off or need to buy or sell livestock. Most women are busy at home.

Sale barns, as they are called in the Midwest, hold general livestock auctions weekly. In Shipshewana, Indiana, the sale barn also hosts a huge flea market on Tuesdays and Wednesdays that draws busloads of tourists from around the Midwest. There's also a livestock auction on Wednesday, attended by locals. The Friday horse sale draws a mostly Amish crowd.

> **CAUTION** **Make No Mistake** _____
>
> "Auction barn" and "sale barn" mean the same thing: a large building holding a sale arena ("sale ring") and livestock pens where farmers bring livestock to sell at regularly scheduled public auctions. The auction barn is paid a fee for its services.
>
> A "farm sale" or "farm auction" is a one-time sale of household goods and farm equipment held on a farm. It's similar to an estate sale, except that the property may be sold as well. The seller hires an auctioneer to organize the sale.

A few miles away, the Topeka auction barn holds its weekly livestock sales on Thursdays, so as not to conflict with Shipshewana's. Twice a year, the sale barn hosts a major national horse sale that draws buyers and sellers from around the country.

Farm auctions are popular entertainment for men and women alike. Large farm sales last all day, and lunch is usually available for purchase, as well as snack foods. Auctions sometimes include just the household goods and farm equipment but other times the property is auctioned off as well.

Farm or estate auctions are advertised in the local paper and other publications to draw big crowds. The auctions are held on the farm being sold, outdoors if weather permits and in the house and barn if not. One or two auctioneers may "call" the sale, going from item to item among the merchandise spread across the farm yard. Small items are displayed on long tables, often grouped together in lots, while furniture and machinery stand on the lawn.

Neighbors gather at farm auctions to see how much articles sell for, to bid on anything that looks useful or attractive, to visit with neighbors, friends, and relatives, and sometimes to express support for the family holding the sale. Farm sales are usually held when someone dies or goes bankrupt, so there's often an undercurrent of sadness for family members and their friends.

Keeping in Touch: Amish Publications

Without telephones, television, or radio, the Amish rely heavily on written communication to stay in touch. Letter writing plays a much bigger part in Amish life than it does in modern culture, and newspapers and magazines published by and for the Amish help bind far-flung settlements into a cohesive cultural group.

Circle Letters

A "circle letter" passes from writer to writer, with each adding his or her own letter to the rest. The Amish use circle letters to feel close to others who share interests or problems. Circle letters may address parenting twins, for example, or widowhood, or the loss of a child to accident or disease. They are support groups for people who live at a distance, chat rooms for those without computers or e-mail.

Amish In Print

Although the Amish only attend school through eighth grade, they are on the whole literate and many enjoy reading. As in all cultures, some individuals show more intellectual curiosity than others and enjoy working with words. As their education has shifted from public to Amish schools, the Amish increasingly have developed their own publications, from newspapers and magazines to school texts, that reflect their culture and serve their needs better than "English" culture publications.

Since the nineteenth century, the Amish have relied on an English-language weekly newspaper called *The Budget* to keep up with doings in Amish settlements "Throughout The Americas," according to its masthead. Published in Sugarcreek, Ohio, since 1890, *The Budget* relies on chatty letters from editorial correspondents to report on weather and crop conditions, visits between settlements, vacations, illnesses, accidents, where church was held last and where it will be next, births, engagements, weddings, funerals, and occasional funny stories.

The Plain Truth

A sampling from an old edition of *The Budget*:

West Farmington, Ohio, June 19, 1994:

> Seems a neighbor lady could not get her husband to tighten her clothes lines. She finally got tired of all this and used some sly tactics. Her husband opened his lunch box one day at work and found this note. 'I'm sorry, you didn't fix my clothesline so you get "no lunch."' He fixed it that evening. She did put a smile face on his note.

Goshen, Indiana, June 16, 1994

> On Monday evening we were at the supper table when a storm came up which included hail. The hail wasn't as big as golf balls but they definitely put marbles to shame.

Entries in *The Budget* offer a peek into Amish culture and a look back in time. Instead of headlines and news stories, the newspaper consists of columns of entries headlined by the hometown and state of the regular correspondent assigned to that area. Writers use abbreviations and colloquial language, and sometimes misspell words. Some write colorful or poetic accounts, and all sign their names.

The Plain Truth

I've changed the names in these excerpts from *The Budget* to protect the subjects' privacy:

Montgomery, Indiana, June 17, 1994:

> A week ago last night when Joe Miller set a tea kettle of boiling water on the bathtub it slid off throwing the scalding contents on Joe's legs and Mandy's feet. Luckily, the baby wasn't nearby. Joe managed to get out to the neighbor's phone and called for help. He was taken to the hospital …. Mandy and baby were taken to her mother … where she was cared for until they could make it alone.

> Elmer Eash had been in the barn with a young bull. The bull was acting playful and bucked Elmer, bursting his colon …. While he was in the hospital his sister Susie and Wilbur Hochstetler brougt (sic) their little David in who had fallen a few ft. from a roof they were changing. He had his arm broken.

The Budget's publisher isn't Amish, and some of its correspondents are former Amish who have been banned. Because of this some writers engage in a little editorializing, occasionally aimed at swaying those still in the faith to leave it, thereby expressing views not in accord with the Amish church. In response, an alternative source of Amish news was created in 1974. *Die Botschaft* (The Message), published by Brookshire Publishers of Lancaster, Pennsylvania, is overseen by Amish deacons who make sure its writers toe the Amish line.

The Diary is a monthly magazine, which, in addition to the kind of reports carried in the weekly newspapers, once specialized in historical information on Amish settlements in America. It publishes old letters, historical documents and genealogies, and reports on historical research conducted by Amish amateur historians. Today it carries very little historical information, focusing instead on community notes like those in *The Budget*. *The Diary* also categorizes major news such as births, deaths, marriages, and accidents in separate sections, making them easier to find.

Two smaller, newer special interest publications are *Farming*, a magazine on small-scale farming published in Mt. Hope, Ohio, and *Plain Communities Business Exchange*, a monthly newspaper for Old Order businesses published in Lampeter, Pennsylvania.

Pathway Publishers, based in Aylmer, Ontario, and with an office in LaGrange, Indiana, publishes books and periodicals for the Old Order Amish and Old Order Mennonites. The founders and owners are Amish farmers who turned to publishing to bring suitable reading materials to others of their faith. They publish without electricity, and all their employees, authors, and illustrators are Amish. Pathway publishes fiction, nonfiction, cookbooks, and a full line of readers and workbooks for Amish schools.

Pathway also publishes magazines, including *Blackboard Bulletin*, the *Young Companion*, and *Family Life*. In addition to fiction, true stories, and editorials, reader input through letters forms a key component of *Family Life*. According to author John Hostetler, a regular feature entitled "What Do You Think" appears in *Family Life* magazine. The column "has covered in-law troubles, zodiac signs and superstitions, the use of nicknames, unwanted baby gifts, new settlements, what to do with offensive salesmen, women working in the fields, vitamin addiction, tourists, borrowing, working in factories, hired girls, hunting, bed-wetting, use of tobacco, conveniences, and other sensitive topics."

Anyone wanting to see inside Amish culture can get a glimpse by reading any of their publications. *The Budget* sometimes can be purchased at restaurants and stores in Amish settlements, including those catering to tourists. In addition, Brad Igou has compiled selections from *Family Life* in the book, *The Amish in Their Own Words*. To get a more up-to-date view, though, the most effective way would be to subscribe to one or more publication. Their addresses are listed in Appendix B.

The Least You Need to Know

- The survival of Amish culture in modern society depends on their ability to teach and enforce conformity within the group.

- Dancing, musical instruments, drinking, and gambling are all forbidden by the Amish.

- The favorite Amish pastime is visiting, which means talking and bantering with friends and neighbors, often while working.

- In addition to work frolics, the Amish create many opportunities to socialize.

- Amish publications and circle letters help unite distant settlements into a single culture.

14

Sight Unseen: The Shadow Side of Community

In This Chapter

- ◆ Shadow behavior
- ◆ Social problems with young people
- ◆ Violence in Amish families
- ◆ Sexual abuse among the Amish

Human communities, like the people who form them, include both positive and negative traits. And just as individuals don't like to examine or even acknowledge their negative traits or behaviors—sometimes called their shadow side—neither does a community.

What is the shadow side of Amish community? It's not much different than the shadow of any other group of people. It includes those who hurt themselves and others with destructive behavior, which they do their best to hide.

It may seem paradoxical that destructive or violent behavior can exist in a religious community that teaches love and nonviolence, and holds its members accountable to God and each other for living those beliefs daily.

Yet what is true of the Amish is true of any church—from Mennonites to Catholics. Religious groups are made up of individual human beings, and therefore always fall short of their ideals.

Shadow behavior is the exception rather than the rule in all societies—if it weren't, we couldn't survive as a species. The reason for shining a light into the shadows isn't to tarnish the reputation of a people, but to acknowledge that problem behavior exists. Recent experiences of the Catholic church in confronting clergy sexual abuse, for instance, have pointed out what happens when people deny a problem exists: It continues and grows.

Shining a Light in the Shadows

All aspects of human life have both positive and negative sides. Well-behaved children raised to obey authority sometimes act out when they outgrow that authority. Close-knit communities create security but also a lack of privacy. The idea of holding each other accountable for living up to our ideals sounds positive. But strict community standards enforced by public confessions and discipline creates shadows in the form of judgmental attitudes and the fear of judgment by neighbors, family, and friends.

> ### Make No Mistake
>
> "If you want to hear all the dirt or other news," says one former Amish man in *True Stories of the X-Amish*, "then attend a quilting session at one of the Amish homes, or attend an auction." As in other rural societies with few outlets for creative energy, gossip is a widely practiced form of entertainment among the Amish.

"What will the neighbors think?" is a commonly heard objection to individual behavior that runs counter to the norm. Jealousy sometimes masquerades as righteousness in complaints about a church member's adherence, or lack thereof, to the rules.

Silence has its shadow, too. Amish culture values actions over words. Feelings usually are acted out rather than spoken. Any thought or feeling considered unrighteous has to be repressed because speaking it will bring the disapproval of the community. But when strong, negative feelings like anger and shame are expressed through action rather than words, those actions are usually destructive.

The shadow of tightly interwoven family relationships is lack of privacy, gossip, and judgment. Quilting bees, barn raisings, and farm auctions help create community harmony. Their shadow side, however, is that along with the pleasant back-and-forth of friendly conversation, these occasions can be rife with gossip and judgment of others.

The shadow of discipline is punishment and vindictiveness. The Amish consider excommunication and shunning to be a form of church discipline. They say they do it to make the person aware of his sin and bring about repentance. But shunning uses silence to inflict emotional wounds. "Shunning with a vengeance" is a phrase used to describe the punitive nature of shunning.

The shadow of patriarchy, or any system that gives power to one subgroup over another, is the unchecked abuse of power. Amish women and children have little power to speak out and make themselves heard when a father or husband is abusive. Men are given more credibility than women, adults more than children, and only older men have the power to discipline younger men.

The shadow of group harmony is that the individuals have to agree or leave, fall in step or be rejected. Amish culture exacts a stiff price for belonging: conformity to group will and practice. Anyone who isn't served or protected by the social order, and says so, faces rejection by the group. There is no procedure, after baptism, for departing peacefully and with good will from Amish society.

> **The Plain Truth** _____
>
> One avenue for Amish women and older children to make their voices heard is through the magazine *Family Life*. The magazine has published many articles and letters from readers speaking out against abuse. Though the Amish condone the physical punishment of children, most Amish people, like the rest of us, don't want to see children hurt or unloved.

Amish culture discourages "rocking the boat," upsetting the power structure, or complex web of relationships that keep the community functioning smoothly. What happens when someone exposes an abuse of power, at home or in the church? As in other hierarchical groups and religious organizations, the person with power is more likely to be believed or supported than the accuser, who may be labeled a troublemaker.

Disagreements with church leaders actually may be easier to air than similar disagreements in families, because they're more public. If enough people witness the leader abusing power, they can protest and be heard, possibly ousting the leader. It's harder for family members to oust an abusive parent, especially in a church community that forbids divorce.

All these shadows make themselves felt in the Amish community, although they're not usually visible from the outside.

The Wild Years: Out of Hand

Upon turning 16, Amish youth in the Lancaster settlement join one of a number of "gangs" with nicknames and distinct identities. (In other large settlements, the gangs are not as organized.) These groups draw members from throughout the settlement

Make No Mistake

Although it refers to a group of young people who hang around together, the word "gang" doesn't have the same negative meaning among the Amish that it does in modern American society.

Ironies and Oddities

Police in Indiana, Ohio, and Pennsylvania have sometimes broken up parties and arrested Amish youth for drinking and using and selling drugs. Lancaster County police asked the Amish leadership to help stop underage Amish drinking because it was contributing to automobile accidents. The Lancaster Amish leadership not only spoke out against teen drinking, they also organized meetings on drug abuse that drew many parents.

into organized activities. Sunday afternoons might see the more traditional groups playing softball or volleyball, ice skating or roller skating, followed by a big supper prepared by members' parents at one farm and a traditional singing held at a different farm. After singing ends at around 10 P.M., the young people hang around to socialize until midnight or later. Most youth stay home on Saturday nights, unless they're dating.

Members of the wild groups, by contrast, socialize on Saturday nights *and* Sunday afternoons and evenings. Many of them drive cars and go out dressed in so-called "worldly" clothes with their hair styled like the "English," to movies or other entertainment, including bars. On Sunday evenings, they organize large "hops" in someone's barn, with beer and dancing to music by Amish bands. These sometimes are planned for a time when parents are away from home, but some parents simply choose not to acknowledge what's going on in their barn.

The issue of "hops" and drinking among the young, and what parents can and should do to prevent these activities, has provoked much discussion over the years among the Amish. Letters on the subject excerpted from *Family Life* magazine in the book *The Amish in Their Own Words* express the views of those who feel that parents must exert more authority to stop wild behavior of the young. That behavior includes drinking, smoking, driving and owning cars, dancing, and "improper courtship activities" resulting in marrying "with purity gone" and pregnancies to prove it.

Having worked so hard to control the thinking, speech, and action of their children up to mid-adolescence, many Amish parents seem to feel helpless to exert any control after that, even though their children continue to live at home. Church rules don't apply to this age group, since they haven't yet become members. Traditionally, parents have simply looked the other way, ignoring youthful acting out rather than taking action against it. Parents don't want to have to draw a line that might force young people to choose between living at home and moving out into the world, where they would no longer be under the influence of their family and community.

Smaller Amish settlements have fewer problems than the larger settlements with wild parties, drinking, driving, and drugs. Where there are fewer young people, they're more likely to remain more closely aligned with their parents than where a large peer group gives them a sense of independent power.

Family Violence

The popular image of the Amish is of a harmonious and peace-loving people, immune from the conflicts of mainstream culture because of their beliefs in moral living, nonresistance, and nonviolence. Like other stereotypes, that one is rooted in truth, but it's far too simplistic to embrace the whole, complex reality. Just as Amish families hide their conflicts to avoid the judgment of other church members, so Amish society (like many groups that aspire to moral purity) hides from the outside world the conflicts between Amish ideals and Amish reality.

Abuse, Patriarchy, and Depression

In his book *Amish Society*, sociologist John Hostetler wrote, "Although the Amish themselves believe that mental illness [such as manic-depressive illnesses] 'runs in a family,' no hard [genetic] evidence has been found to support the Amish folk beliefs."

But mental health experts do know that abuse does "run in a family," learned by each generation from the one before, and also causes depression, post-traumatic stress disorder, and other mental illnesses. Perhaps the mental health problems that the Amish believe run in the family are caused by living conditions and stress related to social conditions, rather than genetic factors. Mental health practitioners and rape crisis centers have confirmed to some researchers that they treat Amish clients for a variety of psychological conditions resulting from abuse. So at least some Amish persons are able to get help coping with family problems from outside their culture.

 The Plain Truth

A woman voiced her views on Amish men who complain about their wives' weight:

> Perhaps the underlying reason a lot of women are overweight is because of a lack of affection and understanding. If they would get all the love they need from their husbands, they wouldn't keep trying to fill that void within themselves with food. If supplying the affection is too much trouble for the husbands, they can just forget about voicing their opinions about the extra fat.

She could have been talking about relationship issues in any modern marriage! In the best Amish marriages, as is true in any culture, partners try to meet each others' needs.

Physical and sexual abuse aren't the only forms of violence that cause depression and other mental health problems. Emotional abuse also takes its toll, and is hard to control in any society that empowers one group of people over another. This is true not only when men dominate women, but when one ethnic or racial group dominates another. Abuse is hard to prove or resist for people without social power. The strict patriarchy of Amish society means that most often the abusers are men, but women also sometimes abuse. And Amish society is by no means alone in this.

Dr. Elvin Coblentz, a psychologist practicing in Ohio, sees Amish women in his practice. He also knows their culture from inside, having grown up Amish himself. He described the effect of repressive Amish culture on women's mental health in the August 1999 issue of *Glamour* magazine:

> It's a husband-dominated society; the woman's needs are minimized, if they're even acknowledged .... One of my patients, an Amish mother of eight, recently said to me, "Happy?! I'm not supposed to be happy. I'm supposed to be quiet and work."

The Plain Truth

Stories of family violence among the Amish usually are told by former Amish members. The reason is obvious: Amish culture divides the world into outsiders and insiders. If you're inside and want to remain among them, you keep to yourself any stories that reflect badly on the community. Some Amish people do report abuse to police, rape crisis counselors, and therapists. Most who tell their stories for publication, though, have already left the Amish community.

The image of the peaceful Amish life is, in some families, fiction. Child abuse and domestic violence abide in Amish homes as well as in homes of the "English." In all families, children learn how to be a parent from their own parents. Those who are loved and respected become loving, respectful parents. Those who are treated as outlets for their parents' anger and frustration, who are never hugged or told by their parents that they are loved, are more likely to treat their own children the same way.

Stress and Anger Among the Amish: Nowhere to Go

Parents lash out at their children because they don't know how to handle their own stress, anger, and pain. Despite the belief that the rapid pace of life makes modern life more stressful than in earlier centuries, there are plenty of stresses in the "simple" Amish life as well. Amish people are under tremendous pressure to avoid community judgment, because the consequences are losing your family, social support, and even livelihood. To avoid that judgment, Amish culture teaches people to …

- Conform to social and religious expectations.

- Avoid attracting attention.

- Conform to church rules or traditions.

- Work as hard as they can, even when there is more work than the adults at hand can physically do.

- Raise many children whether they can afford them or not.

- Keep quiet if they're unhappy and pretend that they are satisfied.

- Hide anger and frustration.

- Avoid showing pride in themselves, their work, or family.

- Remember that they are unworthy of the salvation they seek.

- Avoid intimate contact with the English world to avoid the contamination of ideas that might lead them to question their beliefs or culture.

- Make their children conform to the church's expectations.

- Punish their children for shows of rebellion or independence to maintain family order.

What does an Amish person do with the anger and frustration that can come from trying to meet so many expectations? Some can talk to family members, friends, or church leaders and get a sympathetic response. A good listener may help him or her think through the problem, thereby defusing the anger.

In other cases, the person might be counseled against his feelings and judged for having them. Social expectations among the Amish are strong, and pretty rigid. Some adults are reluctant to admit they don't feel capable of meeting them all.

A frustrated, angry adult is most likely to take those feelings out on his or her spouse or children. A woman may speak sharply to her husband, or not at all. She may strike her children or otherwise abuse them in the name of discipline, and some do. But in story after story of those who have left, the head of the household, the man who must be obeyed by both his wife and his children and who has the authority of the church to use words or force against them if they don't, is usually the abuser.

Words, Whips, Straps, and Pitchforks

The book *True Stories of the X-Amish*, as told to Ottie A. Garrett, records the stories of several individuals and families who left the Old Order Amish community. Although not a scholarly work, the book reflects the voices of people who left the

Make No Mistake

No one claims these stories of abuse are typical of Amish family life, any more than child abuse is typical in non-Amish families. But it does occur, and because the Amish isolate themselves from the rest of society, family violence among them is likely more under-reported than in society as a whole. Certainly not all abused persons leave the Amish and tell their story.

Amish community only after much reflection. Several were young men who left in their late teens; others were adults who left with their spouses and children. Some reported being beaten as children, verbally abused, and made to do dangerous farm work such as driving teams of draft horses alone by the age of eight. Some use their real names; others are given pseudonyms to protect themselves and their families.

One man called Ed reported driving a three-horse team when he was only an 80-pound child and not being able to stop them from taking down 100 yards of fence. "My dad gave me the beating of my life for that, and I can never forget it, as I still have scars from the pitchfork in my rear end simply because I couldn't stop those horses where he wanted them stopped."

"That was just the strict Amish way of correcting their kids," he goes on, "he (his father) always dished out strong punishment. I certainly feel that I was an abused child, probably verbally as much as physically abused." Ed says that he ran away at age 16 not because of the abuse, but because he found the rules of Amish life hypocritical.

"I was so severely punished even when I was innocent, that it just didn't matter to me anymore …. I learned early on to start crying from the first lick because they were determined to make you submissive, forcing you to admit you were wrong whether you had actually done anything or not."

Amish culture condones physical punishment for children. In some Amish families, the punishment goes beyond discipline and becomes abuse.

Family discipline mirrors church discipline, which requires adults to confess when accused of sin, guilty or not, or face excommunication. Perhaps that parallel was stronger in Ed's family than in most because his father was an Amish bishop.

"My second oldest sister," Ed writes, "who was about eight or ten, was beaten so severely that my father damaged her eye. This was all over something she didn't ever do. My father was determined to make her admit to something for which she was not guilty. She was taken to the hospital to have her eye examined and repaired." Whether the doctor asked how the child's eye was hurt, or what tale their father told, he doesn't record, if he knows.

> **The Plain Truth**
>
> For the most part, Amish churches have no hierarchy to which local bishops must answer. Because of this structure, when a bishop abuses power, there is often no higher authority to exercise discipline. The situation isn't common, but when it occurs, it creates a situation in which one abusive person has wide influence.

A different Amish boy, LeRoy, also remembered being beaten with a strap for letting a team of horses knock down a fence post when he was 13. Unlike Ed, LeRoy tried to hide his pain in defiance of his father. That incident led directly to his decision to run away from home and the Amish church.

Manny, another man who grew up as the son of an Amish minister, told the book's author that "by the time (he) was eight years old, he did the plowing by himself. It would take him all day to plow an acre …. And when he didn't do it fast enough to suit his father, he got a whipping with a razor strap. That wasn't an unusual occurrence. His father would whip until he was satisfied, until he got his anger out."

Dan Beachy was another young Amish man whose father's abuse, coupled with questions about the religion, drove him to leave the community when he was 20. "Being the oldest of 15 children, Dan, many times, would be blamed for the mistakes of his younger siblings," according to *True Stories*. As a result, Dan would be beaten severely by his father. His father would strike him with whatever was at hand, usually leather tugs, or straps, sometimes even chains. The one instrument that hurt the worst was number nine wire.

Verbal Abuse: Ridicule and Threats

Sometimes words cut as deeply as wire or straps. "… While beating his son, Dan Beachy's father would yell abusive language," according to *True Stories*. The physical abuse stopped after Dan got old enough to grab the wire from his father's hand, but his father continued to threaten his son with hell for disobeying him.

Ironies and Oddities

"The Amish communities are far from perfect," *True Stories of the X-Amish* records Ed saying. "For those less fortunate, there is criticism and ridicule (from the community), and among those more fortunate or wealthy, there is jealousy and envy with each other …. Gossiping is a favorite hobby of the Amish."

The Amish don't claim perfection, but they do claim a society that's more moral than the world around them. When they fail to live up to that claim, everyone—including the Amish—is disappointed.

Women, as well as children, suffer if their husbands are abusive. Ottie Garrett's wife, Ruth Irene Garrett, also grew up Amish and told her life story to Rick Farrant in the book *Crossing Over: One Woman's Exodus from Amish Life*. She describes her father as "a stern, unforgiving man with stunning white shocks on his scalp and chin and a cold look of disdain that can freeze a person standing." Toward his family he was "dominant—sometimes cruel …"

"For as far back as I can remember," Garrett continues, "my mother, a gentle woman with a round face that flushes easily, was the subject of his persistent ridicule—warranted or not. The children, meanwhile, were held to sometimes impossible standards, any weaknesses they might have—physical or mental—became the subject of my father's scorn."

Although he also punished them physically, Garrett reports, the verbal abuse did the most damage. "It wasn't so much the spankings from his hand or the whippings he carried out with a leather strap," she writes. "It was the cutting words that accompanied his explosive, unpredictable temper …"

"We were all deathly afraid of him, unsure, for the most part, when something was going to send him into a rage."

One of her biggest fears about leaving the Amish was that her father would take out his anger on her mother. "How can I leave mom when I know she will be blamed, abused, scolded, and maybe even hurt because of me?" she wrote to Ottie Garrett, her future husband, before she left the Amish to marry him.

Her letter continues, "There was one time when he was so angry, I became uneasy that he might seriously harm her. Later, I asked her if she's afraid that would happen sometime. She admitted she is afraid and cannot sleep if he walks 'stealthy-like' through the house when he's so angry. She cannot sleep until he is also in bed and she knows he is sleeping."

Where Is the Church?

Of course, the Amish church doesn't condone beating children or wives, or insulting and belittling them. But since there is no national Amish institution, neither is there a central voice to speak or take action on behalf of the Amish community on issues such as abuse.

In recent years, Pathway Publishers has taken a leading role in attempting to both preserve and improve Amish faith, life, and culture. In 2002, *Family Life* magazine began publishing a series of articles titled "Guidelines for Parents." The series included article such as, "Being Worthy Of Your Child's Respect" and "Emotional Security for our Children." Another series, with contributions solicited from readers, was called "Anger! Danger Zone."

Pathway Publishers also publishes books about child and sexual abuse. One booklet on child abuse, offered free through *Family Life*, was titled *Strong Families, Safe Children: An Amish Family Resource Book*. They also distribute the book *Beauty for Ashes: Biblical Help for the Sexually Abused*, published by the Conservative Mennonite Firm, Christian Light Publishers of Harrisonburg, Virginia. A set of booklets titled *Sacred Subjects*, also advertisied in *Family Life* and written by an Amish minister from Indiana, offers sex education from an Amish perspective.

These are signs that the Amish community, like modern society, is coming to terms with the problem of violence in some of its families. But not all communities look favorably upon the efforts of Pathway Publishers to address problems in Amish society.

Some Amish parents don't question the line between spanking and beating, discipline and punishment. Many others, however, try to use corporal punishment judiciously and carefully.

The Pathway Publisher's book *Child Training*, by Joseph Stoll, includes a chapter on spanking. Drawing on letters from Amish parents to *Family Life* magazine, the author writes, "Many readers warned against disciplining when angry, or too severely and unfairly. Children need to be understood, loved, and properly disciplined, but not provoked to anger, ridiculed, or scorned."

Stoll continues, "Hitting on the head, pulling hair, twisting ears, slapping faces, and kicking are abusive practices and have caused permanent injury to babies and young children. Spank a child on his seat where there is the least possibility of physical injury."

And Stoll advises fathers, "… [Y]ou cannot put good judgement there … neither can you pound faith into them with a rod, but you can do your duty as a father with admonishing them with the Word of God and plead with them and pray for them …."

One way Amish leaders who hear of suspected abuse might handle it would be to visit the man in question, counsel him to love his wife as Christ loves the church, as the Apostle Paul counseled, and to temper the discipline of his children with love. But they would be very unlikely to take the matter any further by removing the man from the home or reporting him to police.

The church feels that domestic matters of members should be handled by the church itself, and not reported to outside authorities. Yet this isn't just a matter of wanting to keep dirty laundry private. The Amish are reluctant to report anyone to police, even if they're victimized by someone outside the Amish community.

> **CAUTION**
>
> ### Make No Mistake
>
> What outsiders, including academics who study their culture, interpret as expressions of humility can sometimes be signs of lack of self-esteem.
>
> In *Crossing Over*, Ruth Irene Garrett told co-author Rick Farrant, "My sister and some of my brothers became so submissive, they walked around with their shoulders slumped and heads down, unable to maintain eye contact with people."

Sexual Abuse

Sexual abuse runs in Amish families just as it does in families in other societies. In *True Stories of the X-Amish*, a woman named Mattie remembers a childhood of deprivation, abuse, and fear. "My father was a man governed by his emotions," she recalls. "He was a violent man with quite a temper …. All of us children suffered from his wrath. We were taught to obey and respect our parents, and we did obey. Not one of us children would dare confront him. My mother was not allowed to say much about his behavior. In the Amish communities, the man of the house is the head of the household. My own father took full advantage of his authority."

As she grew up, Mattie's father, an Amish minister, started to sexually abuse her. "He was a preacher in our church, and he would preach sometimes about how it was wrong for boys and girls to do such things as touch each other and go even farther than that …. And yet, he would do these very things to me, his daughter. He would also manage to be alone with me in the barn, and then he would try to molest me."

Although she felt instinctively that it was not right, Mattie said she didn't really understand what her father was doing, or what she could do about it. "He always told me that if I said anything to anybody he would deny it, and of course no one would believe me. They would believe him." She did try talking to a sister about it, who said their mother probably knew what he did, and they shouldn't be talking about it.

"He never got much further than kissing and grabbing," Mattie said, "… but I think he would have if I had not fought him off." Eventually, after she kicked him in self-defense, he stopped molesting her. "I suspect he moved on to one of my sisters. I did try to warn them, but it did not do any good. There wasn't much they could do about it either."

What to Do?

Perhaps one reason people often are reluctant to look at the shadow behavior in their own society or another is that they don't know how to stop it. Denial or avoidance is easier than feeling outraged, disgusted, or helpless. However, that kind of response changes nothing.

One of the most powerful agents of change is one of the simplest: awareness. That's why anyone speaking out, whether Pathway Publishers through its articles on child abuse or an individual telling his or her personal story, often meets with resistance.

No society can be understood by its successes alone. Putting anyone on a pedestal—including the Amish—denies them their right to be fully human. To do justice to a people, one must be willing to see them for who they are, in all their complexity and contradiction. Looking at the dark side of Amish society—or human society—is as necessary to understanding it as looking at the light, the positive, side. Without both, the picture is incomplete.

The Least You Need to Know

- For every positive aspect of a culture, a negative or shadow side exists, and Amish culture is no exception.

- After a childhood rigidly controlled by parents, some Amish young people rebel not only by driving, holding dances, and dressing "English," but also by drinking and even using and selling drugs.

- With few resources for handling their anger and stress, some Amish parents take out anger and frustration on their children.

- Abuse of all types—verbal, physical, and sexual—exists in Amish families as it does in those of other cultures.

- In Amish communities where contact with the outside world is limited, women and children in abusive Amish families have few options for getting help.

You Can't Go Home Again: Leaving the Amish

In This Chapter

◆ The effects of the ban on those who leave

◆ Why people leave

◆ How people leave

◆ The Amish response to those who leave

◆ Stories of those who left

Once Amish, always Amish, or always banned—that's the rule of the church. In the communities that enforce the ban most strictly, those who leave can't really go home again—home as one of the family, welcomed and celebrated and respected—unless they return to the church. And that means confessing their leaving as a sin, asking forgiveness, enduring a period of shunning as penance, and living by rules that forbid marriage if a former or current spouse is still living—even if the couple is divorced and the other spouse doesn't rejoin the church. While many churches used to believe that scripture forbids remarriage while a spouse is living, regardless of circumstances, most have come to recognize divorce. The Amish, however, do not.

Jumping the Fence

Those who choose not to return to the Amish church may be able to visit parents and siblings and attend funerals, but relatives are not allowed to accept anything from any person who is under the ban, or to eat at the same table. Those who leave the church usually won't be invited to family weddings and other celebrations, because those still in the church are only supposed to associate with them when trying to persuade them to return.

The sting of being banned—banished—can last a lifetime.

Irene Garrett describes what being banned is like in her book, *Crossing Over:*

> There is a saying: "You can never go home." And in my case, it's true. Although I may be able to physically return, home will never be the same.

> I am now an outsider—one of those people I once avoided, and once criticized unknowingly.

Make No Mistake

Not all communities, or families, enforce the ban with the same strictness. While churches in Lancaster County, Pennsylvania, practice *Streing Meidung* (strict shunning), in the larger Midwestern settlement the ban is often lifted eventually, especially if the person joins another Anabaptist church. Excommunication, of course, remains in effect, but lifting the ban allows the person to be accepted socially.

That's the biggest difference between belonging to the Amish and being a member of most other Christian churches. The Amish church is not just a church, but a society. Its members can't simply decide to join another church, or even attend Bible study groups run by churches or individuals who aren't Amish. They can't change their lifestyle or religious beliefs and still enjoy a loving relationship with friends and family who remain Amish.

Yet, some people do leave. Reasons given by those who have left include questions about religious rules, intellectual curiosity and to pursue higher education, and the desire to use the Bible—rather than church rules—to guide spiritual growth and life.

A Thirst for Knowledge

"We were only given an eighth grade education, so we pretty much had to stay and depend on the Amish community to survive," said Ed, in *True Stories*. "We were kept ignorant and unlearned, only taught survival within our own realms of life."

The Plain Truth

Although it's seldom openly admitted, the Amish and their Mennonite neighbors harbor a certain distrust of each other's culture, as reflected in some slang terms. Amish youth in Lancaster County, Pennsylvania, may say someone who is too worldly or English has become "Sod." Such a person might be ready to "jump the fence," or leave the Amish church.

A derogatory slang term among Mennonites for someone who has left the Amish is "jerked-over Amishman." Sometimes the "j" is pronounced "ch" in imitation of a Pennsylvania Dutch accent. It means someone who is still a little backward or uncool by modern standards.

In Geuaga County, Ohio, the non-Amish neighbors are referred to as "Yankees" because the first settlers in the area came from New England. In that area, a person leaving the Amish they is said to have "yanked over."

That ignorance, he says, keeps Amish people from leaving even if they want to. "Children are so brainwashed by the time they are four years old; they fear the outside world so much. The English world is portrayed as evil and sinful and a sure way of damnation to an eternal hell."

Ed writes that many who leave their Amish families and communities continue their education, completing the General Equivalency Exam (GED) to earn a high school diploma. A few even go on to college, although without the support of a family, this is hard to do. Earning a living isn't easy for someone with few skills, little job experience, and only an eighth grade education.

Ironies and Oddities

At least two of the three students whose stories are related by John Hostetler in *Amish Society* attended public elementary schools. There they met both teachers and students from "outside" who encouraged and challenged them to continue learning. Their experience supports Amish fears that their children, if educated, might leave the faith.

John Hostetler, in his book *Amish Society*, tells the stories of three Amish young people who left their culture, family, and religion to pursue a love of learning.

Sam

Sam loved school from the start, even though his parents had kept him out of school until he was seven so he would be old enough to quit after eighth grade. Even when his father tried to make him stay home for a day to work, he would sometimes get on the bus at the last minute.

Once Sam finished the eighth grade and had reached age 16, his parents wouldn't allow him to go on to high school. "I felt there was nothing to do but stay home and work for Dad till I was 21," he told Hostetler. "My life was terribly lean during those years."

Sam joined the Amish church, but he was drafted for military service and he left the community for alternative service as a *conscientious objector*. During his alternative service, he made friends with those outside the Amish community. He met many Mennonites, and after he completed his service he went to a Mennonite college. After unsuccessfully trying to retain his Amish affiliation, Sam eventually joined the Mennonite church.

Rebecca

Rebecca, who had loved to read since childhood, became very despondent after she finished grade school. "My dissatisfaction began to show in physical ways," she told Hostetler. "I had no energy, I was anemic. Nothing interested me. I didn't fit in with the Amish young people and I sort of despised them for their lack of learning."

The last straw came when her mother had a late pregnancy. Rebecca, as the oldest of eight, had been "tied down" as her mother's helper through subsequent pregnancies. At age 18, "Finally, I thought, I could begin to see daylight, have a little more time to myself, and to keep the house neat without working so hard. Then I learned that mother was pregnant again, and this was the last straw …. I told father I had had enough."

Unlike many others who left the Amish, Rebecca felt no need to leave in secrecy. She told her father her intentions. Her father offered her a compromise: If she stayed to help her mother through this pregnancy, then she could go to Bible school. Not a college education—a six-week course in Bible studies. But still a leap ahead for a young woman not allowed to attend high school.

"This was enough for me," Rebecca said, "then I could get away and go where there was a library and read." Rebecca did go on to college and didn't join the Amish church. Hostetler writes that her whole family eventually followed her lead and became Mennonite.

> **Vas Es Das?**
>
> A **conscientious objector** (CO) is someone who, for reasons of conscience, objects to joining the military. The government allows men who are members of the churches that historically teach pacifism (Amish, Mennonites, Brethren, and Quakers), to perform alternative public service, such as working as hospital orderlies or in public works programs. Other men can also register as CO's by demonstrating a long-held conviction against killing.

Chris

Chris's eighth grade achievement test showed him to be the best student in the county. Despite the advice of the school principal, who tried to persuade Chris's father to let his son go to high school, his father wouldn't allow it.

A year later, after Chris had repeated eighth grade because he wasn't old enough to quit school, the principal gave Chris ninth grade books and let him take semester tests, which he passed with ease. "But I finally gave up and returned the books," he told Hostetler. "I knew I would never stay Amish because the principal convinced me the Amish should not keep their children home from school. He told me I had brains. He told me I could be more than a farmer." The Amish fear of the effect of public education, especially high school, on their young people proved founded in Chris's case.

> **Ironies and Oddities**
>
> "It is not uncommon," according to Hostetler, "for one or two children in a family to break the tradition with the result that the parents do so later."

After grade school, Chris spent two years at home "brooding" and working as little as possible for his father. "I did a lot of local-diner-and-gas-station-hanging-out with my non-Amish friends," he told Hostetler, "and though I dressed Amish, I fitted in somehow." Eventually, he was able to go to Florida and get work as a hotel waiter, freeing himself from dependence on his father. Once independent, he was able to go on to get a college degree.

While the Amish forbid higher education because it opens the way to the influence of the world, not all discourage learning. Some are well-read, making good use of the local library.

Following the Spirit

Once away from the strict religious requirements of Amish culture, some former Amish persons avoid any religious affiliation. Many others, though, want a deeper spiritual life than they had among the Amish. In Pennsylvania and the midwestern settlements, which are intermingled with Mennonite neighbors, the most common way to leave is to join a Mennonite church. But some who leave the Amish church are attracted by the spiritual vigor of evangelical or fundamentalist churches. This is especially true in newer and smaller settlements such as the one in Missouri, with no large Mennonite community nearby.

Some former Amish people report that the stirrings of doubt about being Amish began when they read the Bible in English for the first time. They could understand

English better than the old German version used by the Amish, and sometimes reached different conclusions about the meaning of scripture than the interpretations handed down by their Amish ministers.

Reading the Bible in English, however, was against the rules of their local Amish churches, as is discussing scripture and biblical questions with non-Amish Christians. (Not all Amish ministers and bishops forbid Bible reading, however, and in some settlements, it's common for Amish people to read the Bible in English. Again, practice varies by church district and settlement.)

Interdenominational Bible study is considered a dangerous exposure to new ideas, interpretations that might conflict with Amish traditions and rules. In some settlements, Amish churches discourage church members from acquiring too much "Bible knowledge." In response, some Amish people wonder what there is to be afraid of. Amish bishop Ura Yoder and his wife Edna had such questions.

The Yoder Family

Ura and Edna Yoder, along with several of their grown children, left the Amish in 1983, according to *True Stories of the X-Amish*. (One son had left four years earlier.) Ura was an Amish bishop in their Missouri church district. He didn't leave because he didn't like the Amish lifestyle, but because the church excommunicated him for preaching what he felt was the truth that he found in the Bible, which sometimes conflicted with traditional Amish beliefs.

"I wanted to preach the Word!" Ura told the author. "Sincerely wanted to preach the Word, because that's what I was ordained to do. And the Bible told me if I preach to please the people, I'm not a servant of Christ."

Ura's differences with Amish doctrine started after he was ordained a minister. Ura felt he had to study the Bible more than he had previously. "… (a)fter I got into the ministry, I got into studying the Bible really deep; and that, according the Amish, was my fault."

After another bishop found Ura's family and like-minded friends discussing the Bible with a Baptist minister in Ura and Edna's home, they were excommunicated along with several of their sons and daughters-in-law. In addition to meeting with the Baptist minister, Ura broke Amish rules by not stopping his son from selling hay to a former church member who was under the ban. "I didn't shun him like the Amish church thought I should," Ura said.

After being banned, Ura and Edna and some of their children joined Baptist churches.

> **The Plain Truth** _____
>
> Unlike some former Amish people who left because they felt restricted by church rules, Ura Yoder was comfortable doing things the Amish way. His argument wasn't with the lifestyle, but with Amish religious beliefs.
>
> In *True Stories of the X-Amish* he says, "If I had went for (electrical) power, equipment, everything—all those privileges; if I had went for that, a thousand times I would have already went back ....
>
> "If the Amish way was the way to get there, to get that free trip to Heaven, why I certainly would not swap it for a tractor.'"

Mike

In *Amish Society*, John Hostetler tells the story of a young Amish man who was drawn away from the church when he got to know a group of evangelical fundamentalist Christians while doing his alternative service.

Mike started out as a strictly obedient Amish man, with a wife at home, determined to represent his religion well to the outsiders. But he couldn't help being struck by the sincerity of spiritual feeling expressed by those around him. He encountered young men singing a spiritual on the train carrying them all to work camp, and a Mennonite minister who led devotions right on the train, with soldiers all around. "I thought, that's just the way it should be. Then I thought to myself, would our Amish preachers have done this? I thought, no."

Mike was also impressed that both the Mennonite preacher and the evangelicals prayed aloud and spontaneously. The Amish read prayers aloud from a prayer book, or recite them silently—they're not taught to pray their own words or thoughts. Mike found it difficult to join in the evangelical prayers, but he admired the sincerity of feeling he heard. Again, he thought, "... well, that's just the way it should be."

Testimony meetings were another new experience. "The boys got up, one after another, with faces aglow, giving Scripture verses and testimony. Each boy said how he was saved, but I thought, no, we do not know whether we are saved until we get over yonder."

Mike had come up against a significant difference in doctrine between the Amish and his born-again Christian friends. The Amish believe a person can hope for salvation and try to live a life deserving of salvation, but never be certain he's done enough. That belief keeps the Amish constantly on guard against breaking a church rule or feeling too secure about themselves. The evangelicals Mike met believed that the Bible said all you have to do is love God, believe in God, and you can know you're saved. For Mike, it was an important distinction.

As he got to know these new Christians, Mike found their standards of behavior to be even higher than the Amish standard he was used to. They didn't smoke, drink, play pool, or go to movies even on the sly. And unlike his friends back home, they didn't tell dirty jokes. "I noticed that their standards in this regard were above mine, but I had the outward appearance. This bothered me."

When he went home next for a visit, he listened more carefully to see if he'd been missing something the Amish preachers were saying. Perhaps they were teaching "salvation by faith," but he found he hadn't missed a thing. "They used the same Scripture verses, but explained it differently and just seemed to explain away the meaning," he told Hostetler.

Back at camp, Mike felt increasingly torn between the spiritual life he was witnessing and the teachings of the Amish. To make matters worse, he knew if he followed his inclinations, he would have to leave his family behind. "If I went home this way, I would be thrown out of church, I would have to part company with my wife."

Eventually Mike did have a conversion experience while at work camp, and after going home he left the Amish church for a Protestant group.

Undercover of Night

Many of those who leave the Amish, especially children of domineering parents or wives of opposed husbands, do so in secret. They're afraid that if family members knew, they would stop them or try to thwart their plans and dreams. Amish runaways may make plans to meet ex-Amish relatives or friends in the middle of the night. Or they may simply start walking and hitch a ride from a passing driver. A few rebellious teenagers who haven't yet joined the church have cars of their own already. Some runaways head for the home of non-Amish relatives, while others fend for themselves, even sleeping outdoors until they can find a way to earn enough to pay for food, new clothing, shelter, and transportation.

No Money, No Home

If they leave while still young, people who leave the church usually go without money or property. Although they work from the time they leave school, it's traditional for Amish young people to turn over all their wages to their father until they turn 21. Their money is considered a contribution to the family. Some fathers save a portion of the money for the child who earned it and return it when he or she turns 21. Others simply use the money themselves. In either case, an Amish young person is lucky to have 5, 10, or 20 dollars in his or her pocket.

Amish people who want to leave their church and culture often go without telling their families, sometimes in the middle of the night. Those who can make arrangements to get a ride from non-Amish friends or relatives.

Martha's Story

One young woman, whom I'll call Martha to protect her identity, wanted to leave her Amish home from the time she was 15, but waited until she was 18 to go. She was afraid to tell her parents she was leaving. "I was afraid they might lock me up to keep me," she said.

Her fears were well-founded. "When Mom and Dad got determined," she said, "they used some force." Her mother had abused the children for years, hitting them with "whatever was at hand," Martha said. Sometimes her mother had punished Martha by locking her in the basement or outside to separate her from the family.

As the second oldest of 11 children, Martha often tried to protect her younger brothers and sisters from their mother's violent temper. "It never hurt as bad when I took it for someone else as when I took it for myself," she said, of her mother's abuse.

The Plain Truth

Sometimes employers who know a young person can't keep his or her wages will add a cash tip for him or her to hide away. Those younger than 21 are likely to know little about how to handle money or how much it takes to live.

Her mother's abuse was at "the top of the list" of reasons she decided to leave her Amish culture, Martha said. She also describes herself as "pretty adventurous," and wanted to go to college. But if she hadn't been abused, she says, "I probably never would have gone." She agreed with an aunt who later said, "All you ever wanted was a good family."

Martha became friends with English neighbors, who offered to help her if she wanted to leave her family. At 18, Martha started teaching at the tiny Amish school built for her siblings and neighbor's children. After the children went home for the day, she would stay at school for some time alone, walking home at suppertime. One afternoon, Martha walked to the home of her English friends instead, hiding there for several days until they moved her to the home of relatives in a nearby town.

She went through the next few years in a daze. She lived with various English families, doing house and farm work for room and board, and sometimes at outside jobs for wages. Her father and other Amish relatives and church members tried to confront her at home and even at work, hoping to persuade her to return to the church. Martha avoided them any way she could, not because she was afraid she would give in to their pressure but because she "just didn't want to feel the guilt" they would inspire.

"They never give up," Martha said. Her family still writes, asking her to come home. "They say, 'Don't get married,'" she said, because that would prevent her from rejoining the Amish.

Martha estimates it took five to seven years for her to get comfortable in the mainstream culture. Ten years after she left the Amish, Martha is self-supporting, has gotten her GED, and has taken some college courses. She has studied writing and hopes to write a book about her life one day.

Visits by the Vanload: The Amish Response

When a church member or Amish child leaves, the Amish swing into action to bring them back. If the family finds out where the runaway is living, they hire English van drivers to bring carloads of relatives, friends, ministers, and bishops to plead, coerce, preach, and harangue. They remind the wayward person that by leaving the Amish, they condemn themselves to hell. The women cry, and sometimes the men do, too, while ordained men preach.

Mother, father, siblings, and extended family portray themselves as brokenhearted—not hard to do, since they believe what they're saying. Reading letters to *Family Life* magazine excerpted in *The Amish in Their Own Words*, one can't doubt the sincerity of some Amish parents who anguish over what they could have done differently to keep their young ones in the faith.

The Plain Truth

"You have said that you will go away. Tomorrow is the day," wrote one parent in a letter published in *Family Life* magazine. "My thoughts go back some 20 years, and sweep and search and grope. If only I could find the seeds (and know) from whence they came, the seeds that separated in your soul and grew and grew and brought such harvest that today we weep …. Do not go away. We need you, and you need us, too."

"Perhaps you think when you have left us that we can just tear out your sheet, and all will be as though you never had been here. But you are young, my child. You cannot realize the bonds that bind, and bind, and bind."

Often enough, wrenching emotional appeals work, as do threatening tirades. The young person, perhaps already homesick, scared, and lonely in an alien world, goes home to safety of church and family.

Those who hold out, though, may receive these visits again and again, along with letters in the same vein, cajoling, berating, and threatening, all in an attempt to bring them back to the church. Emotional manipulation, inducing fear and guilt, is the chief tactic the Amish use to bring the wayward back into the fold.

In other cases, such extremes aren't necessary to persuade a young person to return home. Some simply get homesick or find their yearning for independence gone after spending time alone in the world. Those who leave simply as part of adolescent rebellion and testing of themselves and their elders often return happily to their families, forgiven and ready to join the church.

The Hold-Outs: Excommunication and the Ban

Some subjects of *True Stories* reported having felt since childhood that they would leave the Amish one day. They felt they were meant to live a different life. Having undergone so much to get away, some refuse ever to return, even though it means a lifetime of rejection by their family and home community.

The ban not only forbids those who remain Amish from socializing with the banned person. It also prohibits the Amish from receiving anything from the banned person. This means they can't do business with the banned individual, because a business transaction requires receiving money.

> ### Ironies and Oddities
>
> An Amish person working in a business with a non-Amish owner has less control over whether to do business with the banned person or not. An Amish waitress in a restaurant might not want to serve a banned church member, but she might ask an English waitress to take her place. While an Amish store owner can refuse to sell the banned person merchandise, an Amish clerk in a non-Amish store may get around the difficulty by waiting for the buyer to lay his money on the counter rather than receiving it directly from his hand.

The ban is church-wide, not limited to one settlement. If the excommunicated person moves to a different community or state, the bishop who excommunicated him or her writes to his counterparts in other church districts and settlements across the country asking them to honor the ban. As a result, the person not only won't be served in an Amish-owned store or restaurant, but can't sell goods to the Amish. Thus the ban sometimes creates not only a social stigma but economic hardship as well, diminishing or eliminating the person's livelihood.

The Least You Need to Know

- To change churches, an Amish person has to leave home, family, and community, often at night and in secret.

- The Amish leave their church not only for freedom to choose a modern life, but for religious freedom as well.

- After a person leaves, the Amish use emotional ties, community pressure, and religious beliefs to try to get the person to return before excommunicating them.

- Once excommunicated, the one who left may be shunned for the rest of his or her life by family members who remain Amish, as well as by Amish people across the country, if his or her church district observes strict shunning.

- Those who remain Amish grieve for the person who has gone, believing him or her to have given up the eternal salvation of his or her soul.

Chapter 16

If You Can't Beat 'Em: Adaptations to Modern Life

In This Chapter

- ◆ Economic changes drive social changes
- ◆ Adaptations on the farm
- ◆ The new Amish economy
- ◆ Amish responses to government programs

Amish culture may seem unchanging in comparison to the society around it, but it changes constantly. A generation ago, most Amish homes were heated with wood stoves and had no indoor plumbing. The wash tub and outhouse were everyday realities; chopping and carrying wood were everyday chores. Today, most Amish homes have running water and gas stoves fueled by propane tanks. Newer homes have modern kitchens and bathrooms lit by pressurized gas lamps. Though they still lack central heating, kerosene or gas space heaters have taken the place of wood stoves in many Amish homes.

The Amish don't reject change, but they do want to control it rather than letting it control them. Amish culture values the tried-and-true, whether in housewares or hymns. For them, "traditional" means reliable, proven, wise, based on experience, having stood the test of time. "New" means untested, unreliable, having unforeseen consequences. They fear that rapid change would tear apart their society, and therefore their church.

But change they do.

The Driving Force: Economic Necessity

Most changes in Amish culture in the past 30 years have been driven not by desire for new experiences or an easier life, but by economic necessity.

The Amish population is one of the fastest growing in the country. Between 1970 and 1990 alone, their estimated population in the three largest settlements (church districts near Lancaster County, Pennsylvania; Holmes County, Ohio; and Elkhart County, Indiana) more than doubled in size, from 57,600 to 128,000. Lancaster's Amish settlement had already doubled between 1940 and 1960.

But land, unlike population, doesn't expand. The Amish had to compete for farmland not only with other farmers, but increasingly with industry, housing, and commercial enterprises. Land prices increased dramatically, making it harder for the Amish to buy farms for all their married children.

Some Amish used the historic solution to their problem, moving from heavily populated areas in Pennsylvania, Ohio, and Indiana to more rural communities in Missouri, Wisconsin, Michigan, and Kentucky—or wherever farm land was available and still reasonably priced. As non-Amish farmers gave up the family farm because low market prices made it impossible to make a living, Amish farmers with their low-tech subsistence lifestyle moved in.

The Farm as Foundation of Amish Society

Farming is the traditional occupation for Amish families not only because their forefathers were farmers, but also because farming supports a closely controlled society in several respects, including the following:

- ◆ Living in rural areas allows the Amish to isolate themselves from mainstream society, diminishing its influence on their culture.

- ◆ Sons can learn farming from their fathers, so little formal education (and outside influence) is necessary.

- Farming without electricity and with horses requires a lot of labor, employing not only the father but the entire family. Amish culture values labor-intensive work, because it keeps people busy. The Amish believe "thinking too much" is unhealthy, and best prevented by constant work.

- Children and adolescents can work at home on the farm until adulthood, keeping them under the supervision of their parents as long as possible.

- Farms provide a place to live as well as work, so all of life can be integrated and infused with Amish values, and contact with outsiders kept to a minimum.

The Plain Truth

The Amish put stock in the expression "idleness is the devil's workshop." Amish culture places a higher value on faithfulness to tradition than on intellectual curiosity or self-awareness. Time to reflect, read, and question one's life can encourage dissatisfaction, they believe. Instead, Amish culture recommends physical tasks as a way to stay out of trouble and keep your mind off anything that's making you unhappy.

Farming provided a solid economic and social foundation for Amish life for more than two centuries, but changes in farm technology, markets, and the growing Amish population forced shifts in that foundation.

Farming on Shifting Ground

But farming, like every other aspect of life, changed with increasing speed in the twentieth century. At the beginning of the century, electricity was still a rarity in rural America. By the end of the century, millions of family farmers had gone out of business because of low prices and high production costs, and those still farming relied heavily on electric powered and computerized equipment to make production more efficient.

For Amish farmers to survive economically, they had to be able to compete. Their large families gave them an advantage over non-Amish farmers, as they provided abundant, free labor. And older farmers often owned their farms outright, so as long as they resisted the pressure to expand by borrowing money for more cattle, land, and machinery, their production costs remained lower than most non-Amish.

But the trend of farming for cash had caught up the Amish as well as other American farmers. At the beginning of the twentieth century, the primary object of farming was subsistence living. To provide the family with food and even fiber for clothing, farmers raised a few cows, a few hogs, a small flock of chickens, maybe a handful of sheep, and the hay, corn, pasture, oats, and wheat necessary to feed them and provide bedding for the barn. Extra production was sold to provide cash for anything not grown or made on the farm, such as shoes and heavy machinery.

As industrialization made more machinery and technology available throughout the twentieth century, it became more important to produce cash to purchase machinery that increased production, made work easier, and made life more comfortable. Tractors, hay bailers, corn pickers, combines, automatic feeders, milking parlors, refrigerated milk tanks—not to mention electric appliances and entertainment systems for the home—the list goes on and on.

But as more labor-saving equipment became available, more money was needed to buy it. Farmers could make more money by specializing in a few crops, concentrating on milking large dairy herds or raising thousands of chickens, or hundreds of acres of corn or soybeans, for cash. This specialization, however, made it necessary for farmers to buy more and more of the food and clothing their families needed.

The Amish Response

The Amish responded to these changes slowly at first. By resisting use of expensive machinery, and forbidding electricity and its labor-saving devices in the home and barn, they minimized their need for cash. They could continue subsistence living on their small farms.

> **Ironies and Oddities**
>
> The 1960s back-to-the-land movement decried the effects of industrialization: removing work from home; dividing production into specialized tasks; draining work of purpose, meaning, and satisfaction. They proposed to live more like the Amish—as subsistence farmers, producing most of what they needed from the land, reducing cash purchases. Ironically, Amish culture was changing in response to the very social pressures that back-to-the-landers sought to escape.

From the beginning, though, they made some compromises with mechanical progress. They'd been using gasoline and steam engines on their farms since before the advent of tractors. Steam engines powered threshing machines; gasoline motors ran the blowers used to fill silos with corn silage. When the much smaller and more mobile tractors replaced steam engines, Amish farmers started using them for the same purposes. Rather than try to force their members to give up tractors, the bishops agreed in the early 1920s to allow them as long as they were used at the barn, not in the fields. Rubber tires had to be replaced with steel wheels, to make them less desirable for road use.

This compromise kept horses in the fields and restricted the number of acres an Amish farmer could work. Later, when horse-drawn equipment became scarce, enterprising farmers figured out how to mount gasoline engines to run hay balers and other power equipment, which could be pulled by horses. That compromise has stuck, with the rule in most communities being essentially that anything pulled by horses is okay. Some of the most conservative communities, though, still forbid all engine-driven farm machinery.

Economic pressure played a role again when public health officials in some states demanded that all milk be stored in refrigerated tanks stirred by automatic agitators to keep it uniformly cool. Dairy farming was an essential source of income to many Amish families, so the Amish bishops worked out a deal to allow refrigeration and agitators powered by diesel engines.

As their numbers continued to outgrow the available farmland in the older settlements, and many young families didn't want to leave their home community and the support of an extended family, the Amish devised new strategies. Amish parents began to retire earlier, sometimes supplementing their implement with a small business run from home, turning the farm over to a grown child for raising his or her own family.

The Plain Truth

Moving to new settlements wasn't an easy solution to the lack of land in older settlements, as this 1976 letter to *Family Life* attests:

Can't you see that if you have only one home farm and have seven children, and they each have a family, that you must have enough love for them not to keep them close to you as you would wish, but to let them go? ... Most of those who moved to new settlements did so against the will of at least one set of parents .... Often there were bitter words from relatives that took a long time to be forgotten. I have often wondered why these things couldn't be discussed sanely and sensibly.

Other parents subdivided the farm so it could support more than one family. To make a living on ever-smaller plots of land, some Amish in Lancaster County turned to raising crops such as produce that sold for high prices in nearby cities, or animals such as puppies and chickens that could be raised indoors without the acres devoted to pasture and feed demanded by cows and horses.

Creating New Work, Preserving Traditional Values

Even the formation of newer settlements and updated farming methods couldn't provide enough farming jobs to support all the new Amish families started every year.

"Especially during the 1960s, '70s, and '80s, Amish employment patterns shifted noticeably," according to historian Steven Nolt in his book, *A History of the Amish*.

The shift toward nonfarming jobs took several forms. In the 1960s, a cottage industry grew up repairing old horse-drawn farm equipment and adapting implements and equipment designed for "English" farms to Amish use. Other small industries, run from farm buildings converted to micro-manufacturing facilities, began to develop to fill Amish needs for goods that the rest of society no longer needed.

> **Ironies and Oddities**
>
> A 1988 study showed only 37 percent of Amish household heads in Indiana were still farmers, while 43 percent worked in factories.

At the same time, many Amish men began working in local factories. In Indiana, the recreational vehicle and mobile home industries grew rapidly, spawning factories needing reliable workers. Ohio's rubber industry employed many Amish men.

The Lunch-Pail Problem

In Lancaster, Pennsylvania, especially, the Amish worried about the effect of what they called "the lunch-pail problem" on their church and community. Back in the 1940s, they had excommunicated men for taking factory jobs. By the 1960s, though, those jobs had become an economic necessity.

The lunch-pail problem boiled down to the removal of dad from the farm. For the first time in their history, the Amish were experiencing a division of work from home life, and it made them uneasy. They had four primary concerns:

- A father working away from home lost the opportunity to supervise his children, instill in them the values of the church, discipline them, and teach them adult skills from an early age.

- Working 40 hours a week with both English men and women could erode the Amish values of the men themselves.

- Men working in factories for wages couldn't easily take off a day for a wedding or barn-raising, or other community activities.

- Factory jobs included benefits—health insurance, pensions, life insurance, and so on. The Amish had forbidden commercial insurance because they wanted community members to depend on each other, rather than the outside world, for help in times of need. Mutual aid also enforced mutual dependence, cementing the community together.

In 1982, the Amish magazine *Family Life* asked its readers to comment on the lunch-pail problem. The responses, excerpted in *The Amish in Their Own Words*, showed the wide range of views among the Amish on factory work.

A woman from Missouri wrote, "I have just sent my husband out the door with his lunch pail …. It is not the way we would both like it best. We have three boys, the oldest is ten, and they should have their father at home." But with high interest rates and farm prices, and no savings, buying a farm was beyond their reach.

A person from Indiana wrote about Amish men working in mobile home factories: "Here conditions have come to such a head that many are now compelled to work in factories as the only way to make a living. Some of our factories have such a high percentage of Amish workers that it is no longer exactly rubbing shoulders with the world. It is actually because of the available Amish workforce that many factories have flourished here."

> **The Plain Truth**
>
> A woman wrote to *Family Life*: "There are many blessings to living on a farm. But some of our farms are too big." She laments having to leave her children alone in the house to help her husband in the barn. "In those families where the father carries the lunch pail, at least the children have one parent who stays in the house with them."

Perhaps it's because of their high numbers in the factories that the Indiana Amish have succeeded in maintaining their communities and ethnic identity while working off the farm for non-Amish employers. But even in Indiana, the newer Amish homestead typically includes a building for the "shop"—as any home-based business is called.

Amish Shops and Businesses

Since the 1970s, the Amish in large settlements have been building new homesteads on a few acres at the edge of their farms and supporting them with home-based businesses. These businesses employ family members and sometimes one or more other Amish persons. They provide many of the benefits of farming, allowing the father to continue working at home, engaging the whole family in working together, limiting leisure time, integrating work and home, and providing children with an apprenticeship under their parents' supervision. Starting a business, especially with family labor, costs a lot less than buying and equipping a farm.

The earliest of these Amish *shops* served the Amish community itself. They built, repaired, or modified buggies, wagons, and farm machinery; made harness; sawed lumber; bought, sold, and repaired bicycles where they were allowed; and did custom

Vas Es Das?

When the Amish talk about a **shop,** they don't mean just a retail store where one goes shopping. They mean a workshop where goods are produced and services performed, as well as sold to customers. Many Amish shops are advertised with a roadside sign and open to the public, though not on Sundays. Most new Amish homesteads include an outbuilding for a home shop.

butchering. Local non-Amish people might bring machinery to an Amish welder for repair or buy rag rugs from an Amish woman at her home, but the primary market for these businesses was their own Amish community.

Carpentry and construction had always been among the traditional Amish occupations, and Amish men looking for a way to make a living off the farm often learned these trades. Some formed construction businesses whose crews used modern power tools using either portable generators or electricity available on the building site. Some worked only in the local area, but others traveled out-of-state to build homes and commercial buildings. Related services, such as floor covering and roofing, became staples of the Amish economy as well.

At Home in the World

Small, home-based shops and businesses still form the backbone of Amish entrepreneurship, but they've expanded their markets beyond the Amish community.

Amish retail businesses in town sell goods to the flood of tourists that pours through the larger settlements. Increasingly, the Amish themselves own bakeries, quilt and craft shops, antique stores, and other retail outlets that market to tourists. The signs on their doors that read "Come In, We're Open," as Donald Kraybill points out in *The Riddle of Amish Culture,* show a radical shift in the relationship of the isolationist Amish with the society around them. They're becoming increasingly dependent on commerce with the world beyond their culture to support their growing numbers.

Ironies and Oddities

Instead of working with their husbands on a jointly owned farm, more and more married Amish women have their own employment or their own business. In the long run, this could change the balance of power in Amish marriages and even the culture. But with men holding all leadership roles in the church, that's not likely to happen.

Amish women own a surprising number of businesses, giving them more access to money, independence, and exposure to the outside world. Some are widows or single, but others are married women who sell produce or homemade foods from a roadside stand or weave rag rugs in a shop on the farm while raising their families. Some work with their husbands, but others manage the business themselves, employing their children or other Amish women.

Today, Amish-owned shops dot the countryside in many settlements, inviting the world to buy hand-crafted goods made for tourists and locals alike.

Far more Amish women work in a business than own one. Single Amish women often work in Amish and non-Amish retail stores, restaurants, even banks. Married Amish women still consider homemaking their primary job, but often make money "on the side" producing crafts and quilts for Amish retailers and distributors.

Not all off-farm Amish businesses depend on the tourist trade, and those that remain small sell primarily to local markets. Amish-owned print shops, bookstores, greenhouses, natural foods stores, and fabric stores, for instance, sell to both Amish and non-Amish customers in their local communities.

Some Amish businesses have grown too large to stay on the farm, and have moved into local industrial parks. Some of these, such as makers of furniture and cabinets, have even expanded into factories that ship products across the nation. These businesses don't depend on the tourist trade or local market; instead, they sell wholesale goods to major retailers like Wal-Mart or K-Mart. They use their reputation for quality work to market a range of products including kitchen cabinets, furniture, and wooden gazebos.

Amish Wealth Creates New Tensions

Amish communities have always included both poor and prosperous families. But in the older, more established settlements—especially in Lancaster County—Amish entrepreneurship has exaggerated the differences. In the 1990s, some Lancaster Amish businesses did millions of dollars worth of business a year, turned a 10 percent profit, and paid their owners six-figures incomes, quickly turning them into millionaires. By comparison, many farmers and shop employees in their church might have earned 35,000 dollars or much less.

Donald Kraybill, in his book *The Riddle of Amish Society*, quotes one banker as saying, "The old graybeards have no idea how much money is flowing around in this community."

Ministers and bishops look skeptically at businesses that get too big or appear too successful. They associate success with pride and greed, and pressure business owners not to let their businesses grow too much. "My own people look at my growth as a sign of greed—that I'm not satisfied to limit my volume," one Amish businessman told Kraybill. "… The Old Order Amish are supposed to be a people who do not engage in big business, and I'm right on the borderline right now."

Another entrepreneur told Kraybill, referring to a growing business, "Wait till they start making money, then the church will throw the *Ordnung* at them."

Government vs. the Amish: Tensions, Concessions, and Compromises

The Amish have an interesting relationship with the larger society around them. Although they pride themselves (humbly, of course) on their separation and independence from modern society, in many ways they not only accommodate but even benefit from its provisions.

The Amish try to have as little as possible to do with government, asking their people to refuse Social Security, Medicare, and other government benefits programs. Yet after much controversy and debate, some Amish people have signed up for farm programs that pay farmers not to raise crops, taken out federally subsidized mortgages, and benefited from other government programs.

Make No Mistake

The Amish exemptions were made with the understanding that the Amish would be self-employed farmers and depend on their community's mutual aid, rather than government benefits programs, to help when they needed it. They weren't intended to give Amish businessmen an advantage over the competition.

Amish farmers receive government price supports for their crops, along with non-Amish farmers, helping them stay in business. While sociologist Donald Kraybill marvels at the ability of Amish entrepreneurs to build successful businesses with only an eighth grade education, he also points out an important reason: The federal government exempts Amish employers from paying Social Security taxes (which include payments supporting Medicare, Medicaid, and disability programs) as well as, in some states, workers compensation and unemployment insurance. These exemptions can amount to many thousands of dollars a year in savings, depending on the number of employees. Of course, that could change as more Amish people choose business over farming.

Social Security and Other Benefits

When the federal government first implemented the Social Security program, it applied only to those employed by others. In 1955, Congress amended the program to include the self-employed, including farmers.

The Amish objected to being forced to pay into, and accept benefits from, a government-run program that amounted to insurance. The Amish forbid their members to buy commercial insurance, though they have organized mutual aid programs of their own to protect members against high health care costs and liability suits. Even mutual aid programs caused controversy among those who thought giving and distributing alms to those in need was more biblical.

The Plain Truth

Family Life magazine aired many views on the Amish and insurance in the 1970s and 1980s, including this one:

The biblical way is to support our poor and needy by giving alms. Insurance plans are the way of the world. Our giving of alms must be freewill, spontaneous, generous, and in secret … Alms are to help the needy, not to restore the possessions of the well-to-do.

To the Amish, insurance is a form of gambling, a way of trying to control your own future instead of trusting it to God, and would increase members' dependence on the world while decreasing their dependence on the church community. They believe the Bible requires them to take care of their own, and to cede that responsibility to the government or insurance companies would be a breach of faith.

At first, many Amish refused to pay Social Security taxes. Some relented when the IRS started to seize bank accounts, farms, and even draft horses out of the field, selling them for payment, but others continued to resist. Finally in 1965, when the Medicare program was added to the Social Security Act, a section of the new law allowed self-employed persons to apply for exemption from the tax if they belonged to a religious group that opposed Social Security and provided for their own instead.

That took care of Amish farmers and other self-employed Amish people, but as Amish businesses started to grow and require employees, the Amish faced the same problem. Some organized their businesses to make each participant a self-employed

The Plain Truth _____

Workers compensation insurance and unemployment insurance are run by states, not the federal government, and enforcement varies by state. Pennsylvania, Kentucky, and Wisconsin exempt the Amish from participating in those programs as well.

partner, while other business owners paid the taxes for Amish employees who would never collect their benefits. The employees, too, had to pay their half of the tax, of course.

In 1988, the law was changed again to exempt Amish employees working for Amish employers from contributing to Social Security, saving both employee and employer their respective shares of the tax. Non-Amish employers, though, have to deduct Social Security taxes from their Amish employees' wages and match it with their own half of the payment.

While the Amish have historically avoided farm subsidy programs that would pay them to leave land idle or sell dairy cattle, the gap between the position of the leaders and the behavior of some in the various scattered settlements can be wide. More and more Amish farmers are taking part in government conservation and land preservation programs that pay them to keep farming or make improvements to control erosion or run-off pollution. Others take advantage of government FHA loans to help them buy farms.

Conscientious Objection and Conscription

The majority of Amish men throughout history have refused to go to war, and for many years now, the federal government has honored that refusal. But it wasn't always so.

During World War I, young Amish men and other conscientious objectors were sent to military camps. America had waited until spring of 1917 to enter the war. When Congress passed a draft law to raise an army for the war, it included only a "vague provision for religious conscientious objectors," (CO's) according to historian Steven Nolt. The law didn't include instructions on what the government was to do with those who did manage to convince their draft boards that they couldn't fight because of conscience.

So drafted CO's were sent right along to the same boot camps as drafted soldiers, where commanding officers were expected to make some provision for CO service. In the meantime, the army hoped, the young men might be pressured into changing their minds once surrounded by young soldiers.

In fact, Amish and other CO's in military camps were threatened, beaten, and otherwise abused for refusing to take part in rifle training or, in some cases, wear an army uniform. Nolt tells the story of an Amish farmer from Holmes County, Ohio, named Rudy Yoder who was threatened with death if he didn't put on a uniform and join in military training. Although he was abused throughout his time in the camp, the death threat wasn't carried out.

"Many CO's were made to stand for long periods of time in the sun without refreshment," Nolt writes. "Those who refused to wear military uniforms were at times left in cold, damp cells with no clothing at all. Officers occasionally 'baptized' Amish CO's in camp latrines in mockery of their Anabaptist beliefs .... For the Amish men who endured World War I [military] camp experiences, the memories were powerful and unforgettable."

The Plain Truth

Young draftees weren't the only Amish people coming under fire. The War Department's Military Intelligence Division spied on the Amish, Mennonites, Brethren, and other groups of German descent—especially those whose boys refused to fight. Amish Bishop Manasses E. Bontrager of Kansas was arrested and convicted of "inciting and attempting to incite insubordination, disloyalty and refusal of duty in the military and naval forces of the United States." His crime? He had written a long letter to the *Budget* praising the perseverence of Amish boys in "camp" and exhorting those at home to refuse to buy war bonds and otherwise resist the war machine. *Budget* editor Samuel H. Miller was convicted along with him, and each was fined $500.

By World War II, the fate of conscientious objectors had improved considerably. Mennonite, Brethren, and Religious Society of Friends (Quakers) leaders laid the groundwork in the 1930s by working with government leaders to develop an alternative plan for CO's. The program was underwritten by the peace churches, which managed the program, called Civilian Public Service (CPS). The men lived in camps regulated by the government but run by sponsoring churches. Some worked in forestry and agricultural projects, while others performed social work or served in hospitals. The Amish sponsored one CPS camp in Maryland, doing experimental agricultural projects.

Ironies and Oddities

Historian Steve Nolt points out the irony of the Amish working in CPS camps. "Thus, while the Amish had refused government farm subsidies and social security payments during the depression," he writes, "they later helped to subsidize the government itself by providing free labor for various state and federal projects." The Amish didn't mind giving support for non-military purposes, they only objected to receiving it.

Another alternative to military service for young Amish men during World War II was the farm deferment. Men whose presence was necessary to keep the home farm going could receive farm deferments from the draft, because agriculture was considered a vital industry. Farm products were needed to feed the military as well as civilian population.

The draft didn't end with World War II. As it continued year after year through the 1940s, '50s and '60s, fewer boys became eligible for farm deferments and more had to do alternative service. The law required that the service disrupt the lives of the young men and contribute to the public health or welfare by filling jobs not readily filled from by the job market. It took Amish boys off the farm, often housing them in cities to work in public hospitals, requiring them to wear uniforms rather than Amish clothing, kept them busy only eight hours a day, put a little money in their pockets, and introduced them to non-Amish women and men.

In the minds of the Amish leaders, this was a prescription for disaster—and they were right. Many single young men didn't join the church after they came home again, or if they had been members, they left. Men who were already married to church members took their wives with them when they left for public service, and both lived an essentially non-Amish life, using electricity and other conveniences, being exposed to worldly ideas and entertainment, making English friends. For them, too, it was hard to move back into the life they'd left.

In 1966, the Amish formed the National Amish Steering Committee, a small group of savvy Amish men who negotiated with the government for changes in the regulations. Young men who couldn't get deferments to farm at home could be sent to other Amish settlements to farm there, under the supervision of the Committee.

The negotiations worked so well that the Amish retained the Committee, which continues to intercede with governments on behalf of Amish people and their religious beliefs. Its members testify before congressional committees and negotiate with officials when government regulations threaten traditional Amish values.

The Least You Need to Know

- Amish culture changes slowly, but it does change—especially in response to economic pressures.

- A rapidly growing population and lack of available farm land forced Amish families in the largest settlements to move or look for new ways to make a living.

- By starting small businesses they could run from home, the Amish developed a strong new economic base that preserved their traditional values.

◆ The Amish have negotiated exemptions from many government programs that they feared would make them dependent on the government, including Social Security, Medicare, Medicaid, workers compensation, and unemployment insurance.

◆ During World War I, Amish conscientious objectors who were drafted were placed in military camps, where they were severely abused. By World War II, they could work on Civilian Public Service projects instead.

◆ The National Amish Steering Committee, formed to negotiate Amish alternative service during conscription, continues to represent the Amish viewpoint to the federal and state governments.

Part 5

Fruits of Their Labor: Sampling Amish Culture

Tourism has become a mainstay in the Amish economy in recent decades—to such an extent that cottage industries now support more families than farms do. We look at how the change occurred, and how the Amish accommodate tourists while protecting their privacy. And for those of you who want to visit an Amish community, you'll find a few tips for getting a glimpse of the culture without offending anyone.

Amish cooking has been hyped—sometimes beyond its merits and often beyond recognition. Getting back to basics, we describe Amish cooking, share a few recipes, and invite you to dig in.

Quilts and furniture are probably the two biggest exports of Amish culture, but those made for the mass market are no longer distinctively Amish. Antique Amish furniture and quilts are collected by museums and art dealers, but the newer versions are mostly made to please modern American tastes.

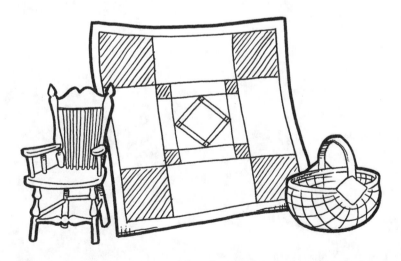

Chapter 17

Outside Looking In: Curiosity About the Amish

In This Chapter

- ◆ Americans discover the Amish
- ◆ How tourism affects Amish life
- ◆ Who interprets the Amish, and why
- ◆ What you can see and what you can't
- ◆ Do's and Don'ts when visiting Amish settlements

Until the early twentieth century, the Amish life didn't appear much different than rural American life in general. Tractors and cars didn't become common on country roads and in small towns until the 1920s. Before that, everyone farmed with horses and rode in carriages. Even in the 1930s, farms and ranches in many parts of America lacked electricity. Only after World War I did American women begin to cut their hair, shorten their skirts, and wear the brightly printed fabrics that became widely available.

As David Weaver-Zercher observes in his book, *The Amish in the American Imagination*, "[I]n 1870 the Amish had far fewer distinguishing marks to set them apart from their neighbors than they would fifty years later, let alone at the end of the twentieth century."

Americans Long for the Simple Life

As twentieth century America replaced the subsistence farm life of pioneers with industrialization, specialized work, and the resulting cash economy, the Amish started to appear quaint by contrast. Within less than a generation, Americans who were leaving the farm and small town in record numbers were already nostalgic for a simpler life that didn't pull them in so many directions at once.

Industrialization required that at least one adult leave home every day to earn money. Homes were increasingly far from the worksite, lengthening the workday by adding a commute, and separating the bread earner's work life from home life. Since most bread earners were men, men's work life was increasingly distant from women's, the life of children from that of their fathers (and later mothers), and the increasing availability of consumer goods exerted continual pressure to keep working more and harder.

No wonder Amish life, with its slower pace, self-employment, and integration of home and family life in one location looked so appealing, as it does to many today. In popular images of Amish life, working Americans found a symbol of that life that they could admire without having to experience the hardships that went with it. With little information available on the Amish, the English world was free to romanticize what they didn't understand.

> **Ironies and Oddities**
>
> By the turn of the twenty-first century, some four million tourists were estimated to visit Lancaster County each year, according to Donald Kraybill in *The Riddle of Amish Culture*. That's about 180 tourists, spending 30,000 dollars, for every Amish resident. The Amish make their greatest contribution to the local economy not through their productivity and buying power, but by the way they live.

Amish culture attracted national attention in 1937, with the resistance by the Amish of East Lampeter Township, Pennsylvania, to their school board's efforts to replace its one-room schools with a larger, consolidated school. *The New York Times* covered the story heavily, as did other national publications produced on the East Coast, where three major cities lay within a short drive of the Lancaster County Amish settlement.

Interest in the Amish has hardly waned since. Amish tourism in Lancaster County grew rapidly after World War II, when the availability of cars and the cash to buy them, along with newly built highways and free weekends encouraged Americans to take to the road. Automobile tourism increased across the country, and for people from New York, Philadelphia, and Baltimore, Lancaster County became a prime destination.

A Mixed Blessing: Tourism Intrudes on Amish Life

For the Amish, tourism has been a mixed, and reluctantly accepted, blessing. While tourists were visiting Lancaster County by the mid-twentieth century, it took decades more for it to move westward to settlements in Ohio, Indiana, Iowa, Missouri, and elsewhere. Some of the newer and smaller settlements are relatively free of tourists. But even there, the accompanying demand for Amish-made products, such as furniture, sold through retail stores in far-away cities creates jobs for the Amish.

The World That Won't Go Away

As we've seen, the Amish place a high value on separation from the world. Their communities focus inward, on their own people, rather than outward on the world around them. Their language, uniform clothing, rejection of education and technology all are designed to distance them from worldly society and increase their identification with each other.

The Amish church discourages social interaction with non-Amish people, fearing that close relationships with nonmembers might lead the Amish to reject the church's rules or marry non-Amish partners. Since either would result in the member's exclusion from both church and family and, they believe, condemn the person to hell, the Amish have strong incentives for keeping the world at a distance.

Despite these incentives to isolation, some Amish people feel a good deal of curiosity about the world and enjoy conversation with people outside their culture. Young Amish people who toy with the idea of leaving their culture for the modern world often welcome the chance to interact with outsiders. Some Amish people do develop friendships with people from other cultures, although they are more likely to feel kinship with those who share some of their beliefs.

What the Amish don't like about tourism is its intrusion into their private lives. They don't like to be asked to pose for photographs, which their religion obliges them to refuse, or to have their photos taken without permission. They dislike being stared at or interrupted in their

> **The Plain Truth**
>
> Increasingly, the Amish enjoy being tourists themselves, sightseeing or visiting friends and relatives in other Amish settlements. Just riding in a hired van or car gives them a break from their ordinary existence, and they enjoy that as much as anybody.

work, unless that work includes selling products to English neighbors and tourists. In Lancaster County, particularly, tourist traffic has become a problem on country roads, making them unsafe at times for Amish buggies.

Having Their Say

What do the Amish say among themselves about tourists? Brad Igou includes a smattering of comments, though none recent, in his book *The Amish In Their Own Words: Amish Writings from 25 Years* of *Family Life Magazine*.

"My wife read to me your article on tourism in Lancaster County, Pennsylvania," wrote one man in 1981. "I listened with interest but also with sadness. The sadness that comes to me is because so many tourists are seeing the Amish [merely] as a culture. I do not believe the Amish could have endured as they have for three hundred years if there were not a deeper reason for not changing with the world."

Other writers also regretted the focus of tourists on the visible symbols of Amish life—the very ones adopted by the Amish to distinguish them from the world—rather than on the religious reasons behind them.

"What did this [inquiring tourist] think our religion was—just a quaint game, a novelty, a museum? Did the man actually learn anything by talking with us?" wrote another Amish reader. "… What is our religion—just buggies, beards, and broad-brimmed hats? Couldn't we somehow have given him a glimpse of the New Testament pattern—a nonconformed church; a strong, close-knit brotherhood of believers …?"

"I guess I'm like the stranger from Texas," the writer concluded. "I have a bunch of questions I would like to have answers to. But I don't think stopping someone at the end of his lane for five minutes is the best way to get them answered."

Mixed Blessing, Part 2: Tourism and the Amish Economy

As we've seen, the Amish population is outgrowing the amount of farmland available in its largest settlements. And while new settlements are being started every year to absorb some of the overflow, the family and community network is so important to most Amish people that they'd rather find new ways of making a living than move.

As noted in the previous chapter, over the past 30 years, this conflict has given rise to a new Amish that depends less on agriculture and more on small, home-based industries and retail shops. The Amish make good entrepreneurs for many of the same reasons that they're successful farmers: They keep their enterprises small, use family labor, forego expensive technology, sell direct to customers as much as possible, work hard, exercise thrift, and avoid paying taxes for government programs they don't use.

So Amish tourism, while it disrupts Amish life and forces more interaction with the world, also helps the Amish preserve their way of life by making it possible for families to subsist in close-knit, rural communities.

In the larger settlements, where tourism has become a major boon to the local, non-Amish economy, the Amish are also taking in some of the cash spent by those who are curious about their way of life. Craft stores selling Amish-made quilts, toys, and decorative items are among the most popular with tourists. They provide a market for small, home-based businesses run by Amish people without exposing them directly to the stares and questions of outsiders.

Single Amish women often work as sales clerks in tourist-themed retail stores or wait tables in restaurants that advertise "Amish-style" cooking. Older women, whose children are grown, sometimes work as cooks or bakers in Amish-themed restaurants or bakeries, or work at home making quilts alone or as part of a business owned by another Amish woman.

Straight from the Farm

Selling produce, eggs, rag rugs, maple syrup and services such as welding directly from home has always been a staple of the Amish farm economy. But until the tourism boom, the market was mostly the neighbors and nearby townspeople who drove out into the countryside to buy fresher, less expensive food and goods they couldn't get in town.

In recent decades, as tourists swarmed through Amish settlements, the Amish have increasingly opened road-side stands and small shops on their farms offering produce, home-canned foods, bakery items, and handcrafted housewares directly to tourists and locals alike.

As Donald Kraybill points out in *The Riddle of Amish Culture*, both the tourists and the Amish benefit from this trend. The Amish get ...

♦ A greater share of the tourist dollar by selling direct rather than through a retailer.

♦ Control of what they sell and how they present their products, skipping the fake "Dutch" decor and misrepresentations of Amish life that non-Amish craft stores often use to attract tourists.

◆ The ability to align their livelihood with their religious beliefs by involving family members, producing items that serve a useful function, operating their shops without electricity, and closing them on Sundays.

Roadside stands are a common sight in Amish settlements, where women often supplement their family income selling garden produce, eggs, baked goods, jams, and jellies.

Tourists benefit from buying directly from the Amish too, gaining …

◆ Some direct contact with the Amish.

◆ A closer look at Amish homesteads.

◆ Access to goods that more authentically represent Amish values and are truly Amish made.

◆ An opportunity to get out of their cars to see, hear, and feel the atmosphere of the countryside directly, rather than simply another retail shopping experience.

As Kraybill notes, however, even direct sales don't provide the "backstage" look at Amish life that many tourists seek. Conversation with the Amish people selling goods is strictly controlled by them to maintain their privacy. They won't respond to questions they feel are too personal, or they'll offer a superficial answer meant to satisfy the tourist without revealing any real information.

For a deeper understanding of Amish culture, ironically, visitors to Amish settlements usually have to depend on the interpretations of the non-Amish.

Interpreting the Amish to the World

As David Weaver-Zercher notes in *The Amish in the American Imagination*, the Amish themselves have been reluctant to explain themselves or their beliefs to outsiders. They've largely left that task to others.

In the second half of the twentieth century, as mainstream interest in the Amish grew, Mennonites frequently felt an urge to set the record straight on Amish religion and culture. Many books on the Amish (including this one) have been written by Mennonite or former Mennonite or Amish scholars and authors. Some early writers wrote to counteract earlier depictions of the Amish as stupid and primitive, while those who wrote later have been more concerned with providing a more balanced picture of Amish life.

Mennonite Perspectives and Prejudices

Although Mennonites may be among the most reliable sources on Amish life, since they share a history, Anabaptist beliefs, and rural communities, they have prejudices as well as insights that color their interpretations of Amish religion and culture.

Living intermingled for centuries, the Amish and Mennonites discovered that good fences *do* actually make good neighbors—or at least make it easier to get along. Each group has erected its social fences, which allow them to maintain cordial relations with neighbors who share basic Anabaptist beliefs and history. However, they also have a tradition of mutual disapproval.

Amish attitudes toward the Mennonites have mellowed somewhat since Jakob Ammann excommunicated the Swiss Brethren (later Mennonite) leaders, consigning them to hell. Though some Amish people might place Mennonites in a separate category from other English people, Amish doctrine still considers Mennonite life and religion less pure and Christian than the Amish way. Even though they believe that only God can judge human souls, the Amish do feel that only those separated from the world are true disciples of Christ.

Despite polite and sometimes friendly exchanges, Mennonites know the Amish disapprove of their lifestyle, consider their dress to be immodest and their leisure activities sinful, and keep their children at a distance so they won't be corrupted. Working together in factories, retail stores, and other businesses may allow Amish and Mennonite people opportunities to get beyond these prejudices and form a personal friendship, but intimate friendships are the exception rather than the rule.

For their part, many Mennonites consider Amish compromises with worldly technology and conveniences hypocritical. For decades, it was Mennonite neighbors who owned the cars that the Amish rode in when necessary and the telephones they used in emergencies, while maintaining their own sense of religious superiority because they didn't own these conveniences.

Among Mennonites, Amish religious beliefs historically have been considered rigid, rule-bound, judgmental, and spiritually deadening rather inspiring. Just as the Amish feel their religion and way of life is spiritually superior to others, Mennonites are apt to feel spiritually superior to the Amish.

Ironies and Oddities

Mennonites have often wanted to help outsiders understand the difference between themselves and the Amish. Since the nineteenth century, the general trend among Mennonites has been away from the kind of rules dictating a conservative, separatist life that their ancestors shared with the Amish. As that shift accelerated in the late twentieth century, many Mennonites who grew up wearing head coverings and plain clothes felt liberated by their church's greater emphasis on inner spiritual experience rather than outer conformity. Having resisted the standards of earlier generations, they don't want the rest of American society to confuse them with the very kind of separatism that they worked so hard to shed. For more on the Mennonites, see Part 6.

So when Mennonites interpret the Amish for a non-Amish audience, they bring all these prejudices and experiences along with them. That's not to say they don't offer insightful or reliable information, because often they do. But no matter how objective they try to be, or how close their relationships with Amish people, they are still trying to portray from the outside what can only truly be understood from inside a culture. And no one, not even a person from within the culture, can speak for an entire people. In every culture, each individual experiences a different truth.

Ersatz Amish: Tourist Attractions

Both Mennonites and other English persons have sometimes exploited tourist interest in the Amish with attractions that claim to depict real Amish life. Some of these depictions come closer than others to the truth, but none can create the experience of actually stepping into Amish life that many tourists seek.

Fake Amish farms populated by a staff of non-Amish people wearing Amish dress, complete with restaurants serving "Amish-style" cooking and gift shops stocked with goods that might or might not have been made by Amish people don't offer much real information. Few Amish people would want many of the knick-knacks sold in most "Amish" craft shops. More and more Amish quilts are made of fabrics and in designs that appeal to tourists but would never be found in an Amish home.

On the other hand, as Donald Kraybill argues in *The Riddle of Amish Culture*, guided tours and tourist attractions provide the Amish with a valuable service: They steer the millions of visitors each year away from Amish homes and off back roads, into facilities created to entertain, if not inform, them. The best offer educational presentations about the Amish and give visitors a chance to ask questions without being rude.

If You Go: What's Worth Seeing and How to Find It

Visiting "Amish Country" (a term invented by English tourism promoters) may not satisfy all your curiosity about the Amish, but with the right approach, you can enjoy yourself *and* learn something.

The way to approach any foreign culture, in my opinion, is humbly. That is, by recognizing what you don't know (the language, the local customs), what you can't learn (how it feels to belong to that culture), and what you can't do (blend in). What can you get out of visiting an Amish settlement and how should you go about it? Here are a few things:

- You can get a solid grounding in Amish and Mennonite history, beliefs, and culture from the few nonprofit educational sites offering information to tourists.

- You can see firsthand what the settlement looks like—the countryside, farms, homesteads, businesses, towns, and people.

- You can hear the Amish speak their language, though you won't understand what they're saying (and it would be rude to ask).

- You can speak at least superficially with a few Amish people, on their terms, in return for buying some of what they sell.

- You can learn something about what interests the Amish by browsing in stores that sell to Amish customers, picking up directories to local Amish businesses, and buying a copy of *The Budget* or other Amish newspapers and magazines.

Don't expect to …

- See an Amish church (they don't exist; the Amish worship in homes).

- Visit an Amish worship service (they're not public).

◆ Find an Amish person with time and inclination to explain why he or she dresses, speaks, works, lives, and worships the way he or she does.

◆ Take photos of the Amish, with or without their permission. (They can't say yes if you ask, and taking them against their will is crude, rude, and can only make you the subject of jokes and disparagement behind your back.)

◆ Tour a real Amish farm. (Real Amish farmers don't give public tours; they're busy farming, and don't need the income enough to welcome the intrusion.)

> **The Plain Truth**
>
> Look for an educational, nonprofit attraction, such as the Menno-Hof museum in Shipshewana, Indiana. Built, staffed, and run by a coalition of Mennonites, Amish Mennonites, and Old Order Amish, Menno-Hof attempts to provide accurate answers to tourists' questions and correct popular misconceptions.
>
> The building, built to resemble a barn, houses a museum, gift and book shop, and gallery space. Tours, led by Mennonite volunteers, start with an introductory video presentation on the Amish, Mennonites, and Hutterites (another Anabaptist plain group). You then move with a group through the museum, stopping for additional presentations on the history and religious belief and practices of the Mennonites and Amish. The information is sound and the presentations colorful and entertaining.
>
> Other intepretive centers can be found in Intercourse, Pennsylvania; Berlin, Ohio; and Arcola, Illinois.

A Few Personal Favorites

Most interactions between the Amish and English people take place in the context of business. You don't need permission to enter a store that's open to the public, ask questions about merchandise, and observe the people around you. Here are a few of my own favorite places to visit for a sense of local culture.

Country Stores

As more Amish have turned from farming to business over the past quarter century, country stores have been popping up in many settlements. The Amish used to have to drive to town to buy groceries, fabric, hardware, and other goods, but when they started their own businesses, they began building them closer to home. Some are general stores, selling groceries, hardware, books, housewares, linens, and other necessities. Others specialize in fabrics, hardware, or health foods. To find them (as well as farm-based shops and roadside stands), drive the quieter country roads near the small towns, or look for a directory to Amish-owned businesses in the area.

You can learn a lot about the culture by look-ing at the items in a store stocked with items that appeal to the Amish market, rather than tourists. It's interesting to browse through the variety of goods, noticing items that are unusual or old-fashioned. In one fabric store, I found a wide selection of Amish clothing for men and boys, plus coverings and bonnets for women and girls made by local women. Since Amish women used to make their own coverings, I'd never had the opportunity to look closely at them before. The variety of fancy dishes and china knick-knacks in several stores sur-prised me.

> **CAUTION**
>
> ### Make No Mistake
>
> If you visit an Amish country store, do buy something to take home—but show respect for the beliefs of those you're vis-iting. *Don't try to buy a head covering or other item that's a religious symbol worn only by the Amish.* You could buy a German Bible, a man's straw hat, tools or housewares without offending, because they can be used by non-Amish people.

Observing (discreetly, of course) the other shoppers in an Amish country store can also give you a glimpse inside Amish culture, without being obtrusive.

Auction Barns

The sale barn remains one of my favorite places to mingle with local people and feel like I'm back home. Ask at a local visitor center or any local business where the local auction barn is located and what day they sell livestock—that's the sale that draws Amish and non-Amish people alike. A horse auction will draw mostly Amish people, so you'll be more conspicuous, but some buyers and sellers will be English.

You can start by walking around the livestock pens, as buyers, sellers, and observers do, sizing up the cattle, horses, or pigs for sale. Then find the auction ring and have a seat in the crowd. Many local people come simply to watch the auction and socialize, so you won't be alone in not bidding. The auctioneer and action around you will offer plenty of local color.

Finally, of course, the sale barn restaurant can't be beat for local food and conversa-tion. I once attended a horse sale at Shipshewana by myself. When I went to the restaurant for lunch, the place was crowded so I was seated at a long table with others (almost all Amish men) eating alone. In that setting, I was able to have a conversation with Amish men who anywhere else would have felt uncomfortable talking to an English woman. And I learned a lot about what to look for in a buggy horse.

Relief Auctions

One area in which Mennonites and the Amish do work together is in what they call *relief.*

The Mennonite Central Committee (MCC) is an organization designed to combine the efforts of various Mennonite and Amish denominations in areas such as disaster relief and economic development in underdeveloped nations.

Vas Es Das? _____

Relief is a traditional term for charity work that relieves the distress of those in need. Unlike missions, the goal of relief work is meeting physical needs rather than evangelizing. Because relief work is a way of living out their faith rather than preaching it, the Amish participate in the relief efforts of Mennonite Central Committee, though they don't undertake mission work.

Ironies and Oddities

Some of the finest handcrafts found in or near Amish settlements aren't made by the Amish or Mennonites. Ten Thousand Villages, an MCC program, operates and supplies shops both in Mennonite areas and in cities across the United States and Canada, providing a market for handmade products that support the families of third-world artisans. (To find out more or locate a store, see their website, www.tenthousandvillages.com).

To satisfy an interest in goods made by Amish and Mennonite men and women, you can't beat the annual Mennonite Central Committee Relief Sales held in many communities across the United States and Canada. (For a listing of dates and locations, go to the MCC website, www.mcc.org, and click on the Relief Sale Board link.)

These are huge events with a festival-like atmosphere. Hundreds of area Mennonite and Amish people donate food items, crafts, quilts, plus many hours of time setting up, selling, and cleaning up after the sale.

You can walk among and talk to local people who work at the sale, sample some of the tastiest samples of their cooking, and buy locally made arts and crafts. High-calorie goodies—doughnuts, pretzels, ice cream, or funnel cakes made on the spot, homemade pies, cakes and cookies are among the favorites. Some goodies are hard to find anywhere else—at some sales, you can even get apple butter cooked in an open kettle over a wood fire.

At these sales, you're welcome to talk to local people and ask questions as well as buy. Here, selling interest in their culture is the point. You're not intruding on their privacy, you're helping to support the charity of their choice, and it's one time most of the people there are willing to put their culture on display in exchange. Those who don't want to talk to tourists are likely to stay away.

The quilt auction is the centerpiece of most MCC Relief Sales. Even if you don't intend to bid, you can wander through the quilt display before the auction starts and examine the patterns and stitching. Some groups of women create their most elaborate piecing and stitching patterns for this event, knowing that the more intricate the quilt, the more money it will bring for helping those in need.

Through these events, the churches and their members who work at these sales are making a statement of belief as well as raising money. Many include a public worship or dedication service either before, during, or after the weekend-long sale to remind everyone that the purpose of the whole big show is to serve God through serving the poor.

Individual settlements may also have local events that offer opportunity to mingle with the Amish. In Lancaster County, the Amish participate in several auctions to support local fire companies. The biggest ones are at Gordonville and Bart (also known as Georgetown).

Another relief agency, Christian Aid Ministries, is heavily supported by Amish and other Plain churches. They have distribution centers in the larger Amish settlements, including one at Leola, in Lancaster County. The center holds an annual open house which draws thousands of people from Plain churches of every stripe.

The Least You Need to Know

- ◆ The Amish prefer isolation from the world, but in the largest settlements, they've come to depend on the tourist market for much of their income.

- ◆ Most tourist attractions aren't run by the Amish, but a few nonprofit informational attractions offer reliable information on Amish religion and culture.

- ◆ One of the few opportunities to interact with Amish people is by stopping at one of the many Amish-owned shops and produce stands on Amish homesteads.

- ◆ Local auction barns and their restaurants offer an opportunity to mingle with Amish and non-Amish local people, listen to a farm auction and sample local food.

- ◆ At an annual MCC Relief Sale, you can buy Amish- and Mennonite-made foods and goods, bid on quilts, and perhaps even take part in a prayer service.

Chapter 18

Dinnertime: Hearty Amish Meals

In This Chapter

- Roots of Amish cuisine
- Plain and simple foods
- Fat and flavor in Amish cooking
- Meats, vegetables, noodles, and breads
- Sweet treats for anytime of day

Traditional Amish cooking comes from Swiss German roots and is very similar to that of Mennonites of all stripes and many Plain groups, such as the Old German Baptist Brethren (Dunkers or Dunkards). The Amish have tended to hold onto some of the older recipes longer than more modern groups, for the simple reason that they don't have electricity and modern methods of preserving foods.

Nowadays, the Amish often combine traditional foods with convenience foods, are apt to buy their bread rather than make it at home, and occasionally enjoy pizza as a family treat. Browsing through a locally published cookbook in an Amish store, you're likely to find recipes calling for Jello, vegetable oil, or cake mix.

Of course, foods, like other aspects of culture, vary from one settlement to another, and some that are still common in Pennsylvania are rarely heard of in Indiana.

Simple Principles

Even though they have adapted some of their recipes and cooking techniques, Amish cooks still follow many principles of traditional Amish cuisine. It is, at its most basic, peasant food from northern climes. Unlike peasant food of the Mediterranean, for instance, Amish cooking is heavy on foods that can be preserved over the winter by canning or cold storage rather than fresh ingredients and uses no herbs and few spices or seasonings. Perhaps it's for this reason that cities aren't filled with trendy restaurants featuring Amish cuisine. Like the rest of their ethnic culture, their cooking is plain and simple. That's not to say it can't be tasty and satisfying, though.

Here are some basic principles behind Amish cooking:

◆ Noon dinner is the big meal on the farm. Traditional Amish dinners include a meat; a starch such as noodles, potatoes, or macaroni; one or more cooked or canned vegetable; bread and butter; jam or apple butter; and often dessert.

◆ Suppers are simpler and lighter. In summer the main course may consist of fruit cobbler, shortcake, or apple dumplings eaten with milk. Soups, cold meats, pickles, applesauce, and other simple dishes are often served at supper.

◆ Meats are served at almost every meal, traditionally cooked slowly for a long time until they fall apart, and are richly flavored. "Rare" is a word rarely found in Amish cookbooks.

◆ Inexpensive cuts of meat may be browned and then cooked in liquid, as in Swiss steak or pot roast.

◆ Amish cooks make homemade bologna—using pork, beef, or a combination— for a quick meat to round out a meal.

◆ Small amounts of smoked meats or meat broth are often used to flavor vegetables, noodles, and other side dishes.

◆ Vegetables are usually cooked until limp—some might say overdone.

◆ Fresh salads exist, but most are more modern inventions. Traditionally, greens such as chard or spinach were often mixed with a hot bacon dressing.

- In summer, fresh fruits and vegetables take on a bigger role in meals, sometimes serving as the main course at supper.

- Flour is the main ingredient in a number of starchy staples, including noodles, pot pie, and dumplings, usually cooked with meat or in meat broth.

- Sweets are a standard part of meals, as is bread and butter. Some families still eat cookies, pie, or cake at most meals, but others serve them less often.

> **Make No Mistake**
>
> Vegetarians beware— Amish cooks use meat to flavor many vegetable and starch dishes. Even a safe-sounding side dish of noodles may be cooked in beef or chicken broth, or green beans boiled with ham or bacon. Lard is the favorite shortening, so even pies, doughnuts, and other pastries may be made with animal products.

The Joy of Fat

Fat could be called the secret weapon of Amish cooking. Sure, it's bad for your heart, but it provides much of the flavor.

Amish cooking was developed by farm women who never had to worry about using too much fat. Fat added flavor to plain foods, kept people warm, and gave them energy for the hard physical work needed on a farm, especially one powered by horses and humans.

> **Ironies and Oddities**
>
> Most Amish women develop full figures as they mature. Genetics plays a part, of course, along with the fact that their culture considers a robust appetite and body healthy. But that figure is also due to the amount of calories—from butter, cream, lard, and meat drippings—in Amish food.

> **The Plain Truth**
>
> Before vegetable shortening and margarine, all cooks used lard and butter for cooking. Most Amish cooks now use some vegetable shortening, but many still use animal fats in traditional recipes. There's no getting around the fact that lard makes the crispest pie crust and gives a fresh flavor to cookies that can't be duplicated. And margarine, of course, can't hold a candle to butter.
>
> So you may decide that the flavor is worth the added cholesterol, as long as these foods aren't an everyday part of your diet. Or you may find exercising worth the extra effort if you remember how good those extra calories you're burning off tasted at the time.

Like most Americans, today's Amish people still enjoy flavor of foods browned in butter, lard, or meat drippings. Fried ham or sausage, chicken, and potatoes frequently appear on the dinner table, and a surprising array of other vegetables also are fried.

And, of course, some of the best desserts and breakfast foods rely on deep frying or contain a good amount of fat mixed with their sugar and flour. Raised doughnuts, crullers, and funnel cakes are all delicious, traditional foods. There's no question the best pie dough is made with lard, and so are, in my opinion, the best sugar cookies.

Dinnertime Staples

Meat and potatoes are the staples of Amish cooking, with a good measure of grains, vegetables, cream, butter, lard, and milk thrown in. Bread and butter and dessert were traditionally served with every meal, although today, with fewer people farming, the Amish are lightening up their diets like the rest of society.

Dinner on the Hoof

Amish main dishes tend to be a meat seasoned with salt and pepper and either roasted, fried, or boiled. Both beef and chicken are often stewed, and noodles or dumplings added in the final stage of cooking. Beef roasts usually are baked until deeply browned on the outside and well-done, sometimes with water in the bottom of the pan. Even so, the meat comes out a little dry, but richly flavored.

Less tender cuts are cooked with moist heat, and some older recipes call for boiling the meat before turning roasting it in the oven. Stewed meat and chicken is cooked, often with chopped onion, salt, and pepper, until it falls off the bones and makes a rich broth. The cook removes the bones, and may finish the dish with noodles or dumplings. Or for stew, she adds vegetables and cooks it some more, then may finish it with dumplings or squares of dough for pot pie.

Eat Your Veggies

Most Amish women cook—some might say *overcook*—their vegetables. This tradition may have resulted from having to rely on canned vegetables most of the year, since the Amish have traditionally lived in climates with cold winters. During the summer, women raise and can or pickle bushel upon bushel of green beans, corn, tomatoes, cucumbers and other vegetables. In the winter, they usually just open a can of vegetables and heated them with minimal preparation.

The Plain Truth

Schnitz und Knepp (dried apples and dumplings) is a traditional Amish dish. The following recipe comes from *Amish Cooking*:

1 quart dried apples (schnitz)

3 lbs. ham

2 TB. brown sugar

2 cups flour

1 tsp. salt

¼ teaspoon pepper

4 tsp. baking powder

1 egg, well beaten

Milk

3 TB. melted butter

Wash the dried apples then cover them with water to soak overnight. Cover the ham with boiling water and boil it for 3 hours. Add the apples and the water in which they were soaked, and boil it for 1 hour longer. Add the brown sugar.

Make the dumplings by sifting together the flour, salt, pepper, and baking powder. Stir in the beaten egg, milk (enough to make a fairly moist, stiff batter), and butter. Drop the batter by the tablespoon into the hot ham and apples. Cover and cook for 15 minutes. Serve hot.

The water bath canner remains standard equipment in Amish homes, where women can vegetables, fruits, pickles, relishes, and even meat.

Relishes—vegetables chopped and mixed with vinegar, spices and sometimes sugar—as well as pickles and sauces like ketchup or chili sauce all lend themselves to canning. Cabbage can be cured into sauerkraut, chopped and pickled as part of a relish, or kept with winter squash and other hardy vegetables in a cool cellar for cooking during the winter.

> **Ironies and Oddities**
>
> Dried corn is a winter treat. It's prepared by cutting corn from the cob, mixing it with cream and sugar, and drying it in a pan in a low oven. The result is a toasty, nutty tasting grain that you can occasionally find in Amish stores. Soaked, boiled, or baked in water to cover, and finished with cream, butter, and a little flour, it's delicious.

Even in summer, fresh vegetables are usually cooked quite thoroughly before serving. Because they raise their vegetables at home, traditional Amish cooks often enjoy a wider range of vegetables than other cooks commonly use. Kohlrabi, salsify, lima, and other shell beans, parsnips, chard, endive, and spinach are commonly found in home gardens, along with green and wax beans, tomatoes, potatoes, carrots, cucumbers, corn, and sometimes summer squash, eggplant, and peppers.

> **The Plain Truth**
>
> If you've only eaten your asparagus steamed or sautéed, then you'll probably be surprised by how delicious it is fried, as in the following recipe:
>
> Wash asparagus stalks and slice thinly lengthwise with a sharp paring knife. (This takes a great deal of patience!) Toss slices with flour to coat. Over medium-low heat, melt enough butter in a skillet to cover the bottom generously (don't worry about having too much) and add asparagus strips. Sprinkle with salt and pepper, and turn frequently to avoid burning. Cook to a rich golden color. Devour.

The Staff of Life: Wheat and Other Grains

To feed a large family on a small budget, Amish cooks use a lot of starches. Noodles dough requires only flour, a few eggs and water, and can be dried and cooked later, or cut into squares and boiled with meat to make pot pie. Starches help stretch a small amount of meat into a hearty, filling meal.

Biscuit dough is one of the most inexpensive and versatile starches available. Using only flour, shortening, baking powder, salt, and milk, a cook can bake the dough into biscuits; steam it atop a stew for dumplings; layer it over fruit and sugar to make cobbler; roll it thin and cut it into squares for wrapping apple halves to make apple dumplings; or add a little sugar and extra shortening to bake shortcake.

Amish women cook corn meal in water until it thickens into mush, which is either served with milk and sugar for breakfast or supper, or chilled in a loaf pan until it solidifies. The mush is then sliced, fried until brown, and served with maple syrup or molasses for breakfast. Scrapple is a variation of corn meal mush flavored with pork sausage, then chilled and fried as a main dish.

Bread, of course, is the most reliable starch of all and is still served at every meal, often with homemade apple butter, jam or jelly as well as butter. *The Mennonite Community Cookbook* describes the traditional "Grandma" baking bread using a liquid yeast "sponge" that she kept in the cellar. Twice a week, according to the book, she would mix up a gallon of liquids, including the yeast, and blend it into enough flour to make a workable dough, which she kneaded and let rise overnight. The next day she would shape and bake 12 to 14 loaves of bread in an outdoor, wood-fired oven.

Some Amish women still bake bread at home, but commercial yeast is widely used, as are propane gas stoves. In some settlements, women still may bake bread in woodstoves, but at least they don't have to go outside to do it.

The Plain Truth

My great aunt Mertie showed me how to make noodles when I was a child. When the dough was rolled out, Aunt Mertie would dry the sheets of dough by spreading them on dish towels hung over the backs of her kitchen chairs. Here's her recipe:

Measure white flour onto a bread board. Make a nest in the center. Using a fork, mix one egg with one tablespoon of water for every cupful of flour and pour the mixture into the nest in the flour. Starting with the fork, work the liquid into the flour. When the dough gets stiff, work it with your hands and adjust flour and water as needed to make a stiff dough that doesn't stick to your hands. It should be almost dry but not crumbly.

Knead dough and divide into portions about the size of your fist. Work each portion into a ball and roll it out on the bread board. The sheet of dough should be thin, but strong enough to hang together when you pick it up.

Place each sheet of dough on a clean dishtowel until partially dry but not crunchy. Cut noodles to desired thickness. For very thin noodles, cut in long strips two inches wide, stack strips, and cut crosswise into thin strips. Separate noodles and allow to dry completely until crisp, like store-bought noodles, or cook while still slightly pliable.

Time for Dessert!

Now for the goodies, the crown jewels of Amish cuisine: desserts. Or, more properly, sweets. Because Amish farm families don't save the goodies for last. They may start their day with *kaffe kuchen*, pancakes with syrup, doughnuts, or a slice of pie. Traditionally, women baked once or twice a week, producing the many pies, cakes, cookies, doughnuts, and other sweets that were—and in many cases still are—considered as essential as the family's bread.

No question about it, Amish cooks excel at combining three staple ingredients—sugar, fat, and white flour—in many delicious ways.

Vas Es Das?

Kuchen, is Pennsylvania German for cake. It's commonly found in Amish and Mennonite cookbooks, but often attached to foods we wouldn't consider cakes. *Mennonite Community Cookbook* includes recipes for *Roll Kuchen* (crullers), *Streusel Kuchen* (raised coffee cake), *Leb Kuchen* (Old-Fashioned Ginger Cookies), and even *Geburtstagkuchen* and *Kaffe* (birthday cake and coffee).

When they bake their own bread, they often save some of the yeast dough for making into *kaffe kuchen* or cinnamon rolls, or deep fry it into doughnuts or crullers. While the fat is hot, they might make funnel cakes—a thin batter poured through a funnel into deep fat, fried brown, and sprinkled with powdered sugar.

In summer, Amish cooks combine the three staples (flour, sugar, and fat) with fresh fruit to create pies, cobblers, dumplings, and shortcakes. Made with sweetened biscuit dough, cobblers, dumplings, and shortcakes traditionally are served as a main dish with milk and sugar, rather than topped with whipped cream for dessert.

Old Recipes, Modern Ingredients

As technology changes everything else in our lives, it has changed what we eat as well. The oldest Amish recipes called for "blubs" of molasses from a barrel, a few cents worth of ingredients, and other measurements we can't approximate today.

Today's commercially ground flours, for instance, may not absorb the same amount of liquids as the locally ground flours our great-grandmothers used. They had no prob-

Ironies and Oddities

Why are they so good at making sweets? In a society in which taverns, dancing, and playing music have always been off-limits, how else to lift their spirits or drown their sorrows but in calories—and lots of them?

lems adjusting for different flours; many old recipes simply left out the flour, expecting the cook to work in enough to make the right kind of dough or batter. When adapting an old recipe, modern cooks have to take the flour measurements with a grain of salt.

For all early American settlers, sugar and molasses were expensive and the stores were harder to reach than they are today, so they were used more sparingly. Many of the old cookies called for more flour and less sugar than typical modern recipes, for example.

Old recipes for baked goods called for the most common spices, such as nutmeg, cinnamon, allspice, and ginger. But sometimes ingredients weren't in the cupboard or were too expensive to buy, so the cook had to make do. The cookbook *Heavenly Recipes* includes a recipe for Grandma's "gingerless" gingerbread flavored with cinnamon rather than ginger.

Even baking pans have changed. The first time I tried an old recipe for butterscotch pie (included later), it only filled my pie crust about half full. I remembered then that old "pie plates" were much more shallow than the glass pie pan I was using. Along with everything else, American society has "super-sized" its desserts in the years since our ancestors settled the country.

> **Make No Mistake**
>
> Though the recipes included in this book have been adapted to modern, commercially available ingredients, some still require you to use your own judgment about exactly how much flour will make the perfect dough. Feel free to adapt recipes to your taste by adding or substituting ingredients. Cooks know that no recipe can ever replace expertise; that's what makes cooking an art!

Cakes

Cakes are popular Amish desserts. Handwritten recipe collections often start with a section of cake recipes. Many of these historic recipes are for simple, everyday fare rather than elaborate layer cakes. Because sugar wasn't a readily available commodity in colonial America, many old cake recipes weren't frosted.

One of those would be gingerbread, which we consider a dessert today. But some traditional cookbooks place it with breads rather than cakes, and it may have originally been more like a sweet bread. My father used to spread gingerbread with butter before eating it (which actually tastes quite good and bears out the principle that adding butter to anything improves it.)

Along with gingerbread, other traditional Amish and Mennonite cakes such as apple butter cake and applesauce cake rely for flavor on a little cinnamon, some ginger and nutmeg, and fruit in forms that could be canned for winter use. Some of the old cake recipes in my family collection simply call for "flavoring." By using vanilla, lemon, maple, or other flavorings, the cook could make a variety of cakes from one recipe.

Recipes such as busy day cake and lightening cake attest to the expectation women felt to produce a steady supply of desserts, in addition to all their other work.

The Plain Truth _____

Like many old recipes, this one for soft gingerbread from my great aunt Mertie's handwritten collection included only a list of ingredients. I've added baking directions, and recommend using fresh grated ginger instead of the dried variety for the best flavor.

1 cup butter

1 cup sugar

4 eggs

1 cup molasses

1 cup milk or cream

2½ cups flour

1 tsp. cinnamon

1 tsp. ground ginger or 1 TB. grated fresh ginger root

2 tsps. soda

Cream butter. Add sugar gradually and beat until fluffy. Add eggs and beat well. Add molasses and cream, and blend into mixture. If using fresh ginger, add it and blend well. Sift dry ingredients (if using fresh ginger, stir into sifted dry ingredients) and add gradually to liquids. Bake in a greased and floured 9×13 pan at 350°F for 30 to 35 minutes until center tests done.

Cookies

The big, soft sugar cookies like my own grandmother used to bake using her mother's recipe were relatively easy to make and provided an inexpensive treat. Amish cookbooks and recipe collections contain many recipes for both sugar cookies and ginger or molasses cookies, perhaps the two most popular varieties historically. Most of the ginger cookies are soft or chewy, descendents of *leb kuchen* or "ginger cakes" as the early cookies were called. But recipes for ginger snaps and other crisp cookies fill the cookbooks as well.

Many of the old cookie recipes make enough cookies to feed families of 10 or more, so if you make them today, you might want to cut them in half.

Pies

Pioneer women may have listed cakes first in their recipe collections, and cookies may have made their name immortal, but it's pie that most people associate with Amish cooking. And rightly so.

The Plain Truth

This is my Grandma Rensberger's recipe for her mother's sour cream sugar cookies. On baking day, her mother stored these cookies in a clean bucket covered with a dishtowel, which she hung inside the cellar door. "All day long," Grandma told me, "you'd hear the screen door slap with the kids coming in and out to get those cookies." For the best flavor, make sure you use lard. Grandma's recipe had no directions, so I've added those and adapted it to modern ingredients.

1 cup lard

2 cups sugar

3 eggs

1 cup sour cream

2 tsps. baking soda

2 tsps. baking powder

4½ cups flour (approximately)

Cream lard with sugar, beat in eggs and add sour cream. Sift soda and baking powder with three cups of flour, and mix into the dough. Add remaining flour gradually to make a soft but not sticky dough; too much will make cookies dry. Chill overnight. Just before rolling out, knead in a little more flour if needed to make dough easy to handle. Cut with large, round cookie cutters and bake at 400°F about 5 minutes. Cookies should be firm enough to spring back when touched, but not browned.

Even the best cakes and cookies can't hold a candle to the taste of pie. It's the combination of a rich, crisp crust and sweet filling, either creamy rich or bursting with fruit, that makes pie so special. In the old days, pie was as much a part of the daily menu as other desserts. Amish women feeding big families might bake a dozen or two every week.

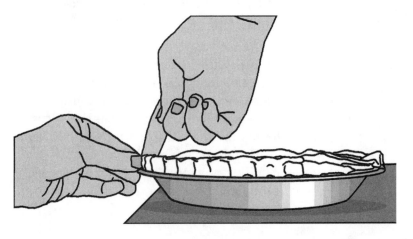

A traditional crimped edge gives pie crust a beautiful finish.

The Plain Truth _____

Making pie crust has been made out to be difficult, but it doesn't have to be. The beauty of this recipe, is that it blends an egg into the flour with the water. The egg helps to bind the water and flour, and guarantees a tender crust.

6 cups flour

1 TB. sugar

1 TB. salt

2 cups lard (or vegetable shortening)

1 egg in a cup filled with water

In a large bowl, stir together flour, sugar, and salt. Cut in lard or shortening. Break the egg into a liquid measuring cup and beat it to a uniform yellow color. Add water to the egg to equal one cup total. Pour the liquid over the flour and mix it in with a fork. Knead the dough just enough to form a smooth ball. Refrigerate at least one hour. Makes four pie crusts.

The key to a tender crust is not to handle it too much. Shape enough dough for one crust into a ball, flatten it on a bread board or clean counter sprinkled with flour, and roll it with a floured rolling pin to make a circle about ⅛ to ¼ inch thick. Lay the crust in a pie pan and trim the edges so they hang about ½ inch over the edge. Don't reuse scraps of pie dough, unless you want to make a miniature pie for your children.

You can freeze extra pie crusts by laying each between two sheets of waxed paper and folding them in halves or quarters. Store them in plastic freezer bags and thaw before using.

While fruit pies are certainly popular and delicious, it's the cream pies that are among most distinctively Amish. Almost all the pie recipes in traditional cookbooks are for cream or crumb pies; cooks are expected to know how to make fruit pies by heart.

Ironies and Oddities

Pie fashion varies by settlement and each generation adds its own twists to traditional recipes. Shoo fly, a molasses-and-crumb pie that's popular in Pennsylvania and has become one of the best known Amish recipes, doesn't show up as often in Indiana, except in tourist restaurants.

The exception is fruit pies with cream or eggs mixed in, or those that take extra preparation, such as grape pie or apple snitz pie.

Most cream pie recipes use very few ingredients other than cream, flour, and sugar. Old-fashioned cream pie is so common in the Indiana Amish and Mennonite community that local restaurants often just use the abbreviation "O.F. Cream" on their daily lists of pies. Butterscotch is another traditional favorite, requiring no more than butter, brown sugar, eggs, flour, and milk to make a rich, creamy pie.

Mary Emma Showalter wrote in her introduction to pies in *Mennonite Community Cookbook*, "Although we have no way of tracing their history, we are convinced that some of these recipes were brought by memory from the old country. Among the most popular ones are the crumb pies and open-faced sour cream fruit pies, including apple, peach, and raisin."

The Plain Truth

This old recipe for butterscotch pie only made enough for about a modern 8-inch pie. To fill my 10-inch glass pan, I doubled the recipe:

1 baked 8-inch pie crust

(For a 9 or 10-inch pie, double the recipe.)

1 ½ cups milk

1 egg

2 heaping TB. flour

Butter the size of a walnut (about 2–3 TB.), softened

1 cup brown sugar, firmly packed

In a heavy sauce pan, heat milk over medium heat until steaming, stirring occasionally. Meanwhile, beat egg and set aside. Mix flour, butter, and brown sugar with a fork. Mix in egg. Whisk mixture into hot milk. Turn heat to low and continue whisking until mixture starts to boil. Cool slightly and pour into pie crust. Chill and top with whipped cream.

Finding Recipes Today

In pioneer days, a few Amish women wrote down recipes they didn't use frequently, so they could remember the ingredients. All they needed was a list of ingredients and maybe approximate measurements; they knew by heart how to make bread, cakes, cookies, noodles, and all manner of other filling foods. Some of those notebooks exist today as family heirlooms.

Today, commercial publishers sell Amish cookbooks with standardized measurements and directions. Some are more authentic than others, and some of the most authentically Amish don't necessarily have the most ethnic recipes. That's because the Amish don't live in a museum, but continue to adopt new ideas and

Make No Mistake

One of the myths perpetuated by tourist establishments is that Amish meals include "seven sweets and seven sours." However, sociologist John Hostetler, who grew up Amish, writes in *Amish Society*, "The only place I have ever eaten the seven sweets and sours is in a tourist hotel."

The Plain Truth

The newest source of Amish and Mennonite recipes, is the Internet. A search for the name of a recipe or simply "Amish recipes" will turn up dozens of choices. Some come from cookbooks, but many are submitted by individuals to recipe-sharing sites. So even though you're using an electronic tool to find them, the recipes still come from someone's recipe box or grandmother's handwritten notebook.

foods from the culture around them. Pizza has become popular, and some Midwestern Amish communities hold "haystack" suppers as fundraisers, serving a dish derived from taco salad.

Amish Cooking, compiled by "a Committee of Amish Women" and published by Amish-owned Pathway Publishing, is as authentically Amish as you'll find. Yet the recipes are a mixture of the old and contemporary, as you can tell by the chapter titled, "Meats, Sauces, Pizza and Meat Curing."

In the country stores and tourist shops of Amish settlements, you can also find locally self-published cookbooks with the favorite recipes of a large family or a church group. These, too, include both traditional and more modern favorites. More personal and less professional than either of the two above, these books give a glimpse into the lives, assumptions, and syntax of the groups that write them. They often include, as cookbooks historically did, household hints that provide a glimpse into the life of a homemaker as well.

The Least You Need to Know

- Many traditional Amish recipes are based on the dried, smoked, pickled, and canned foods that Amish and early Mennonite women had available during cold weather months.

- Modern Amish cooks combine traditional foods with more contemporary recipes, some using convenience foods.

- Grains form a staple in the Amish diet, taking many forms including bread, biscuits, muffins, noodles, and corn meal mush.

- Some of the best foods in Amish and Mennonite cooking are the sweets—doughnuts, cakes, cookies, and pies.

- Ingredients have changed over the years, so some of the oldest and most traditional recipes have to be adapted for use today.

Chapter 19

Collectibles and Hand Crafts: Furniture and Quilts

In This Chapter

- ◆ "Amish-made" in the marketplace
- ◆ Amish crafts become collectible folk art
- ◆ Amish furniture of today and yesterday
- ◆ Handmade quilt patterns and colors

As country style furniture, textiles, and home decor became popular in the United States over the past two decades, so did anything made by Amish people. The image of woodworkers using old-fashioned hand tools to create traditionally styled furniture, although not always accurate, certainly appeals to buyers.

Mainstream interest in Amish culture has spilled over into anything made by the Amish. That's because consumers associate Amish craftsmanship with Amish values: quality, honesty, thrift, and hard work. Although as noted by the "Amish Marketplace" website, one of many selling Amish-made products, "… not all Amish quilters are skilled and not all Amish quilts are of high quality," many retailers—like many consumers—don't make that distinction.

Furniture and quilts are the two most widely marketed products made by the Amish to support or supplement their family income. Some can be purchased directly from the people making them, but most tourists prefer to shop in stores that carry a wide array of products from many producers in one location. Not only do they get more choice with less effort, but they also may feel more comfortable walking away without making a purchase than they would buying directly from the Amish craftsperson.

But it's not just tourist shops in Amish settlements that sell Amish-made products anymore. Increasingly, furniture stores across the nation advertise Amish furniture, and Amish goods and crafts with Amish themes—whether or not made by the Amish—can be ordered from merchant websites. Some sites offer custom-made quilts or furniture in your choice of styles, patterns, sizes, woods, or colors.

Collectible Culture

As the Amish have started manufacturing furniture and quilts for sale, examples of their traditional and historic styles—first in furniture, and later quilts—have became valuable as collectors' items. Today, the finest pieces of furniture, most from the nineteenth century and before, are housed in art museums and private collections. The motifs hand painted on many of them—birds, tulips, and so on—were identified as "Pennsylvania Dutch" and widely copied on all kinds of furniture and housewares in the mid-twentieth century.

> **CAUTION**
>
> **Make No Mistake**
>
> Consumers often believe that Amish values translate into fairly-priced, high quality, handcrafted goods made to last. But with so many Amish people producing goods today, chances are not all will live up to that reputation. Your best bet is to buy directly from a home-run shop—and even then, inspect before you buy. Don't assume "Amish" is a guarantee of quality.

The oldest and most traditional Amish quilts, most made between the late nineteenth century and 1940, are distinctive for their dark, sometimes bold, colors and abstract, geometric designs. Most of them now grace the walls of museums, corporate offices, and private collectors. Amish quilts sold today use the print fabrics and intricate patterns that are traditional to other—non-Amish—cultures that settled the Appalachian mountains and the Midwest.

If you value quality of workmanship and attention to detail, then Amish-made furniture and quilts are a good investment. But don't confuse them with the older, ethnic styles that are now considered folk art rather than household goods.

Amish Furniture as Folk Art

Around the 1920s, early American folk art became popular with urban collectors. Furniture and housewares that had been created for practical use became artifacts in museum collections. The Pennsylvania Dutch decorative arts became a subject of interest among antique collectors as well as art historians.

The Plain Truth

Although "Pennsylvania German" and "Pennsylvania Dutch" are terms for the Amish language, they also refer to a wider culture formed by a whole array of German-speaking peoples who settled in that state. In addition to the Amish and Mennonites, Moravians, members of the German Reformed Church, and Lutherans brought the Germanic culture with them to Pennsylvania.

They applied artistic designs to everyday objects, such as furniture, textiles, pottery, ironwork, pewter, and baptismal/marriage certificates. These articles, created for use in homes, schools, and churches from the mid-eighteenth through mid-nineteenth century, now are collectively referred to as Pennsylvania German or Pennsylvania Dutch folk art.

As author Eve Wheatcroft Granick points out in *The Amish Quilt*, so few Amish people lived in eastern Pennsylvania before 1840, it's doubtful they contributed much original work to the production of Pennsylvania German arts. "We have only a few items of verifiable Amish origin," she writes, "… that date to the years before the 1840s …. One of the most significant contributions the Amish made to Pennsylvania Dutch culture appears to be the persistence with which they preserved traditional forms long after other Pennsylvania Germans had abandoned them …."

The Lancaster Amish, in particular, kept the old arts alive. "In this community more than in any other Amish settlement," Granick writes, "the traditions of Pennsylvania Dutch culture and art are heavily intertwined with the Amish way of life."

Amish and Mennonite Develop Distinctive Styles

According to an article published by the Mennonite Historical Society of Canada in the *Canadian Mennonite Encyclopedia Online*, early American Amish and Mennonite furniture stood out more for its decoration than the way it was built. Swiss Mennonites in eighteenth century America applied a technique called *sulfur inlay* to unpainted furniture. The encyclopedia describes 22 surviving pieces as "constructed in the heavy Swiss-German manner" decorated with "crowns, tulips, stars, urns, birds." Similar designs were also applied to linens and other textiles. "Although the

Vas Es Das?

Sulfur inlay is a process used by Pennsylvania German furniture makers to produce designs in wood. According to the Philadelphia Museum of Art, "The technique of sulfur inlay, in which molten material is poured into incised areas of decoration, has been documented among a small group of eighteenth-century Delaware Valley furniture."

sulfur inlay technique may have been brought to Switzerland," the article concludes, "it was more likely developed in Pennsylvania."

When art collectors began tracking down antique blanket chests, tall case clocks, dressers, and other furniture and accessories, they researched the history of each. Collectors were able to identify early furniture makers and classify their work into "schools" of craftsmen using similar designs.

Starting in the mid-nineteenth century, a group of Amish-Mennonite furniture makers in the village of Soap Hollow in Somerset County, Pennsylvania, developed a distinctive style of painted furniture. According to the Canadian Mennonite Encyclopedia Online, "Soap Hollow furniture is often painted red with black and gold trim. Some pieces … have a yellow ground and tan, brown and bright green decoration." The article also notes that Soap Hollow decorations, dates, and initials are stenciled on the background rather than drawn free-hand. In the late 1800s, two Soap Hollow furniture makers emigrated to Michigan and took their distinctive furniture style with them to the Midwest.

Another Pennsylvania Amish furniture maker, Henry Lapp, lived in Lancaster County in the late nineteenth century. He became well-known for his plain, painted furniture as well as wood grain patterns. Lapp was deaf and could speak very little, which may be one reason he became skilled in the solitary pursuit of woodworking rather than the farming engaged in by most Amish men. The Philadelphia Museum of Art has his order book, which shows water color paintings of the furniture pieces he could offer customers.

In Indiana, two Amish furniture makers also brought the old Germanic style of furniture making with them when they moved west. One, Samuel M. Miller of LaGrange County, carried on the style of painted furniture made in Somerset County, Pennsylvania. M.H. Hochstetler lived further west, near the town of Nappanee, where he made painted furniture around the turn of the twentieth century. Nappanee became known as a furniture-manufacturing center, although most of its furniture wasn't made by Amish craftsmen.

Amish Furniture Today

The Amish are still making furniture today, although they use power tools (run on electricity, if the factory or shop is owned by a non-Amish person, or by air pressure or hydraulic power if it's an Amish-owned shop) instead of doing everything by hand. They work both in small, farm-based shops and in larger factories in industrial parks. Some businesses are family-owned, while others are owned by Mennonites or other English people who employ Amish craftsmen.

But the furniture they manufacture is no longer distinctively Amish—or more accurately, Pennsylvania German. Instead, they make home furniture in styles popular with mainstream America—mission, Shaker, traditional country, and others. Amish furniture can be purchased directly from local makers in Amish settlements.

But today you don't have to visit the shop of a furniture maker to buy Amish-made products. Large distributors who represent Amish craftsmen sell their furniture through commercial furniture stores across the country and even take orders over the Internet. Amish craftsmen still custom-make furniture, usually offering certain styles and pieces and letting the customer specify the wood, finish, and size of piece wanted. Some websites let you order custom-made pieces as well.

From Bed Cover to Wall Hanging: Amish Quilts

Like furniture, Amish quilts fall into two categories: traditional and contemporary. Unlike furniture, though, traditional Amish quilts developed a distinctively Amish style that wasn't shared by their German neighbors.

Most traditional Amish quilts made between 1880 and 1940 share the following characteristics:

- Bold, solid colors
- Striking color combinations
- Stark, geometric patterns
- Tiny, precise quilting stitches
- Black used for borders and background
- Wool (Lancaster County) or cotton (Mifflin County and Midwest) fabrics
- A few, well-defined patterns, which were consistent within a settlement

Making a Quilt

Quilts come in two varieties, those with solid tops and those that are pieced. Solid top quilts emphasize the decorative nature of the quilting itself, while pieced quilts achieve their beauty from the combination of colors and shapes that make up their pattern.

Women making pieced quilts start with paper patterns that they pin to the fabric. They cut around those pieces and sew them together in a prescribed order to form the top of the quilt. When making quilts for home use, women traditionally used scraps of fabric left over from making clothing and parts of discarded clothing that weren't too worn or faded. They would buy fabric for the backing, or underside, of the quilt.

It's the layer between the top and bottom that makes a quilt warm. The earliest Amish quilts sometimes had only another layer of fabric between top and bottom, but cotton batting became more common in the late nineteenth century. By mid-twentieth century, the cotton batting was being replaced by the thicker, warmer, and easier to wash and dry polyester batting.

> **The Plain Truth**
>
> Skilled quilters use many small, closely placed stitches to create the pattern. The thinner cotton bats of old quilts allowed quilters to place their stitches more closely than they can when stitching through thicker polyester bats, so the type of filling has affected the quality of the quilting.

The final stage of quilt making is the quilting itself. While the pieced pattern usually stands out most on a quilt, the stitching pattern says more about the quality of the quilt. Stitching patterns can be quite elaborate, and quilts with larger plain areas usually feature more detailed stitching patterns. Quilters first draw the quilting pattern onto the fabric using a template, repeating the pattern throughout the quilt. Then they stitch along the lines.

Early Amish Quilts

Traditional quilt styles varied by settlement. Lancaster County, Pennsylvania, quilts are in some ways distinct from those made by the more conservative Amish groups in Mifflin county, as are quilts made in Ohio, Indiana, and elsewhere.

In addition to variations in pattern, fabric use also varied by settlement. The Lancaster Amish favored wools, the Mifflin County Amish mixed in cottons, and the Midwestern Amish women tended to use less expensive cottons almost exclusively. In her fine, detailed book, *The Amish Quilt*, Eve Wheatcroft Granick points out that in quilt styles, as in all forms of cultural expression, the Amish deliberately chose what was out of fashion with mainstream Americans.

The earliest Amish quilt tops were solid rather than pieced, as plain as the clothing worn by their creators. The only fancy work was in the stitching patterns that held together top, bottom, and filling. According to Granick, some of the most conservative Amish and Old Order Mennonite districts still prohibit pieced quilts as unnecessarily fancy.

When Amish women finally started making pieced quilts in the 1870's, they first chose outdated quilt patterns. "In Lancaster, Amish women worked out variations of the Medallion Square," Granick writes in *The Amish Quilt*. "This design had been virtually forgotten after the 1850s by other American women." This pattern features large blocks of fabric that together form a single pattern, rather than the many blocks repeating a pattern that were so popular in later quilts.

Making solid-top quilts and pieced quilts with large areas of solid fabric required women to buy fabric just for quilt making. Rachel and Kenneth Pellman, in their book *A Treasury of Amish Quilts*, suggest that was one reason the long-established—and comparatively wealthy—families of Lancaster County could choose to make plainer quilts than their Amish sisters in the Midwest. Whether because quilt styles had changed by the time the Midwestern settlements were established, or because they were less conservative than the Lancaster Amish or had less money to buy fabric, Midwestern Amish women chose quilt patterns made up of many small pieces cut from fabric remnants and old clothing.

> ### Ironies and Oddities
>
> Today, we think of the Amish as having a long history of quilt making. But Amish women were actually among the last American women to start quilting, just over a century ago. Quilt making was practiced in ancient times, and American housewives quilted throughout the nineteenth century. But Amish women continued to use traditional German bedding—blankets, coverlets, and featherbeds—until the late 1800s.

> ### Ironies and Oddities
>
> The most conservative Amish and Mennonite churches consider patchwork unnecessarily fancy. In *The Amish Quilt*, Eve Wheatcroft Granick writes, "In some of the most conservative Amish groups in Indiana and Canada, the making of pieced designs has been specifically forbidden by church rules, from the nineteenth century to the present day. This prohibition … is practiced among some of the old Order Mennonites as well."

Even in the Midwest, though, Amish women chose "simple and repetitive block designs," according to Granick, while mainstream American homemakers were sewing more elaborate patterns, sometimes embellished with appliqué. Amish quilt fashions continued to evolve, but consistently lagged behind English styles by 20 years or more, until recent decades.

Identifying Amish Quilts by Pattern, Colors, and Stitching

Before the 1940s, Amish quilts stood out for their distinct ethnic choices of pattern, color, and stitching. Each settlement's quilts showed slight differences as well, because Amish women used patterns and stitching templates easily available from relatives or neighbors.

Lancaster County Quilts

Quilt patterns favored by the Lancaster County Amish include ...

Ironies and Oddities
Diamond in the Square or Center Diamond was also sometimes called the Cape pattern, because the center diamond is surrounded by large, triangular pieces. "That name comes from the fact that dresses wore out, but capes seldom did," according to *A Treasury of Amish Quilts.* Quilters could recycle their triangular capes by using them to fill in around the diamond in a new quilt.

- Center Diamond (also called Diamond in the Square)
- Center Square
- Bars
- Sunshine and Shadow
- Nine Patch and Double Nine Patch
- Baskets
- Log Cabin
- Crazy Quilt
- Lone Star
- Irish Chains

Black and deep shades of blue are the dominant colors in many Amish quilts, forming borders and backgrounds that contrast with brightly colored pieced goods. Though Granick says black was more common in the Midwest and rarely used in Lancaster County quilts, other authors include examples of early Lancaster quilts in which black plays a prominent role.

Some colors were used in quilts that weren't worn by Amish women, indicating that quilters purchased the fabrics just for quilting. Women sometimes bought bundles of fabric that included many colors, and used the ones they couldn't wear for making bedclothes.

In the nineteenth century, Lancaster Amish quilters favored brown, rust, wine, olive and forest green, gray, medium to dark blues, and purple.

Diamond in the Square, sometimes also called the Cape pattern, is a traditional Amish quilt pattern from Lancaster County, Pennsylvania.

In the twentieth century, manufacturers started using new dyes that resulted in brighter colors. Lancaster quilts from the first half of the twentieth century feature royal and medium blues, purples, shades of red from brilliant to wine, pink, aqua and teal, and olive and bright greens.

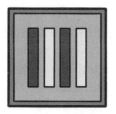 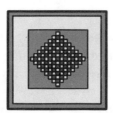 

 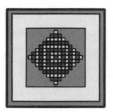

Traditional quilt patterns from Lancaster County. Top row, left to right: Bars, Sunshine and Shadow, Nine-Patch. Bottom row, left to right: Baskets, Around the World

The pattern of quilt stitching in traditional Amish quilts varies by settlement as well. Lancaster County quilters used wide borders around their quilts, as well as large open spaces in the early examples. Both to hold their cotton bats firmly in place and for decoration, quilters filled those open spaces with thousands of tiny stitches in elaborate patterns. The subtle beauty of intricate quilting may be considered the true artistry of a quilt, even more than color and piecing.

Lancaster Amish women used quilting patterns that drew upon Pennsylvania Dutch arts and crafts, such as hearts, tulips, hexes, and stars. Other patterns show images of nature: vines, fruit leaves, fruits, ferns, roses, and other flowers. Geometric patterns were common in the earliest quilts, but more elaborate stitching became popular in the heyday, only to give way to less demanding motifs in later years.

Mifflin County Quilts

The Amish living in Mifflin County, Pennsylvania from the 1790s gradually developed different styles from the Old Order Amish of Lancaster County. Beginning in the mid-1800s, several Mifflin County groups left the Old Order to form the Byler and Peachy Amish. In the 1880s, the Byler group split again and a bishop from Nebraska came to help the dissenters organize a new church, which therefore became known as the Nebraska Amish. The quilt styles of each group reflect their differences from each other and the Lancaster Old Order Amish.

The most commonly used designs were variations on the Four-Patch and Nine-Patch patterns. Other patterns moved into more elaborate piecework, such as was developing among the Midwestern Amish. Jacob's Ladder, Irish Chain, Shoofly, Baskets, Log Cabins, Crazy Patches, and Tumbling Blocks can all be found on Mifflin County quilts.

Nebraska Amish quilters had the most limited choice of patterns and muted colors in Mifflin County. Piecework was restricted to the colors they wore: browns and blues, purples, plums, black, and red or green from young girls' dresses. Phyllis Pellman Good writes in her book, *Quilts from Two Valleys*, that the only color the Nebraska Amish could buy just for quilting was tan, which was used for backgrounds and borders. Their quilting patterns were equally conservative, mostly straight rows, chains, fans, and blackberry leaf vines.

The Byler Amish, by contrast, did more intricate piecing and used more vivid colors than the Nebraska Amish, including pinks, oranges, shades of green, and black. Blackberry leaf vines, chains, hearts, and fans were also popular quilting patterns of the Byler church.

The Peachey Amish, the most liberal group, also made quilts with the least apparent restrictions. They used the widest variety of patterns, and their color choices included bright blues and purples, golden yellow, pink, bright greens, and orange in addition to the more subdued blacks, blues, and browns. They particularly liked to place bright colors next to each other for a sometimes startling effect.

Midwestern Amish Quilts

As the Amish moved westward, they settled in areas already populated by non-Amish neighbors, and they had more interaction with people outside their church than in the larger Pennsylvania settlements. Midwestern Amish quilts reflect this interaction, using a wider array of patterns, set off by blue or black borders or backgrounds.

While there were some differences between the quilts made by Amish women in Ohio and Indiana, for the most part they were very similar. The more conservative Ohio Amish groups were more likely to choose plainer quilt patterns, but their more liberal cousins were known for adopting intricate patterns and producing them in endless variation. Some pieced the back as well as the top of the quilt, making it reversible.

Indiana Amish women made more fan quilts than in other settlements. They sometimes arranged the fans inside solid-color blocks, while the fans zigzagged diagonally across other quilt tops, their edges decorated with turkey track embroidery.

And of course the Amish carried their quilting far beyond Indiana, to Illinois, Michigan, Iowa, Missouri, Kansas, Wisconsin, and other states.

Traditional quilt patterns popular with the Midwestern Amish included:

Shoofly

Nine Patch

Ohio Double Inside Border Plain Quilt (Ohio)

Railroad Crossing (especially Ohio)

Log Cabin

String Stars

Roman Stripes

Spiderweb

Double Wedding Ring

Fan (Indiana)

Variable Stars

Rolling Stone (Indiana)

Baskets (Indiana)

Bow Ties (Indiana)

Swallow Tail (Indiana)

Double T (Indiana)

Hole in the Barn Door (Indiana)

Lone Star	Garden Maze
Broken Star	Hummingbird
Streak of Lightening	Ohio Star
Ocean Waves	Le Moyne Star
Zigzags	Rabbit's Paw
Indiana Puzzle	

Before the twentieth century, when black and dark blue became popular background colors for Midwestern Amish quilts, Ohio Amish women preferred blues, browns, and reds for background colors. Indiana women favored indigo, browns, tans, greens, and later burgundy, golden yellow, oranges, shades of blue, and lavender. Indiana quilters were more likely to use bright reds, bought specifically for their quilts, than Amish women in other states.

Blue and white quilts enjoyed popularity in Ohio and Mifflin County for around two decades following 1920, and to a lesser extent in Indiana. According to Granick, Indiana quilt makers, unlike Amish women elsewhere, did occasionally slip a striped, dotted, or plaid printed fabric into their quilts. Though unusual, it showed the somewhat looser rules of the Indiana Amish regarding quilt patterns.

The Plain Truth

Common quilting patterns throughout the Midwest include rope, twist, flower, and leaf border designs, diagonal lines, straight, and grid lines, and quilting along piecework seams.

While less restricted in their patterns and fabrics, Granick notes that the Amish from Indiana westward didn't show the same quality in their quilt stitching that their cousins in Pennsylvania and Ohio practiced. As the Amish left their established communities and moved westward, their stitches became longer and fewer, quilting designs less intricate. Life on the prairie probably didn't lend itself to the hours of elaborate needlework that were possible in more established, prosperous eastern settlements.

The Amish Quilting Industry Today

By the 1950s, Amish women throughout the country started adopting the quilt styles that the rest of American women were abandoning for ready-made and synthetic blankets. Amish women added white, pastels, and bright colors to their quilts, adopted even more patterns and sometimes even adding embroidery.

Amish women also seemed to adopt some of the color preferences of mainstream culture. Overall, the quilts took on the lighter look of English quilts, with colors more closely matched rather than in stark contrast to each other.

Now many Amish women make quilts for sale to English customers. Some specialize in cutting pieces and others in quilting, rather than making an entire quilt. One woman then coordinates production and sells the finished products. This specialization of labor mimics the factory system, making production efficient, yet allows Amish women to remain at home.

> **Ironies and Oddities**
>
> In the last two to three decades, traditional Amish quilts became so popular that they have moved out of cedar chests and off Amish clotheslines into the collections of museums and individuals.

With Amish-made quilts so popular, Amish women also make them to donate to charity auctions, such as the Relief Sales run by Mennonite Central Committee around the country (see Chapter 17). These auctions provide an opportunity to look at hundreds of quilts made by local Amish and Mennonite women, admire their handiwork, and buy one for a good cause.

The Least You Need to Know

- ◆ Furniture making and quilting are both traditional to Amish culture.

- ◆ Today, the Amish make furniture and quilts in styles that appeal to American consumers rather than in traditional Amish styles.

- ◆ Pennsylvania German or Pennsylvania Dutch folk art was created by a whole array of settlers of German descent, but some of its designs were carried on longer by the Amish than others.

- ◆ Traditional Amish furniture and quilts are now highly sought after by antiques and art dealers, and most are held by museums and private collectors.

- ◆ Contemporary Amish-made furniture and quilts can be purchased from local craftspeople, in tourist and specialty shops near Amish settlements, and nationwide through stores and websites.

Part 6

Beyond the Old Order: Where Have All the Mennonites Gone?

What happened to all those Mennonites after the Amish left? What have they been up to since? The basic functions of life: growing and dividing.

Over the past century, the largest body of Mennonites went from being almost as distinctive as the Amish to blending into the American mainstream. Now they're uniting with the next largest group (which once was considered the radical fringe) to form a big new denomination called Mennonite Church USA.

Mennonite life is never quiet for long, though, despite their image, and already controversies threaten attempts at unity.

Chapter 20

The Rest of the Story: Mennonite Growth and Divisions

In This Chapter

- Amish Mennonites splinter away
- A conservative movement among Conservatives
- Old Mennonites, the original namesake
- General Conference Mennonites
- The Russian Mennonite saga
- Reversing their history, some Mennonites reunite

When last we visited Mennonite history, it was 1865 and the conservative minority among the Amish (later known as the Old Order Amish) had just split from their progressive brethren, who called themselves Amish Mennonites. Since then, we've followed the course of the Old Order Amish, but what ever became of the Amish Mennonites? We've looked at similarities between the Old Order Amish and the Old Order Mennonites, but who are all those other people who call themselves Mennonite today? Where did they come from, and how are they related?

A seemingly simple question like, "What is a Mennonite?" has many answers, none of them complete. Every attempted answer is bound to leave out some nuance of belief or practice, because so many people lay claim to that name, which they inherited from their forebears or adopted and carried forward.

Traditional, Transitional, Transformational

Authors Donald Kraybill and C. Nelson Hostetter provide a useful way of classifying Mennonite groups in their book *Anabaptist World USA*. They divide Mennonites into three groups:

- **Traditional:** Old Order and similar groups (covered in the Chapter 4 of this book)
- **Transitional:** retaining some plain dress and customs, but speaking English and driving cars
- **Transformational:** seeking to transform the world rather than separate from it

In Chapter 4, we looked at traditional Anabaptist groups, because they are similar to the Old Order Amish. In Part 6, we'll take a closer look at transitional and transformational Mennonite groups.

What Became of the Amish Mennonites?

The disagreements didn't end when the more progressive Amish Mennonites parted ways with the Old Order Amish. Still to be decided by the progressives were several central doctrines: the importance of a direct experience of God for Christian conversion or baptism, church education, missions, and so on.

The Amish church had never been evangelical—its members would explain their faith if asked, but made no attempt to convert others to their faith. They let their lives stand as their testimony that living according to Christian principles could result in a better life, as well as better people.

However, the Protestant revivalist movement in America was going strong in the latter half of the nineteenth century, and as the Amish Mennonites continued to call annual meetings of their ministers to help shape the new church, they were forced to consider questions regarding the role of evangelicalism in their faith.

One question was how important spiritual experience was as opposed to living a moral life. The revivalists stressed the importance of direct spiritual experience, an emotional contact with the Holy Spirit, or God, so powerful it inspired outward changes in one's life. The traditional Amish view was that it was enough for a person to decide to make those changes, although what they called "regeneration" from within would certainly help a person stay on the straight and narrow path.

Ironies and Oddities

A Wisconsin newspaper article was accompanied by a photo of men and women in plain dress, identified as Mennonites. The article quoted a college professor from a Mennonite college, noting that he himself was a Mennonite.

Yes, he was Mennonite—but not like those in the photo. "Plain" Mennonites don't go to college or sponsor them, earn doctorates, or teach college.

Egly Amish

One group of Old Order Amish—who became known as the Egly Amish—was strongly influenced by American evangelicalism at the same time that Amish Mennonites were splitting away from the Old Order for different reasons. The Egly Amish valued a conversion experience of the Spirit, feeling that conforming to outer rules was an empty practice in comparison. One bishop, Henry Egly, went so far as to say that no one could really be considered a Christian, and eligible for baptism, without such an experience. He refused to baptize anybody who hadn't experienced directly the presence of God.

Egly's own congregation couldn't agree to back him, but others among the Amish Mennonites were drawn to his teaching. He led those who were willing to follow into his own denomination, the Egly Amish. They emphasized individual faith, but kept some of the more conservative Amish traditions such as plain dress and, for a time, German language services.

After Egly's death in 1890, they dropped many of their Amish traditions, including plain dress, and gradually became more like fundamentalist Christian churches. The group called itself the Defenseless Mennonite Church from 1897 until 1948, when it adopted the name Evangelical Mennonite Church to reflect its increasingly evangelical nature. The change also reflected a drift away from the Anabaptist belief in nonresistance to violence, and a greater identification with other evangelical Christian churches that participate in the military. As part of that drift, the Evengelical Mennonites left behind their plain dress, as well.

> **The Plain Truth** _____
>
> When Shipshewana, Indiana, became a destination for tourists curious about the Amish and Mennonites, local churches built a museum called Menno-Hof to explain their history and beliefs. One exhibit features a timeline 79 inches long showing Amish and Mennonites church divisions between 1525 and 1975, a span of 450 years. Though an accurate count is difficult because some groups later merged with others, the timeline records 16 splits among the Swiss Brethren and 21 divisions among the Mennonites for a total of 37 splits, an average of one every 2.13 inches—or approximately every 12 years!

Stuckey Mennonites

Another split occurred in 1872, resulting in yet another Mennonite group named for its leader. This time, it was Illinois Bishop Joseph Stuckey, who allowed congregations under his supervision much more latitude in dress and other lifestyle rules than his more conservative brethren. A far more serious issue, though, was that his churches accepted excommunicated members from Amish congregations. This ran counter to tradition, and Amish bishops felt it undermined their own ability to discipline their churches by giving members an alternative. Most Amish Mennonite leaders agreed.

The last straw was a poem written by a member of Stuckey's congregation, Joseph Joder, that celebrated his belief in _universalism_, the belief that a loving God will save all of humanity, not just Christians—or more specifically, just Amish or Amish Mennonites. This belief would mean the end to the threat of hell and punishment as a motivating factor for Christian behavior, ministers feared, and ran counter to traditional beliefs.

> **Vas Es Das?** _____
>
> **Universalism** was a belief spread through the Midwest by circuit-riding preachers in the mid-nineteenth century. They taught that all human beings, even those who commit evil, will be saved by God out of love for humanity. Central Illinois had several Universalist churches, and the belief found some support among the Amish there before the uproar over Joseph Joder's poem.

Stuckey taught that only God, not church discipline, could change an errant person's heart. He didn't agree with Joder, but he wouldn't excommunicate him, either. The wider community of Amish Mennonite ministers, who were already suspicious of his liberalism, decided Stuckey had gone too far. They cut off fellowship with him and congregations supporting him. Those congregations became known as the Stuckey Amish, representing the liberal fringe of formerly-Amish congregants when it came to church discipline.

For half a century after Stuckey's death in 1902, his followers operated their own church conference. But even during his lifetime, Stuckey had felt affinity for the General Conference Mennonite Church, established in 1860 by progressive Mennonites who wanted a church more open to change (more on General Conference Mennonites later in this chapter). Eventually, in 1946, the former Stuckey Amish officially joined the General Conference Mennonite Church.

Conservative (Amish) Mennonites

When the Old Order Amish dropped away from the Amish Mennonites, some people found themselves dissatisfied with both groups. In 1910, they founded yet another group on the middle ground: the Conservative Amish Mennonites. Members who had come from the Amish Mennonites considered themselves conservative, while those who left the Old Order Amish were the liberals of their home communities. They met in the middle, adopting practices of both groups. Though they …

♦ Built meetinghouses.

♦ Engaged in overseas missions.

♦ Adopted Sunday schools.

They also …

♦ Worshiped in German.

♦ Dressed much like their Amish relatives.

> **Make No Mistake**
>
> With so many Amish, Mennonites, and other Anabaptists, it's impossible to include the history, beliefs, and practices of them all in this book. Not only are there dozens of Amish and Mennonite groups, but their practices change over time in response to the society around them and the desires of their members. And with every change, it seems, comes new divisions and the formation of yet another group.

As the group evolved through the decades, its practices gradually became more like the Mennonites and less like the Amish. For example …

♦ English, not German, became the language of worship.

♦ Women started using small prints for their dresses.

♦ Women's head coverings shrank in size and lost their ribbons.

♦ Some women stopped pinning up their hair and some even cut it.

♦ Men switched from hooks-and-eyes on their coats to buttons.

♦ Men stopped wearing beards.

In 1954, the conference dropped the word "Amish," becoming the Conservative Mennonite Conference.

Although many women in the Conservative Mennonite Conference no longer wear a prayer covering, older women often do. Their clothing, though modest, is no longer plain.

Mainstream Amish Mennonites

With the evangelicals, progressives, and conservatives stripped away, the remaining Amish Mennonites represented the mainstream. Between 1888 and 1893, their independent congregations organized themselves into three regional conferences.

They supported higher education, which early in the twentieth century meant high school, still a rarity for most Americans. The Mennonites and Amish Mennonites started a private high school in Goshen, Indiana, which later became Goshen College.

Other joint projects with the Mennonites finally led to the Amish Mennonite conferences merging into the Mennonite Church over the decade from 1917 to 1927. Most Mennonite Church congregations in much of the Midwest were formerly Amish Mennonite.

Conservative Mennonite Movement

As they drifted closer in lifestyle to the Mennonite Church, the Conservative Mennonite Conference became too progressive for many of its members. Starting in the 1950s, a number of Conservative churches resisted the trend by leaving to form small affiliations under a variety of names. Author Stephen Scott refers to this trend as "the conservative Mennonite movement."

Although not their official name, "conservative Mennonites" is an apt description of these churches. While they vary in their degree of conservatism, all hold a number of beliefs in common, including the following:

♦ They believe in the Bible as inspired by God, interpret every word literally, and consider it the central authority in guiding Christian life.

♦ They support education through their own schools, which often end with tenth grade. They don't believe in higher education, and instead of colleges, they sponsor Bible institutes where students can study the Bible and related religious topics.

♦ Conservatives support mission outreach and the publication of evangelical, Sunday school, and other religious materials.

♦ Electricity and telephones are accepted; television is outlawed; radios are tolerated by some groups but not others.

♦ Conservatives drive cars and worship in churches.

Seeing themselves as members of the kingdom of God, conservative Mennonites have no part in the doings of any earthly nation. That's why they don't …

Make No Mistake

Don't confuse "conservative Mennonites" with "Conservative Mennonites." The "conservative Mennonite movement" describes a trend among former members of the officially named Conservative Mennonite Conference against the progressive drift of that denomination during the twentieth century. Those who left may be described as "conservative Mennonites," but the term "Conservative Mennonite" means a member of the Conservative Mennonite Conference.

The Plain Truth

The clothing of members of the conservative Mennonite movement is generally plain, but it varies by group. Women's head coverings, though, are required, not as an article of dress but as a religious symbol. They're made of white net and worn over uncut hair. In general, as with other Amish and Mennonites, the more conservative the group, the larger the covering.

- Vote.

- Serve on juries.

- Participate in government in any way.

- Join the military.

Yet these conservative Mennonites also see government as being put in place by God to rule the un-Christian, by force if necessary, and believe Christians have to obey all laws that don't conflict with biblical teaching.

Who's On First? "Old" Mennonites: The Real Thing

Amid the proliferation of splinter groups carrying the name "Mennonite," there has long been only one official Mennonite Church. Descended from the Swiss Mennonites who emigrated from Europe before the Amish, these were the mainstream Mennonites and by far the largest group. To distinguish them from the newer General Conference Mennonites, founded in 1860, the Mennonite Church was commonly called the "Old" Mennonites.

They maintained the Anabaptist beliefs in adult baptism, nonresistance to violence, and separation of church and state. They also believed in living out their faith, but how they did that changed gradually through the years.

Hard work and frugality were values the Old Mennonites carried on from their forebears. Until perhaps the 1960s, they still continued to separate themselves from the world somewhat by wearing conservative, but not plain, clothing. The women wore "prayer coverings" to church, although those were small and often perched on short hairstyles. Piano accompaniment to their four-part hymn singing came to be accepted in Mennonite churches, where decades earlier this had been a divisive issue.

The social upheaval of the 1960s challenged Mennonites along with the rest of society to change. Young women started wearing prayer coverings that were lacy circles pinned over flowing locks. Younger people updated their clothing styles, and more and more left the farm for college or work in factories and businesses. Nonresistance began to be replaced by active war resistance. Eventually they came to look and act very similar to the rest of American society.

The Plain Truth

Like young people across America in the 1960s, Mennonite youth pushed for social change. They challenged Mennonites to go beyond traditional nonresistance to violence and to become active peace witnesses. During the Vietnam War, while most Mennonite men chose alternative service, a few chose the more radical course of draft resistance.

General Conference Mennonites

Although the largest Mennonite body, the Mennonite Church was not the most liberal. That place on the spectrum was held by the General Conference Mennonite Church. Founded in 1860 by a handful of liberal Mennonite churches from Pennsylvania and Iowa, this progressive church ...

◆ Supported higher education.

◆ Started missions among the Native Americans and abroad.

◆ Developed an educated, professional ministry.

◆ Maintained the Amish tradition of congregational autonomy—but without the bishops and the *Ordnung* to force uniformity.

The General Conference, or GC as it was called for short, remained a small group of congregations until 1874. That's when several thousand descendents of the original Dutch Mennonites, who had found refuge in Russia in the eighteenth century, moved to the United States. The political climate in Russia had turned against them, and they were fleeing persecution. They settled on the Midwestern and Canadian plains, where General Conference churches were most common, increasing their membership and adding diversity to their ethnic mix.

The Plain Truth

After 150 years in Russia, Mennonites there had become distinct from those who settled in the United States. The tsars let Mennonites set up their own church-states. Russian Mennonites in turn supported the tsars, and even their armies, though they didn't fight themselves. Mennonites became the ruling class and enjoyed advantages over other Russians. Mennonites grew prosperous, and many enjoyed the material pleasures of the world. Eventually, Russian Mennonites became more of an ethnic group than one based on religious conviction.

The Mennonite Sojourn in Russia

While Mennonites in North America were growing, prospering, arguing, changing names and affiliations, another large group of Mennonites were living a completely different story in Russia.

The Mennonites in North America had mostly come from the Swiss German Anabaptists. But Anabaptists in the Netherlands represented a different branch of the family tree.

The Plain Truth

Historically, property laws in Europe often discriminated against Mennonites, and they had to pay heavy taxes in lieu of military service. These were two factors that led them to seek refuge in Russia.

While the Swiss Germans had retreated into the countryside, becoming farmers, the Dutch had remained an urban people. Looking all over central Europe for a homeland since the early days of Anabaptist persecution, they were offered temporary safe haven by one local ruler or another, because their hard work and successful farming practices made them a boon to the local economy. But sooner or later, a new ruler would come into power or the Mennonite refusal to join the army would cause them to suffer persecution again.

In the late 1700s, Dutch Mennonites living in Prussia were looking for a new home. Catherine the Great, empress of Russia, offered settlers 165 acres of farm land per family, plus religious freedom and a guarantee that they wouldn't have to serve in the Russian military—ever. The government offered them the opportunity to live in settlements where they could control their own education and local government, and even suspended taxation until the newcomers could get settled.

Starting in 1789, the Mennonites began settling in Russia, where they lived for 150 years. Living in isolated areas, they set up their own self-governing villages rather than individual farms. They prospered, developing industries as well as farms and large estates, and achieved a degree of social status they hadn't known elsewhere.

Ironies and Oddities

Though they had to leave their property behind, one thing the Russian Mennonites did bring with them from the Russian steppes was winter wheat. They introduced the crop in Kansas in 1874. Winter wheat grew well on the Great Plains, and was soon adopted by other farmers. Today, it's a staple of the U.S. farm economy.

As in America, reformers who wanted to return to a stricter and more spiritual religious life formed a new Mennonite branch. The Mennonite Brethren Church originated as a revivalistic group in Russia who wanted spiritual reform. They moved to the western United States and Canada.

After the Russian government moved to rescind the exemption of Mennonites from military service in 1871, Canada and the United States both invited the Russian Mennonites to come farm their plains. The governments offered free land, religious freedom, the right to control their children's education and, in Canada, military exemption. The United States didn't guarantee military exemption, but the warmer climate and fertile land attracted many Russian Mennonites anyway. About 10,000 Russian Mennonites and Hutterites settled in the Midwest and Great Plains states, and another 8,000 in Manitoba, Canada from 1874 through the 1880s.

During and after the Russian Revolution in 1917, those Mennonites who had stayed in Russia suffered increasing hardship. Their property was seized, and they were organized into collective farms. Many of the men were arrested or exiled, and disease and famine threatened the rest. Mennonite Central Committee (MCC) was organized in 1920 by American and Canadian Mennonites to coordinate distribution of food and other help to Russian Mennonites.

Between 1923 and 1929, another 22,000 Russian Mennonites were allowed to leave the Soviet Union for Canada, which was more open to their immigration than other countries. A few thousand more were able to leave for Paraguay and Brazil.

The last big emigration of Russian Mennonites from the Soviet Union took place at the end of World War II. While Germany temporarily occupied parts of the Soviet Union, 35,000 Russian Mennonites left for Germany. Only 12,000 managed to reach western Germany before the Soviet army caught them. After the fall of the Germans to the Allies, about half those Russian Mennonites were able to emigrate to Canada and half to Paraguay and other South American countries.

Most of the Russian Mennonites who settled in the United States joined the General Conference Mennonite Church. They were in general more urban and progressive than the Swiss German Mennonites who had established the older settlements in Pennsylvania and the Midwest.

Although the General Conference maintained its Anabaptist beliefs, its members believed they could be "in the world but not of the world," as Jesus commanded. They believed that dressing differently was missing the point; it was spiritual nonconformity to the world that mattered.

The Least You Need to Know

- The Amish Mennonites no longer exist as a group. They further divided into more conservative and more liberal groups, until the main body joined the Mennonite Church.

- The more conservative churches that left the Amish Mennonites formed the Conservative Mennonite Conference.

◆ Since coming to America, the ("Old") Mennonite Church remained the largest body of Mennonites and held a position in the middle of the conservative-to-progressive spectrum.

◆ Those who felt the Mennonite Church was too conservative formed the General Conference Mennonite Church in the nineteenth century.

21

Shaking It Up: A Century of Change

In This Chapter

- ◆ Mennonites resist modernization
- ◆ Evolution from congregations to national denominations
- ◆ Repairing an old split
- ◆ Education helps modernize the church
- ◆ Changing values

A dramatic shift occurred—very slowly, of course—among the majority of Mennonites during the twentieth century. Gradually, they changed meaning of "Mennonite" from an ethnic identity to a religious affiliation.

Throughout Mennonite history, the Mennonite Church has been the largest group of Mennonites. Noticeably more conservative than the next largest group, the General Conference Mennonite Church, author Stephen Scott notes that at the dawn of the twentieth century, "Members of the Mennonite Church were still 'Plain People.'" Women wore cape dresses and head coverings and men wore standing collar suit coats. Ministers, deacons, and bishops were still unpaid lay people chosen by lot.

Men and women still sat separately for church services. Throughout most of the century, the church maintained a long (and growing) list of what was forbidden, from wedding rings to divorce to television.

By the end of the century, though, a wave of modernity had swept through the Mennonite Church that made its members virtually indistinguishable from both members of the more progressive General Conference and the rest of American society. They had built colleges to educate their children, opened seminaries and hired professional clergy, accepted divorce and remarriage, and expanded into American cities and countries around the world. By the end of the twentieth century, most Mennonites lived modern lives.

As noted in the previous chapter, finally their beliefs and practices had become so similar that the members of the Mennonite Church decided to merge with the General Conference Mennonite Church, rather than continue as two separate organizations.

What had become of their differences? How had the Old Mennonites changed so much in the course of a hundred years that they felt comfortable reuniting with the group who had left less than 150 years ago?

Vas Es Das?

Protracted meetings, later known as revival meetings, were church services held over several days at a host church. They often featured a visiting preacher, and were inspired by the more evangelistic camp meetings held by Methodist and other churches. Also known as tent meetings, they were often sponsored by several churches and held in tents or at special camp facilities to accommodate the crowds.

Holding Off the Modern World

Until the 1940s, nineteenth century leadership had a firm grip on the Mennonite Church. They kept firm to the middle road, between the rigid traditionalists of the Old Order Mennonite groups and the hot-heads who had formed the loose affiliation called the General Conference Mennonite Church. The Mennonite Church had adopted some of the revivalist ways of the late nineteenth century evangelical movement, holding revival or *protracted meetings*, replacing the deadly-slow German hymns with faster-paced gospel songs, holding Sunday school, and even changing the language of worship from German to English so converts could fit in more easily.

The Flag of Plainness

Yet the male leaders of the early twentieth century Mennonite Church held fast to their authority, and prescribed strict codes of dress and behavior that had to be followed by all members. The plain dress that had been encouraged in the nineteenth century became mandatory in the early twentieth century. Mennonite women parted their uncut hair down the middle and pinned it up, although they didn't have to pull it quite as tightly to their scalps as Amish women, to judge from old photographs. Otherwise, their appearance was very similar to the Amish, except they didn't have to tie the strings on their white prayer coverings. They did, however, wear a type of cape dress and apron, and a black bonnet over their covering for going outdoors.

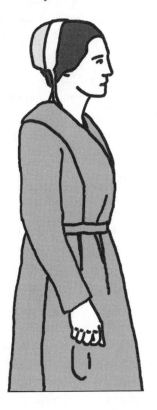 

Members of the Mennonite Church (Old Mennonites) began the twenty-first century as a Plain people, but by 1999, most had dropped all semblance of plain dress.

Like the Amish, Mennonites didn't all comply with the rules to the same degree. Ordained men and their wives were held most strictly to the code, and women's dress was more distinctive than men's. The most conservative Mennonites, who lived in Pennsylvania, Virginia, and Maryland, adhered most strictly to the dress code, while Midwestern Mennonites dressed less plainly. The head covering, that most distinctive flag of plainness, was discarded first in the West (except in Oregon) and Midwest, and lingered longest in the East.

Just Plain Living

Dress wasn't the only area of life ruled by the Mennonite Church. Entertainment was strictly controlled. Radio was banned at first, as was television, even before it

The Plain Truth

Team sports were considered too competitive and encouraged close contact between boys, so Mennonite schools didn't sponsor teams until the 1950s.

became commonly available. Movies, of course, were off limits, and so was live theater.

Dancing was forbidden because it involved touching between men and women, could be considered unnecessary and frivolous, and focused attention on the body in a way that made Mennonites uncomfortable. Although musical instruments could be enjoyed at home, pianos and organs weren't allowed in church.

To enforce a strict code of dress and behavior, the Mennonite Church needed a structure that gave authority to the people at the top. Until 1898, no national organization of Mennonite churches existed, although almost all congregations belonged to a regional conference.

The Rise of National Church Institutions

The General Conference had been the first to invite Mennonite congregations across the country to organize, starting in 1860. They didn't start out to form a new denomination—just the opposite: The original idea was to unite all Mennonite churches, whatever their differences and idiosyncrasies, under one umbrella organization.

Ironies and Oddities

The General Conference Mennonite founders didn't originally intend to create a separate denomination. Instead, they hoped to change the Mennonite history of in-fighting by uniting the many factions of Mennonites to accomplish the more fundamental goal of spreading Anabaptist Christianity. But as not all churches would agree to overlook their differences, what started as a conference on unity led to yet another church split.

Churches could choose to belong to the General Conference while retaining their own local governance. The Conference didn't seek to dictate rules of dress or behavior, or define too closely what it meant to be Mennonite. The loose affiliation of churches worked in a democratic manner, with churches electing delegates who met at annual meetings to vote on developing joint projects including missions, schools, and church publications.

The General Conference emphasis on missions was somewhat foreign to Mennonite churches, which until then mostly had focused on preserving the faith rather than spreading it. Only a minority of Mennonite churches chose to join the General Conference.

By 1898, though, the Mennonite Church regional conferences decided to unite into one national conference for the purpose of building national institutions. But significant differences existed between the national Mennonite Church and the General Conference Mennonite Church.

The Mennonite Church created a national structure of top-down authority to enforce a strict code of dress and behavior. Only ordained men could attend the biennial meetings where church doctrine was decided and spelled out in official statements. The national body (the General Conference or later General Assembly) had authority over regional conferences, which in turn could discipline local congregations, where ordained men were in charge of making sure members met the requirements. To be a member of the Mennonite Church, you had to follow the rules.

> **CAUTION**
>
> **Make No Mistake**
>
> Did they run out of names, or just imagination? Or did they confuse everyone on purpose? When the Mennonite Church held its first national meeting in 1898, they called it the Mennonite Church General Conference—sure to be confused with the unrelated General Conference Mennonite Church. And it was, for almost a century, until the Mennonite Church renamed its meeting the Mennonite General Assembly.

Modernity Creeps Into the Mennonite Church

In the mid-1940s, a new generation of Mennonite men rose to take the place of the rigid traditionalists who had led the church since the beginning of the century. Instead of rising from the uneducated ranks of local ordained ministers and bishops, some of the most prominent leaders were college educated.

They led the church through a period of growing acceptance of modern life that continued through the end of the century. Churches changed from ordaining unpaid, untrained pastors to professional, trained clergy. Plain dress was gradually dropped. Churches bought pianos and organs, church sponsored schools and colleges took up team sports; and movies, theater productions, and dancing eventually all became acceptable for Mennonite Church members.

Accompanying these changes in lifestyle was a more fundamental shift away from top-down authority to a more democratic structure for decision making. By 1971, the church changed both the name and nature of its national meeting.

Renamed the Mennonite Church General Assembly, the meeting allowed lay delegates for the first time, including women. Congregations got more local autonomy, diminishing the disciplinary role of the regional and national conferences. The role of bishops was changed from disciplinarian to advisor, or in some cases was eliminated altogether. Some regional conferences even started ordaining women ministers.

Some churches resisted, of course. The most conservative left the Mennonite Church and formed new, smaller organizations or remained independent. These churches make up what some have called the Conservative Mennonite Movement of the late twentieth century.

Why did the largest body of Mennonites modernize so rapidly over the last 60 years? What were the social causes that led them to change their definition of what it means to be a Mennonite?

School's In: Mennonites Build Colleges and Seminaries

The longest and most deeply held attitudes among Mennonites and the Amish often are rooted in the searing experiences of early Anabaptists in Europe. The persecution that threatened them with imprisonment, torture, and death and pursued them from country to country for more than a hundred years left lasting impressions on their culture.

In his book *Mennonite Society*, sociologist Calvin Redekop points out that while many of the most influential Anabaptist leaders were well-educated, so were their persecutors. "It was the 'learned professors and doctors' who provided the rational justification of the rejection, prosecution, and oppression of the Anabaptists," Redekop writes. They presented the legal and religious case against the Anabaptists that allowed the state to make their persecution official policy. So along with a distrust of governments, Anabaptists developed an early distrust of higher education.

The Plain Truth

Mennonites developed their distrust of education early. Menno Simons, the early Anabaptist leader for whom the denomination is named, wrote, "I repeat, do not hear, do not follow, and do not believe the many learned ones who let themselves be called doctors, lords, and masters, for they mind but flesh and blood."

They had rejected the intellectual debates of Catholic theologians who manipulated church doctrine to ensure their own power and wealthy. The Anabaptists wanted to get back to the basics of Christianity that made the early Christian church vital and easily embraced by uneducated multitudes. They didn't want a religion that gave the wealthy and educated minority power over the uneducated majority of farmers and tradesmen. That's why they chose an uneducated, volunteer, part-time ministry over a professional clergy supported by the church.

That choice was reinforced by the persecution that forced them to scatter to remote rural areas.

Education has always been more available in urban areas, and the money to pay for it produced by the cash economy of cities. On scattered farms, early Mennonites were able to survive and preserve their religion. When they became a rural people, Mennonites put off a pursuit of higher education for close to 400 years.

Higher Education Becomes a Priority at Last

By the end of the nineteenth century, American Mennonites faced a very different threat than their Anabaptist forebears in sixteenth century Europe. Mennonites had been in the United States for more than 200 years, and nobody was chasing them anymore. The government by and large left them alone, as did the Catholics and Protestants. Mennonites owned land and small businesses, and in a nation still largely rural composed of farmers, they fit in and prospered. Their life was a little more restricted by church rules than the lives of neighbors who were neither Mennonite nor Amish, but the differences weren't all that noticeable.

With stability, the threat of persecution was replaced by the threat of stagnation. A religion that had begun as a radical rebellion against authoritarian religious rule had become set in its own ways. When people are threatened with death and destruction, their first concern is survival not only of their lives but their way of life. When neither is threatened, they have time to consider how they themselves would like to alter that way of life.

Revivalism

In the late nineteenth century, the Protestant revivalist style of worship and emphasis on Christian conversion experiences seemed like a breath of fresh air to many Mennonites. They, like the Amish today, still sang its slow, German hymns in unison. Preachers spoke without emotion, in measured tones that some found unconvincing. Shows of religious fervor were discouraged along with all other emotional displays. Ordained men made and enforced the rules, interpreted the scriptures, and their goal was the continuation of tradition rather than renewal.

The ideas and religious fervor of the revivalists was spread through Sunday school materials and publications promoting evangelism, and by traveling preachers who held community-wide tent meetings. Some Mennonites felt their own churches were too inward-focused, neglecting their Christian duty to both spread the faith and serve the physical needs of the poor and sick in the world. They also felt the Mennonite churches could use a little of the spirit of those revival meetings.

To accomplish this would take a new generation of preachers trained in preaching and theology, like those of the Protestants. In their first 200 years in America, Mennonites hadn't founded a single college or Bible school to train their ministers. They had never before felt a need for trained ministers. But those who wanted change in the church and a new emphasis on mission service to the world saw higher education as instrumental to both, and if they couldn't get the training at Mennonite schools, they would get it from other denominations.

Secular Education

Another fact of life in nineteenth century America was that the country was gradually becoming more settled, so people could turn their attention and spend their resources on cultural institutions and experiences. Most people still had limited opportunities to go to school, but more institutes and colleges were springing up across the country to train teachers, doctors, nurses, scientists, lawyers, and other professionals. Of course, Mennonites were still mostly farmers, but some professions, such as teaching or medicine, were acceptable ways of making a living, too.

The Plain Truth

Conservative religious people often seek to limit or control their children's education to prevent them from leaving their religious tradition or changing it by introducing new ideas. They know that with higher education comes a wider awareness of people and ideas outside one's immediate experience. That awareness often leads to a greater understanding, tolerance, and acceptance of differing points of view. This is why the Amish continue to forbid education beyond the eighth grade, and why those with a strong enough desire to learn sometimes leave their families to satisfy that longing.

The Light Dawns

In his 1909 Mennonite history, professor C. Henry Smith of Goshen College wrote that of those bright young men who had left Mennonite homes for college during the nineteenth century, few returned to their Mennonite faith. "They," he wrote, "had been trained away from many of their earlier religious beliefs" and having little inclination to return to the religion that had not supported their ambitions in the first place. "It finally began to dawn upon a few of the leaders of the denomination that if this process were to continue indefinitely, the Mennonites must ever play an insignificant role in the religious world," Smith continued.

So to keep their young people from seeking a secular education and losing them to the world, as well as to bring fresh thinking into the church and prepare young people for mission work, Mennonites slowly began to found their own educational institutions.

At first these were Bible schools meant to train students for ministry and mission. The General Conference made a stab at starting such a school in Ohio in 1868, but it closed just 10 years later. In 1882, though, General Conference Mennonites in Kansas opened the Mennonite Seminary in Halstead. In 1893, it moved to Newton, Kansas, and was renamed Bethel College. A second General Conference college, Bluffton College in Bluffton, Ohio, was founded in 1899.

The more conservative Mennonite Church came to support higher education a little later, and only over the objections of its most conservative members in Pennsylvania and elsewhere. "Goshen College," according to professor Smith, writing just a few years after its founding, "owes its existence to the efforts of a few of the more liberal minded leaders" of the Mennonite Church. They expanded a private Mennonite school, The Elkhart Institute, which had been founded in Elkhart, Indiana, in 1895 to offer business and teacher training, into a church college. In 1902, the college was moved to the more centrally located county seat, Goshen, and renamed Goshen College. The Mennonite Church soon took over running the school, and today Goshen is the largest Mennonite college. Other Mennonite Church colleges were founded in Hesston, Kansas (Hesston College, 1909), and Harrisonburg, Virginia (Eastern Mennonite College, now Eastern Mennonite University, 1917).

Ironies and Oddities

The Mennonite Brethren Church, an evangelical branch founded in a schism in Russia and later brought to the United States, also sponsors colleges in Fresno, California (Fresno Pacific University), and Hillsboro, Kansas (Tabor College, founded in 1908). The Mennonite Brethren are third largest Mennonite organization in the United States, generally more theologically conservative than the other two (although they don't follow traditional Mennonite practices) and more influenced by American evangelical and fundamentalist denominations.

In 1970, the Mennonite Church and General Conference Mennonite Church combined their two seminaries, which had been located in Goshen, Indiana, and Chicago, respectively, into the Associated Mennonite Biblical Seminaries in Elkhart, Indiana. The Mennonite Church also supported Eastern Mennonite Seminary in Harrisonburg, Virginia, while the Mennonite Brethren support Mennonite Brethren Biblical Seminary in Fresno, California.

In recent decades, Mennonite colleges have even started offering some graduate courses, particularly in education. Eastern Mennonite Seminary, together with Eastern Mennonite College, became known as Eastern Mennonite University. The same is true of the schools in Fresno, where the seminary and college were combined into Fresno Pacific University.

Throughout the history of Mennonite higher education, conflicts have arisen between conservative and liberal branches of the denominations over what should be taught, how much of the faculty and student body should be Mennonite, the role of colleges in preserving Mennonite faith and heritage, and other issues. Gradually, after the last of the baby boomers had graduated and enrollment declined, even those surrounded by the most heavily Mennonite communities began admitting more non-Mennonite students to survive.

Nonresistance Opens the Door to Modernization

In addition to higher education, two other social factors had a major modernizing influence on Mennonites during the twentieth century. One was urbanization, which affected all of American society during that period and will be discussed in the next chapter.

The other, ironically, was World War II. Just as the war gave young Americans serving in the military a chance to meet people and hear ideas from around the country and abroad, it also widened the world for Mennonite men who chose alternative service instead.

World War II proved to be a watershed event in Mennonite history. According to Mennonite sociologist Calvin Redekop in his book *Mennonite Society*, few U.S. and Canadian Mennonite men had served in the military in World War I, choosing instead to declare themselves conscientious objectors. In the United States, they were placed them in military camps to do noncombatant work, where they often were severely abused or even tortured. *Through Fire and Water: An Overview of Mennonite History* by Harry Loewen and Steven Nolt reports that in contrast, over half (54 percent) of American Mennonites who were drafted during World War II chose to join the military either as combatants or noncombatants, although both were opposed by their church. Many of those who joined may not have come back home to Mennonite churches, since feeling would still have run strong against their choice.

But more significantly for the church, the 46 percent of drafted American Mennonite men who did perform alternative service in the *Civilian Public Service (CPS)* program brought new perspectives back home with them. The war forced young men out of their ethnic communities, where everyone shared the same heritage and religious teaching, and into the world and new experiences. Although they kept their identity as Mennonites, they saw some of the needs of others beyond their ethnic group. They exchanged ideas with people from different backgrounds and learned how others saw and experienced the world.

Vas Es Das? _____

Civilian Public Service or **CPS** was a government program created during World War II to give draftees who objected to military service because of religious conviction or conscience a chance to perform public service instead. They worked on forestry projects, in public psychiatric hospitals, and other assignments that promoted the public good.

When those young Mennonites came back to their home communities, they brought new ideas with them. Their appetite for higher education and an active role in the world had increased. A few years later, they became the new generation of church leaders, and changed it significantly. They brought a focus on serving the physical needs of humanity at large, rather than just other Mennonites, for instance. They also had gotten to know Christians from other denominations, other cultures, ethnicities, and races. That experience contributed to a gradual broadening of the Mennonite worldview to embrace those outside their narrow ethnic community.

In his book *Mennonites in the Global Village*, Canadian sociologist Leo Driedger compares the attitudes and values of Mennonites born before and after World War II. Reporting on a survey, Driedger writes "… [P]ost-Second World War Mennonites score higher on political action and concern for racial justice. They wanted a more significant role for women in Church leadership, for example, and a more equal partnership in marriage. They were much more involved in the larger community. Values are changing … to greater concern for justice, politics and communication in a larger, more open circle, beyond the in-group."

Later, during the Vietnam War, another generational shift occurred among Mennonites. Like others of their generation, young Mennonites took an active role in protesting the war and the draft. A great controversy arose among Mennonites over whether political protest was consistent with their tradition of humility and obedience to government. The traditional Mennonite public persona was one of meekness and nonresistance, rather than nonviolent resistance as advocated by the younger generation.

As the Vietnam generation assumed leadership in the decades after the war, Mennonite organizations advocated active peacemaking rather than simply nonresistance to violence. An almost imperceptible shift to anyone outside the church, this important change showed the developing Mennonite conviction that it wasn't enough for Christians to separate themselves from the world so they could live pure lives, as their Anabaptist heritage taught. The most progressive Mennonites were feeling called to work toward transforming the world itself, for the benefit of all. That change in attitude would remain a driving force that would carry the church into the twenty-first century.

The Least You Need to Know

- The Mennonite Church, the largest Mennonite denomination until its merger with the General Conference Mennonite Church, moved from plain to mainstream over the course of the twentieth century.

- While General Conference Mennonite churches were loosely affiliated and congregations remained autonomous, the Mennonite Church created a national organization to spell out beliefs and enforce rules of behavior and dress that all members had to follow.

- Both Mennonite denominations established colleges and seminaries during the twentieth century, creating a professional clergy, providing training for the growing Mennonite professional class, and creating an educated class that continued to push for greater liberalization.

- After World War II, when a new generation took over who had been exposed to the world through alternative service, the Mennonite Church gradually became more liberal.

- The Vietnam War stirred more active protest among Mennonite youth than earlier wars, and was a defining moment in the move from advocating pacifism and nonresistance to active peacemaking by the church.

22

Mennonite Church USA: Mainstream Mennonites Today

In This Chapter

- ◆ Would you know one if you saw one?
- ◆ Mennonite churches and worship
- ◆ Urban and minority Mennonites
- ◆ Global growth
- ◆ Controversies and social issues among modern Mennonites

In the last quarter of the twentieth century, the Old Mennonites (Mennonite Church, or MC), who were never very far behind in matters of dress and lifestyle, gradually conformed more and more to the society around them. Differences between Old Mennonite and General Conference (GC) churches came to seem less and less important to many of their members. Eventually, in 1995, the Mennonite Church voted to explore merging with the General Conference.

Today, the two churches are near that goal, and expect to be fully integrated into a new official institution, Mennonite Church USA, in 2003.

Two Churches Meet in the Middle

As you learned in the two previous chapters, the Mennonite Church (MC) had a different relationship with members and local congregations than the General Conference (GC) Mennonite Church. The Mennonite Church began life as a top-down affiliation of regional conferences that set policy at the national level, to be enforced at the regional and local level. Members were expected to follow policy, at least to the extent that regional and local bishops chose to enforce it, in order to be members.

Over time, the reins were loosened and congregations gained more autonomy to accept or reject policy statements issued by their regional conferences. Yet even then, the conferences were expected to maintain some authority and discipline member congregations that got too radical.

The General Conference, on the other hand, was an affiliation of autonomous local congregations that neither set rules nor enforced standards. There were no bishops, and no need for them, since there was no national doctrine or policy to enforce. Individualism, which the Amish and others feared as a threat to community life, was far more evident in the structure of the GC than the Mennonite Church.

When the majority of congregations on both bodies voted to join forces, they started a long process of integrating those two different governance styles as well as the variations in belief and practice under one umbrella organization. In the end, they agreed to meet on middle ground.

"Seeking balance" is what one church official called it. John E. Sharp, an ordained Mennonite minister, currently serves as director of the Mennonite Church USA Historical Committee in Goshen, Indiana. According to Sharp, some General Conference regional bodies were leaning toward developing some kind of accountability so congregations weren't as free to go off in directions the rest of the church would find objectionable. At the same time, Old Mennonite (MC) churches had been moving toward greater autonomy for congregations, and many had already rid themselves of their bishops (although most probably wouldn't describe it that way) or redefined their roles.

New Rules for a New Church

In the new church, congregations are accountable to regional conferences, which themselves are members of the denomination. While the denomination sets vision and direction for the church, it doesn't try to force regional conferences to follow suit.

Power in the new church is held by the regional conferences. As they did under the old MC and GC denominations, regional conferences hold annual meetings attended by delegates from member churches. Representation is apportioned by church size. If conference leaders and a majority of churches in the conference disagree with one congregation's policies or behavior, delegates can vote to expel the offending congregation from membership. Regional conference policy can only be changed when enough congregations themselves demand change.

> **Ironies and Oddities**
>
> Who says Mennonites aren't politically savvy? Rather than ask for a straight up-or-down vote on joining the new church, MC USA asked regional conferences whether they wanted to join right now. That way, "No" only meant "Not now." Rather than take no for an answer, the new church made conferences who declined to join "provisional members" until January 31, 2007—in case they change their minds.

Under the MC USA organization plan, MC and GC regional conferences voted whether to join the new church by its inception date, February 1, 2002. The leaders of the new denomination hoped that former MC and GC conferences that shared the same geographic region would merge their organizations, but the full merger could take years.

The key, says Sharp, is that relationships between church bodies have to be built on trust. "Authority lies where it's given, or conferred," he says, meaning that if congregations choose to bolt, they will.

Holdouts and Holdovers

Some congregations have opted not to join the new church, even before the merger process was complete. Congregations at the extremes of Mennonite belief and practice, whether liberal or conservative, have feared their voices would be drowned out in the new denomination. So far, conservative congregations seem to be leaving voluntarily. Some liberal churches are holding back from joining the new denomination and others are being expelled by regional conferences.

According to Donald Kraybill and C. Nelson Hostetter in their almanac, *Anabaptist World USA*, "Several clusters of congregations in various parts of the country withdrew from the Mennonite Church to protest the merger and/or because they felt the new church would become too lenient on issues such as homosexuality and other matters of biblical interpretation." A number of eastern churches have already withdrawn from their conferences to join a new affiliation, the Alliance of Mennonite Evangelical Congregations.

Depending on how many congregations leave the fold, either voluntarily or not, this latest merger may result in more reshuffling than reunification. That would hardly be a surprise, given Mennonite history.

> **CAUTION** **Make No Mistake** _____
>
> Do Mennonites reflect a diversity of opinion, or just stubborn insistence on only associating with people who support their own opinion (what you might call a "my way or the highway" theology)? Either way, it's hardly surprising that some congregations are refusing to compromise on issues they believe to be make-or-break religious tenets. It's their Mennonite heritage.
>
> For the majority of churches that choose to join MC USA, though, the denomination gives them a new, larger, and perhaps more visible presence in the world.

So Who Are Mennonites Today

With all changes Mennonites have made in the past quarter century, particularly the convergence of the MC and GC into a single organization, it has become increasingly difficult to define what it means to be Mennonite. Why are Mennonites so hard to define, when the Amish are so easy? One reason is that the Amish have maintained their ethnic identity along with their religious faith. They form new settlements when their many children need more room to live and work. Very few people join the Amish from another culture or religion. Not only would they have to embrace Amish religious beliefs and adapt their clothes, transportation, home, and maybe their job to Amish standards, they'd even have to learn a new language.

On the other hand, anybody can be a Mennonite. Over the course of the twentieth century, the most progressive groups gradually removed many of the cultural barriers that made it difficult for others to feel at home. Even some of the conservative groups actively seek to share their religion and welcome new members, although their dress and restrictions on lifestyle might prove a barrier for some.

In _Anabaptist World USA_, Donald Kraybill and C. Nelson Hostetter say that roughly two-thirds of Anabaptists they classify as "transformational" seek to assimilate into the larger culture along with disseminating their faith beyond the original Mennonite ethnic groups. While the goal of traditional and transitional groups—those who retain plain dress and customs—is to preserve their religious identity by separating from the world, transformational groups seek to transform the world itself by their presence in it.

A key difference of belief separating transformational Mennonites from their more traditional cousins is that of ultimate spiritual authority. While traditional Anabaptist groups grant religious leaders and the group as a whole spiritual authority over individual members, transformational groups—the more modern Mennonites and other Anabaptists—"usually grant individual conscience priority over the collective authority of the church," according to Kraybill and Hostetter. In other words, each member is ultimately responsible to his or her own conscience rather than the church. This belief places more importance on developing a personal theology and moral code than on following group doctrine.

What Makes a Mennonite a Mennonite?

So what makes a Mennonite a Mennonite today? Most would probably say it's their Anabaptist faith rather than cultural identity. So today there are not only traditional "ethnic Mennonites" (those born into the Swiss-German or Dutch-Russian Mennonite culture and faith), but also Hispanic Mennonites, African American Mennonites, Chinese and Japanese and Korean Mennonites and many more—and that's in North America alone.

The reason Mennonites have "lost" much of their ethnic distinctiveness is more complicated than simply allowing themselves to be seduced by modern society. There remains in Mennonite churches a constant tension between adapting to the world and maintaining Anabaptist beliefs, and even some Mennonites feel that materialism is behind most of their changes. But there's more to it than that. Over the last half century, progressive Mennonites have tried to separate their ethnic identity from their religious beliefs, allowing the faith to be expressed in many languages and customs.

> **CAUTION**
>
> **Make No Mistake**
>
> Anybody can be a Mennonite in theory—but barriers still exist for noncelibate homosexuals and members of the military. Some churches have been expelled from regional conferences for accepting practicing gay members, while others threaten to leave because the church position isn't strict enough. Churches near a U.S. naval base in Virginia have faced the same kind of controversy over accepting members of the armed forces.

In the nineteenth and early twentieth centuries, the issue of whether and how to share their faith with others was a divisive one in Mennonite churches. Many of those who championed mission work, whether at home or abroad, saw that asking outsiders to change their clothing, hairstyles, and language as a condition of joining the church would make evangelism difficult. Some leaders began to make a distinction between the Swiss-German and Dutch-Russian culture of ethnic Mennonites and the Anabaptist beliefs on which their religion was founded.

Can You Spot a Mennonite?

Nowadays, to find out if someone is a Mennonite, you'd have to talk to him or her. At the heart of the Mennonite religion are the core Anabaptist beliefs. Like the founding Anabaptists, of course, Mennonites share basic Christian beliefs with Catholics and Protestants.

Mennonites, like many Christians, believe in …

   ◆ Three aspects of God (Creator, Christ, and Holy Spirit, or Father, Son, and Holy Ghost, or the Trinity).

   ◆ The divinity of Jesus, as the human embodiment of the Christ.

   ◆ The Bible as the inspired word of God.

As Anabaptists, American Mennonites further believe in …

   ◆ Adult baptism.

   ◆ Rejection of violence, expressed by some as a peace witness.

   ◆ A life of service to those in need.

   ◆ Modeling daily behavior on the example of Jesus.

   ◆ Separation of church and state.

Ironies and Oddities

Talking about "ethnic Mennonites" can get tricky. Mennonites sometimes refer to those born into the traditional Swiss-German or Dutch-Russian Mennonite culture as "ethnic Mennonites" to distinguish them from newer converts. They don't use the term to mean Mennonites from other ethnic groups such as African Americans or Hispanics.

Unlike some of their forebears though, most Mennonites today no longer practice foot washing. They also practice open communion, unlike their forebears, who only allowed members in good standing with the church to take communion. Both traditional practices are still followed by more conservative Mennonite groups.

Rules of dress and behavior that had once been considered important ways of demonstrating the Anabaptist values of simplicity, modesty, and nonconformity to the world have lost their relevance for modern Mennonites. Instead of emphasizing appearance, Mennonites today try to express their beliefs through service.

Mennonite Church USA identifies the following Mennonite values:

◆ Strong commitment to community.

◆ Interest in social issues and peacemaking.

◆ Voluntary service to those who have experienced hardship and loss in floods, tornadoes, and other disasters.

◆ Mission outreach.

Churches Buildings and Worship Services

Of course, church building styles and worship services vary as much as Mennonites themselves. Following the historic pattern, the oldest churches are more formal and conservative, especially those in rural areas of the eastern United States. As you move west, rural churches get more progressive. Urban congregations in all parts of the country, many of which are also the newest congregations, tend to be more informal, culturally diverse, and theologically liberal.

As you might expect of churches that grew out of the Anabaptist rebellion against excessive church wealth and power, Mennonite churches tend to be fairly simple. Although they no longer meet in homes, as early Anabaptists did and the Amish still do today, Mennonites churches still reflect the theology that "church" is not the building, but the people who gather there. Even among modern Mennonites, a few congregations call the building a "meeting house."

Mennonite church sanctuaries are simple spaces, usually with light-colored walls, clear windows, wooden pews, and a simple wooden pulpit.

Inside, the sanctuary walls are plain white or cream, and usually windows are clear, although a few churches have added stained glass. A wooden pulpit stands on a dais at the front of the church, sometimes with a simple wooden cross on the wall behind it. There may be a table in front of the dais, sometimes holding flowers or a seasonal decoration, but no formal altar in the "high church" tradition. Candles and candle lighting are not usually part of a Mennonite church service, except for a special occasion such as an Advent or Christmas service.

Services include hymns sung by the congregation in four-part harmony, sometimes accompanied by a piano or organ, but often *a capella*. "Special music" may include soloists or small groups and other instruments. Even in large churches with choirs, congregational singing remains an important part of worship, because it involves all church members as participants rather than spectators.

The Plain Truth

In church services, ministers dress similarly to their congregations rather than wearing symbolic religious garb. In the more formal churches, men wear suits and women wear dresses or slacks, though young people generally dress more casually. In less formal congregations, men may wear casual pants or jeans, and women wear casual dresses, pants, or jeans.

Mennonites believe in "the priesthood of all believers," meaning that no one needs an intermediary between himself or herself and God. Mennonite ministers are paid professionals who preach, teach, and lead the congregation, but they don't function as spiritual intermediaries as Catholic priests, for example, do. Although the majority of Mennonite ministers are still men, women are increasingly common among the clergy.

Services usually include an opening prayer, scripture reading, several hymns, a sermon of 20 to 30 minutes, followed by a prayer, announcements, another hymn, and a closing benediction. Many churches now also include a "sharing time" in the service, inviting members to share a concern for prayer or a happy event for thanksgiving.

Children are an integral part of Mennonites church activities, and the tradition of sending children to Sunday school while parents stay home is foreign to Mennonite experience. Many congregations now include a children's story before the sermon. Larger congregations provide childcare for young children during the sermon, but older children are usually expected to sit with their parents during church. Sunday school is held before or after church services, with classes for adults as well as children.

Mennonites traditionally hold communion twice a year, often on World Communion Sunday in the fall, and on the Thursday before Easter in the spring. Some churches hold communion more often. All baptized Christians are welcome to participate in communion; children don't take part before baptism.

Make No Mistake

Instead of wine, Mennonite churches use grape juice in their communion to represent the blood of Jesus Christ, and bread to represent the body. Mennonites don't believe, as do Catholics, in transubstantiation—that the juice and bread change into the blood and body of Christ when blessed by the minister. Instead, they see communion as a symbolic way to remember Jesus' death, and to express unity and harmony among members.

Some congregations practice foot washing following communion. These include both traditional congregations, which never dropped the practice, and churches that have reinstated foot washing as one of the few rituals Mennonites have.

Visiting remains almost as important to Mennonites as to their Amish cousins as a way to build community, an important concept to Mennonite congregations. Most people stay around after church to talk, sometimes over coffee and refreshments, and many congregations hold regular potluck meals after church for more socializing.

Bigger Trends: Moving on Up to the City

In 1985, a book called *The Muppie Manual: The Mennonite Professional's Handbook for Humility and Success* by Emerson Lesher poked fun at the new class of Mennonite professionals trying to reconcile their Anabaptist heritage with the competitive demands and materialistic goals of urban professional life. The term "muppie" (Mennonite urban professional) stuck, and so did the growth of Mennonites in the city.

According to sociologist Leo Driedger in *Mennonites in the Global Village*, 90 percent of Mennonites lived in rural areas (on farms, in the countryside, or in small towns) before World War II. "More than half of North American Mennonites are now urban," he writes.

Looking at changes in populations figures between 1972 and 1989, Driedger finds that Mennonites along the highly urban East Coast of the United States increasingly lived in the "urban" countryside—no longer farming, but still commuting to jobs from homes beyond the suburbs.

The Midwest showed the least change, with two-thirds still living on farms or in small villages of under 2,500 people. The Plains states had the largest percentage of Mennonites still farming, while the Pacific had the most urban Mennonite population, with 83 percent living in small, medium, or large cities.

Muppie Values and Beliefs

Along with living and working in cities comes exposure to the values of modern city life, where individualism, competition, and professional jobs are rewarded more than community, cooperation, and jobs that require more physical labor and less education. How has moving off the farm affected Mennonite values and beliefs?

Not surprisingly, urban professional Mennonites were less fundamentalist in their theology and less orthodox in their moral beliefs and behaviors than those still in rural areas. "[U]rban Mennonites are indeed more open and more socially concerned, and reach out more" than their rural counterparts, Driedger writes. Muppies were also more politically active, open to cooperation with other Christians and to the larger society, and more concerned with pacifism. "Twice as many muppies also strongly endorsed a greater role for women in the work of the church, expressed concern for racial equality, and had more sympathy for the poor," Driedger writes. With exposure to the world, he concludes, comes less concern for preserving one's ethnic or religious group and more for the needs of others.

Urban Mennonites also reported feeling more conflict between their faith and society than those still living in rural areas. Living in the midst of a Mennonite settlement, you are less likely to be confronted every day with the contrast between Anabaptist values (humility, community, cooperation, and nonviolence) and the values of modern American society than you are in the city.

All one has to do, of course, is turn on the television to be inundated by American values, but you can always choose not to turn on the television. For those who have to travel to work everyday and share an office with many who share the mainstream values, the contrast is harder to ignore.

Minority Positions

Early Mennonite mission efforts focused on helping other minorities in the United States who were discriminated against and as a result lived in dire poverty. Native Americans, Hispanics, and African Americans were among the first groups Mennonites reached out to, and today they, along with Asian Americans, represent the fastest growing segment in Mennonite congregations in the United States.

Today, people of color and cultural minorities make up about 25 percent of the membership of MC USA. Some African Americans, Africans, Asians, Hispanics, Native Americans, and Asian Americans belong to multicultural congregations. Many others belong to Mennonite churches where most members share their cultural heritage and language.

Hispanic Mennonites, for example, originated as a distinct cultural group within the Mennonite Church in Chicago. According to a September 2001 article by Gilberto Flores in *Mennonite Life*, rural Mennonites who had migrated to the city met Latin American immigrants there and introduced them to Mennonite beliefs. The first Hispanic Mennonite was baptized in Chicago in 1932, and from there, Hispanic Mennonites developed a network of churches across the country. Those churches conduct their own missionary work in Hispanic communities, providing support to new Spanish-speaking immigrants. Like any minority, Hispanic Mennonites still struggle for full recognition and participation in Mennonite church institutions.

> ⚠️ **CAUTION**
>
> ### Make No Mistake
>
> While the main body of Mennonites has embraced all races and ethnicities, there are still conservative communities in which a long Mennonite pedigree helps one be accepted. These are usually the long-established Mennonite enclaves where people expect to know your grandparents, aunts, uncles, in-laws, and cousins. There are still ethnic Swiss-German and Dutch-Russian Mennonites who not only value their own heritage, but consider themselves the "real" Mennonites.

Urbanization has contributed to minority growth in the church, of course, because most Americans belonging to ethnic and racial minorities live in or near cities. Yet most new urban churches aren't in the city itself, but in nearby suburbs. New, inner city churches are largely supported by the Mennonite Mission Network.

For the church as a whole, with its rural heritage and culture, the cultural gap is even wider. For generations, rural Anabaptists have associated cities with worldly excess, resulting in modern times in crime, poverty, drug abuse, and homelessness. While some cultures see cities as desirable places to live, centers of culture and learning, Anabaptists have worked to keep from losing their children to city life, fearing it would erode their morals.

With its focus on missions and social service, the institutional church offers programs it hopes will help bridge the gap between traditional Swiss-German and Dutch-Russian ethnic Mennonite cultures and the church's future. Yet the ghosts of Anabaptists fleeing persecution in the cities for the sanctuary of the countryside still haunts the church culture, even if its population no longer is as rural or ethnically uniform as it once was.

Mennonite Global Growth

While Mennonites originated in Europe and flourished in North America, they have spread their Anabaptist beliefs to every continent. Over a million Mennonites live in 60 countries, and North Americans are no longer a majority. The fastest-growing Mennonite populations are in Africa, Asia, and Latin America.

The Plain Truth

Mennonite World Conference, an organization made up of the more liberal Mennonite Church bodies, along with Brethren in Christ Churches, counts 1.2 million members. Of those, fewer than half (443,918) live in North America. Africa is the continent with the next largest population, at 405,979.

If you slice the world in half along the equator, you'd find roughly 50 percent more members in the southern hemisphere as in the northern. But who wants to slice the world in half? The whole point of Mennonite World Conference is to bring the world closer together. Through programs, publications, networks, and a conference every six years, MWC provides venues for Mennonites from the developing world to express their viewpoints to those in the developed world.

What do they have to say? John Sharp of MC USA says many of them find Mennonites in the United States and Canada "far too liberal and lax."

"Many of them have endured—and some still endure—persecution," Sharp says. "It gives them passion for their faith." By contrast, they think North American Mennonites "care too little about evangelism and justice, and too much about materialism and individualism."

He says the world conferences provide Mennonites from every continent an opportunity to learn from each other, to give and receive "encouragement and, if needed, admonition."

Controversies and Social Issues Among Modern Mennonites

Social issues such as the role of women, child abuse, domestic violence, homosexuality, and unwanted pregnancies haven't been invented by modern society. They're as old as human kind, and as present in traditional cultures—including the Old Order and conservative Anabaptist groups—as they are anywhere else.

Mennonites who have chosen to actively participate in modern society are less able than their conservative brethren to hide from their own social ills. As society has started to face the problems of abuse and issues of tolerance, Mennonites, though often reluctantly and somewhat late to the game, have had to struggle with those issues, too.

The Appearance of Peace

American society as a whole gives social issues a variety public airings and reactions: media investigations, talk shows, policy debates, support groups, self-help books, legislation, compassion, backlashes, and even occasional violence. Individual Mennonites are exposed to and take part in those cultural activities, but the response of the church and culture are peculiarly Mennonite.

Central to Mennonite culture is the Anabaptist principle which is that spiritual life can't be segregated from daily life. Mennonite community evolved as a way to interweave the two, and its power can't be overstated. The weekly ritual of attending worship service and Sunday school is buttressed by weekly Bible and issue discussion groups, work projects, church outings, potluck dinners, and other social occasions, making church the social as well as religious foundation for Mennonite lives.

But as Mennonites and the Amish developed a culture meant to express Anabaptist religious teachings, they didn't always interpret those teachings accurately. Instead of distinguishing between anger and a violent reaction to it, the culture lumped the emotion together with the response, labeling both sinful. Uniformity and unanimity were mistaken for purity and harmony. Peace was equated with lack of conflict.

Over generations, those values created a culture of secrecy and repression. Arguing with, or even challenging the opinion of a powerful church member or faction, threatened the perception of community peace and purity. Conflicts were to be avoided or kept secret, and anyone who spoke of them met with stony silence, rejection, shaming, and shunning, usually not as an official church act but as a social tactic used to enforce church uniformity. As long as no one expressed any conflict with another member of the community, everyone could believe they were a righteous community living in peace.

The appearance of peace became more valued than the real thing. Not only could victims of violence or injustice not confront their abusers, but anyone who had committed an error felt he had to hide it from the church at all costs, or lose his entire social and religious identity. As one survivor who was severely abused by his father put it, "At one point I actually felt anger at the church on behalf of Dad, because it was all so squeaky clean and righteous, no one who had done what he had in life could possibly have come forward."

Every time a new group came along insisting on its right to be heard, it broke the unspoken Mennonite rule against rocking the boat. Peace and justice were ideals addressed through foreign service, not in the local congregation. Progressive Mennonites wanted to extend that work to include ordaining women as well as men, welcoming gay, lesbian, and bisexual members into the church, and learning to prevent family violence and sexual abuse and helping survivors heal. But they faced an uphill battle against the traditions of Mennonite culture.

The Role of Women in the Church: Front and Center

From an Anabaptist tradition in which women weren't even allowed to speak in church, Mennonite women have moved all the way to the pulpit. In 1973, the Mennonite Church installed its first woman minister, Emma Richards, in Lombard, Illinois, a Chicago suburb. The General Conference church followed suit three years later, installing Marilyn Miller as pastor in Arvada, Colorado.

Over the past century, Mennonite women have come a long way, from being silenced in church to public ministry.

Today, 356 women serve as pastors in MC USA churches, representing 15 percent of the total. (In Canada, the percentage is higher, reaching 24 percent.) Roughly half the students entering seminary in recent years have been women. Even so, acceptance of women ministers has been slow in coming and isn't complete. Some regional church conferences refuse to ordain women even now.

Jane Miller Leatherman, who is studying for a career in ministry at Associated Mennonite Biblical Seminary, observes that the current freshman class has more young women than previous classes. So far, most Mennonite women seminary students have been, like Leatherman herself, making a middle-age career change. "Conditions weren't conducive for women to choose ministry when we were younger," she says.

The Plain Truth

Jane Leatherman recounted a story of a woman seminary student whose education was paid for by an older Mennonite woman in her home church. "I often sense that there are older women who might have wanted to go into ministry if they'd had the chance," Leatherman says, "and those women today support younger women who are able to live out that dream."

Pioneering women ministers faced skepticism and sometimes outright hostility, but after nearly 30 years, church leadership and most members of the new MC USA support women's role as pastors.

Women's Issues and Family Violence

As women ascended to leadership in the church, they began to make their voices heard on issues of concern to them. In 1973, MCC set up a task force devoted to women's issues. Starting in the late '80s, the organization made available information on wife battering, sexual abuse, and pastoral sexual misconduct. In 1990, it held its first conference on child abuse in California, and started a support network for adult survivors of sexual abuse.

Recent work includes educational materials on pornography, guidelines on preventing pastor sexual abuse, and a newsletter on the continued problem of violence against women. In addition to abuse issues, MCC has addressed issues of reproductive issues, including abortion, which the church opposes.

Sexual Abuse

Along with the rest of American society, Mennonites in the late 1980s and '90s began to hear stories of sexual abuse in their midst. Like most Americans, Mennonites were reluctant to believe the stories of survivors. They didn't understand repressed memories or the process of healing from childhood trauma.

Accounts of child sexual abuse of one member by another, especially when the perpetrator was still alive to deny the accusation, raised enormous conflict within families and churches. Sometimes, both were still members of the same church. For those congregations, supporting the victim meant risking tearing apart the fabric of an institution that was at the center of their lives. It also raised the question of the church's responsibility in creating the social environment that had allowed the abuse to occur and remain hidden.

Jane Leatherman, the seminary student, grew up in a Mennonite family. It took her more than 30 years to remember that her mother's father had sexually abused her as a child. She feared her mother wouldn't believe those memories, but not only did her mother believe her, she related incidents that supported those memories.

Her mother wasn't the only one who wasn't surprised. Others in the Mennonite community who had known Jane's grandparents also offered insight. One man told Jane that her grandfather had a reputation for being "sleazy" with women. "I just never thought he would do it to a child," he told Jane after hearing about her abuse.

Jane's own congregation was less supportive. Although their initial response to her revelations surprised her with its warmth and sympathy, it soon became clear that some wanted her to forgive and get over it so they didn't have to think about sexual abuse anymore. No one in the church understood the lengthy process of healing from emotional trauma or how to support survivors.

In the early 1990s, sexual abuse was a very visible issue at church-sponsored conferences and in Mennonite publications. By late in the decade, though, the issue had faded from public view. Asked whether the church has taken steps to prevent child sexual abuse, support survivors, and help perpetrators seek treatment, Jane Leatherman said, "The church hasn't done anything marvelous to counteract it. They haven't learned about sexual abuse and decided what to do about it."

> **Ironies and Oddities**
>
> According to Beth Graybill, director of MCC U.S. Women's Concerns Desk, which has organized conferences and published educational materials on sexual abuse, "MCC intended for local church conferences to pick up the abuse work. Some have, in fact, formed local task forces to continue education on the issue, but few hosted their own conferences."

Physical and Emotional Abuse

Physical and emotional abuse occur in Mennonite families as they do throughout society, but many in Mennonite communities still prefer to hear about it happening somewhere else rather than among their own. As a result, those abused as children are sometimes revictimized by their church communities.

Paul (a pseudonym chosen to protect him and his family's privacy) grew up in a Mennonite family in central Illinois. His parents raised four children, and Paul's father abused them all. Paul believes his older brother took the brunt of the physical abuse; his younger sisters were sexually abused from infancy. Their father used humiliation and terror to control the whole family.

"I was the one who fought back," Paul says. The beatings stopped when he got big enough to grab his father and throw him to the floor.

Paul left home at 19, but returned years later to take over the family farm. A disagreement with leaders in his local Mennonite church served as the impetus for Paul to begin therapy, where he discovered long-suppressed pain from childhood and learned how to heal from it. He also joined a different Mennonite church. But even so, Paul says, he never talked about his abuse or healing in his new church. "I didn't trust the minister," he says, or the confidentiality of Mennonite church culture.

Paul's marriage had long lacked affection, and as he healed from his childhood trauma, Paul found his wife became angrier and more abusive. "I think she was afraid," he says, that his emotional changes would end the marriage. "She needed to convince me that I couldn't heal or change, that I was no good and she would have to take care of me," he says. Eventually, the abuse became not only verbal and emotional but sexual as well.

In 1992, Paul spoke at an MCC conference about his abuse and mentioned, obliquely, the effect on his troubled marriage. When he read the same presentation to his home church, "Nobody knew how to deal with it," he says, because both child abuse and marital trouble were still taboo subjects in many Mennonite churches. But soon a handful of people came to tell him privately about their own abuse, saying that they couldn't go to the church leadership for counsel or support.

When Paul finally ended his marriage, the church ministers called him to account for filing for divorce. Many Mennonite churches still believe that members are accountable to the church for actions they consider against biblical teachings, such as divorce.

Paul tried to explain his actions, describing the years of emotional abuse and lack of love, the rages and verbal abuse, and the sexual abuse. The ministers refused to believe him, citing his wife's denials. Church members followed their lead; some stopped talking to Paul, as though he were being shunned.

Eventually Paul left his Mennonite church. "Some people in the church are willing to deal with [abuse]," he says, "but only if a man is the perpetrator, the victim is female, and it's no one among them."

Today, he has remarried and attends an interfaith group with a wide variety of beliefs, where he feels accepted. Yet he refers to himself as "an Anabaptist living in exile," and hopes one day to find an open-minded Mennonite church in another community. "I don't have any use for how [Mennonite] people treat each other," he says, "but when I look at the deeper theology, that's what I claim."

Welcome or Not: Gays and Lesbians in the Church

The most visible and divisive issue in the Mennonite church today is whether to grant church membership to noncelibate gays, lesbians, and bisexual people. According to Gloria Nafziger of the Brethren Mennonite Council for Lesbian, Gay, Bisexual and Transgender Interests (BMC), "noncelibate" really means those in a committed relationship, since congregations don't know whether single people are sexually active or not. "It's another example of the importance of keeping the silence" in Mennonite culture, Nafziger says.

Disagreements over whether to welcome homosexual members remain a major stumbling block to regional church conferences joining the new Mennonite Church USA, according to John E. Sharp, director of the church's Historical Committee. The national denomination hasn't set a policy on homosexual membership, and doesn't force its regional conferences to conform to national policy on other issues such as ordaining women, on which policy does exist.

Yet some conservative congregations believe the national organization *should* have a policy—forbidding churches to accept gay and lesbian members. They don't want to join a church that they fear will dilute their power to exclude members who don't follow what they view as scriptural Christian tenets.

Ironies and Oddities

The oldest Mennonite Church in America, Germantown Mennonite Church in Philadelphia, was expelled twice by former MC and GC conferences with which it was affiliated for welcoming gays and lesbians. The first expulsion, in 1998, was from the former Mennonite Church; the second, from the former General Conference, took place in 2002, after Germantown ordained a gay man so he could work as a chaplain.

The document they use to define those tenets is the Mennonite Confession of Faith adopted in 1995 by the MC and GC denominations before their merger. The statement defines marriage as union between "one man and one woman for life." It goes on to say, "According to Scripture, right sexual union takes place only within the marriage relationship."

Based on that statement, regional conferences formerly belonging to both MC and GC denominations have expelled (or "dismembered" as some congregations prefer to call it) churches for accepting into membership persons in homosexual relationships.

Other churches are in various states of limbo, not yet expelled but banned from voting at church conferences. One congregation voluntarily withdrew from conversation with its regional conference for three years, giving itself a "sabbatical." Two churches were expelled from their MC regional conference, then reinstated several years later after conference leadership had changed and the churches agreed to accept the Mennonite Confession of Faith, without specifying whether they demanded all members live by it.

Still other congregations have issued welcoming statements without being expelled from their regional conferences. But discussions taking place now could change their status in the future.

As Mennonites continue to debate and divide, one thing that doesn't change is the range of expression that Anabaptists find for their faith. From the plain dress of the Old Order Amish, Old Order Mennonites, and many smaller branches, to the focus of the most liberal churches on promoting peace and social justice, all share the belief that faith is a daily reality, not a Sunday ritual.

The Least You Need to Know

- ◆ Mennonite Church USA is the name of the new denomination formed by the merger of the Mennonite Church and the much smaller General Conference Mennonite Church.

- ◆ The increasing numbers of urban Mennonites bring a broader worldview to the church with more emphasis on social justice and active peacemaking.

- ◆ Anabaptist rejection of church wealth and ceremony, as well as the value placed on community, are evident in the simple decor, lack of ritual, emphasis on congregational singing and love of fellowship found in Mennonite churches today.

- ◆ North American Mennonites are now a minority worldwide, with the fastest growing churches in Africa, Asia, and Latin America.

- ◆ Modern Mennonites face the same social issues as American society in general.

- ◆ Today, the single most divisive issue in Mennonite churches is whether to welcome noncelibate gay, lesbian, and bisexual members.

Appendix A

Words to Know

Amish   Followers of an Anabaptist Christian religious group founded by Jakob Ammann in Switzerland in 1693. Today approximately 180,000 Amish persons live in the United States.

Anabaptists   Church reformers in sixteenth century Switzerland who insisted that only adults who chose to follow the biblical teachings of Jesus Christ could be baptized. Although they had been baptized as infants by the Catholic Church, they defied the Catholic Church, Protestant reformers, and civil authorities by baptizing each other again (*ana-* means *again*). Both Mennonites and the Amish trace their origins to that first Anabaptist meeting on January 21, 1525.

Ausbund das ist Etliche schone Christliche Lieder, or ***An Excellent Selection of Some Beautiful Christian Songs***   The full name of the Amish hymn book. It contains only word, not music, for songs written by early Anabaptist martyrs while in prison. The book also includes some of their stories of martyrdom. It's commonly called the *Ausbund*.

ban   The Amish term for excommunication of those who refuse to confess and repent of sin when confronted by the church. The German word *bann* means "excommunication." Former church members who are "under the ban" are also *shunned* (see following definition).

baptism   A Christian rite or sacrament dedicating a person's life to the service of God. Baptism is inspired by the biblical account of Jesus asking to be baptized in the Jordan River to symbolize his dedication to God.

In some churches, persons being baptized are immersed in water, but most perform baptism by pouring water over the person's head.

buggy   Technically, an open carriage such as those sometimes seen in Pennsylvania, but in most Amish settlements the word is used by the English to refer to the standard, covered Amish carriage.

charge   A statement "laid upon" an ordained man detailing the duties he is expected to perform. For a bishop it includes performing baptisms, communion, weddings, ordinations, and excommunications. Ministers or preachers are charged with preaching, reading, and praying with the church. Deacons assist ministers at services, collect and distribute alms for the poor, are sent by the bishop to speak with those suspected of breaking church rules, and act as an intermediary between prospective bridegrooms and the bride's parents.

Civilian Public Service or **CPS**   A government program created during World War II to give draftees who objected to military service because of religious conviction or conscience a chance to perform public service instead. They worked on forestry projects, public psychiatric hospitals, and other assignments that promoted the public good.

communion   Sometimes also called The Lord's Supper, a Christian sacrament or sacred ritual based on the words of Jesus in the biblical account of the Last Supper. Christian groups vary widely in the frequency with which they celebrate communion. For Catholics, it's the heart of every mass. Some Anabaptists celebrate communion only once a year, on Thursday of Holy Week, which coincides with the Jewish Passover, the night that Jesus ate his last supper on earth.

covering   *See* kapp.

dat   Pennsylvania German for dad or father.

excommunication   Expelling a person from church membership (also referred to as placing a person "under the ban.") In the case of the Amish, excommunication is often accompanied by shunning, which means that church members may not associate socially with the ex-member. Spouses who remain in the church are not supposed to have sexual relations with an excommunicated spouse.

Grossdaadi haus   The Pennsylvania German term for "grandfather house" often attached to a farm house.

Holy Kiss   An old custom based on the Apostle Paul's instructions to the early Christian church at Corinth, "Greet one another with a holy kiss." (I Cor. 16:20) The Holy Kiss is only exchanged between people of the same gender.

kapp   The small, white cap with long ribbon strings that Amish women wear on the back of their heads to hide their hair and show submission to God and men. Also called prayer covering, covering, head covering, and prayer veiling, and worn by conservative Mennonite and Brethren women.

kuchen   Pennsylvania German for cake. It's commonly found in Amish and Mennonite cookbooks, but often attached to foods we wouldn't consider cakes. *Mennonite Community Cookbook* includes recipes for *Roll Kuchen* (crullers), *Streusel Kuchen* (raised coffee cake), *Leb Kuchen* (Old-Fashioined Ginger Cookies), and even *Geburtstagkuchen* and *Kaffe* (birthday cake and coffee).

knepp   Dumplings, which appear in many recipes for both main dishes and desserts.

Lob Lied   The second hymn sung at every Amish church service, in every district throughout the country. It's a hymn of praise, and begins "Oh Father God, we praise thee." After thanking God, the hymn goes on to pray for the ministers to be able to speak God's teachings, then for the congregation to be open to receiving their words, and finally for God to be present.

mam   The Pennsylvania German word for mom or mother.

Mennonites   Members of an Anabaptist group originating in Switzerland in 1525 and later named for a Dutch preacher leader named Menno Simons. Mennonites share many of the beliefs of the Amish (who broke with the Mennonites in 1693 because they felt the group was becoming too much like worldly society), but accept more aspects of modern life and grant more individual freedom to members. There are many Mennonite denominations, whose lifestyles vary from almost as conservative as Amish to indistinguishable from mainstream society.

nonconformed   The word the Amish apply to the relationship of their culture to the world around them, based the Apostle Paul's command to the early Christians at Rome: "… Be ye not conformed to this world: but be ye transformed by the renewing of your mind, that ye may prove what is that good, and acceptable, and perfect, will of God." (Romans 12:2)

nonconformity   To choose to be different from other people, or choose not to follow the rules of others. For the Amish, it has the particular meaning of being unlike non-Amish people in order to emphasize that they see themselves as "true Christians," and therefore unlike the rest of society.

Ordnung   German for "order," and refers to the traditions and rules that regulate Amish church life. It is largely oral, handed down from generation to generation, though some parts of it have been written from time to time. It can vary from settlement to settlement, but agrees on basic, biblical principles that govern Amish choices and customs.

Pennsylvania Dutch A popular term for the German dialect spoken by the Amish, more accurately called *Pennsylvania German*. "Pennsylvania" refers to the colony where most early Amish (and Mennonite) settlers lived and where the language was most frequently heard. *Deutsch*, the German word for "German," sounded like "Dutch" to English speakers, so they started referring to the language by that name. The Pennsylvania German word for the language is *Deitsch*. There is no relationship between Pennsylvania German and the real Dutch language spoken in the Netherlands. Nevertheless, English speakers in areas where the Amish live generally refer to their language simply as "Dutch."

Pennsylvania German The correct term for the German dialect spoken by the Amish. *See also* Pennsylvania Dutch.

Protestant Reformation The name of the movement led by Martin Luther and others in Europe starting in 1517 who challenged the doctrines and practices of the Catholic Church of the time. Among changes demanded by protestors were the use of biblical teaching rather than church law as the foundation for church decisions, church services conducted in the language of the people rather than Latin, an end to the selling of indulgences, and allowing priests to marry. Protestant denominations today, including the Lutherans founded by Martin Luther, trace their roots to the Protestant Reformation.

protracted meetings Later known as revival meetings, these were church services held over several days at a host church. They often featured a visiting preacher, and were inspired by the more evangelistic camp meetings held by Methodist and other churches. Also known as tent meetings, they were often sponsored by several churches and held in tents or at special camp facilities to accommodate the crowds.

regeneration A term used by the Amish to mean a spiritual renewal or rebirth brought about by the influence of the Holy Spirit. Evangelical Christians use the term "born again" to mean a similar change, though the Amish believe regeneration occurs over time, rather than in a single, powerful conversion experience.

shop An Amish workshop where goods are produced and services performed. Often these shops also sell directly to customers, and many are advertised with roadside signs. Most new Amish homesteads include an outbuilding for a shop.

shunning Practice used by the Amish to discipline former church members who have been excommunicated from the church for refusing to confess and repent. It dates back from early Anabaptist days, and was one of the key points in the division between Amish and the group that became the Mennonites, who do not practice shunning. The Amish base their practice on scriptures including II Thessalonians 3:14–15: "If any man obey not our word by this epistle, note that man, and have no company with him, that he may be ashamed. Yet count him not as an enemy, but admonish him as a brother."

True-Hearted People   Also called Half-Anabaptists, these were people who helped the early Anabaptists in Europe, often sheltering, hiding, and feeding them in the face of severe persecution. Some were relatives who had not joined the Anabaptist movement, but protected their family members from the authorities. The question of their salvation was one of the dividing issues between the forerunners of the Mennonites and the Amish.

universalism   A belief spread through the Midwest by circuit-riding preachers in the mid-nineteenth century. They taught that all human beings, even those who commit evil, will be saved by God out of love for humanity.

Where to Learn More

Books

Bishop, Robert and Elizabeth Safanda. *A Gallery of Amish Quilts: Design Diversity from a Plain People*. New York: E.P. Dutton, 1976.

Committee of Amish Women, compilers. *Amish Cooking*. Scottsdale, PA: Herald Press, 1992.

Fisher, Sara E. and Rachel K. Stahl. *The Amish School*. Intercourse, PA: Good Books, 1986.

Good, Merle and Phyllis Pellman Good. *20 Most Asked Questions About the Amish and Mennonites*. Intercourse, PA: Good Books, 1995.

Hostetler, John A., compiler. *Amish Roots: A Treasury of History, Wisdom, and Lore*. Baltimore, MD: The Johns Hopkins University Press, 1989.

——— *Amish Society*. Fourth Edition. Baltimore, MD: The Johns Hopkins University Press, 1993.

——— and Gertrude Enders Huntington. *Amish Children: Education in the Family, School, and Community*. New York: Harcourt Brace and Jovanovich, 1992.

Garrett, Ruth Irene with Rick Farrant. *Crossing Over: One Woman's Exodus from Amish Life*. San Francisco, CA: Harper Collins San Francisco, 2003.

Garrett, O.A. ed. *True Stories of the X-Amish*. Horse Cave, KY: New Leben, Inc, 1998.

Good, Phyllis Pellman. *Quilts from Two Valleys: Amish Quilts from the Big Valley, Mennonite Quilts from the Shenandoah Valley*. Intercourse, PA: Good Books, 1999.

Granick, Eve Wheatcroft. *The Amish Quilt*. Intercourse, PA: Good Books, 1989.

Igou, Brad, compiler. *The Amish in Their Own Words: Amish Writings from 25 Years of Family Life Magazine*. Scottsdale, PA: Herald Press, 1999.

Kraybill, Donald B., ed. *The Amish and the State*. Baltimore, MD: The Johns Hopkins University Press, 1993.

—— and Carl F. Bowman. *On the Backroad to Heaven: Old Order Hutterites, Mennonites, Amish, and Brethren*. Baltimore, MD: The Johns Hopkins University Press, 2001.

——. *The Riddle of Amish Culture*. Revised Edition. Baltimore, MD: The Johns Hopkins University Press, 2001.

—— and C. Nelson Hostetter. *Anabaptist World USA*. Scottsdale, PA: Herald Press, 2001.

—— and Steven M. Nolt. *Amish Enterprise: From Plows to Profits*. Baltimore, MD: The Johns Hopkins University Press, 1995.

—— and Marc A. Olshan. Eds. *The Amish Struggle with Modernity*. Hanover: University Press of New England, 1994.

Loewen, Harry and Steven Nolt, with Carol Duerksen and Elwood Yoder. *Through Fire & Water: An Overview of Mennonite History*. Scottsdale, PA: Herald Press, 1996.

Niemeyer, Lucian and Donald B. Kraybill. *Old Order Amish: Their Enduring Way of Life*. Baltimore, MD: Johns Hopkins University Press, 1993.

Nolt, Steven M. *A History of the Amish*. Intercourse, PA: Good Books, 1992.

Pellman, Rachel and Kenneth. *A Treasury of Amish Quilts*. Intercourse, PA: Good Books, 1990.

Pottinger, David. *Quilts from the Indiana Amish: A Regional Collection*. New York: E.P. Dutton, in association with the Museum of American Folk Art, 1983.

Scott, Stephen. *Amish Houses & Barns*. Intercourse, PA: Good Books, 1992.

———. *The Amish Wedding and Other Special Occasions of the Old Order Communities*. People's Place Booklet #8. Intercourse, PA: Good Books, 1988.

———. *An Introductin to Old Order and Conservative Mennonite Groups*. People's Place Book #12. Intercourse, PA: Good Books, 1996.

———. *Plain Buggies: Amish, Mennonite and Brethren Horse-Drawn Transportation*. Intercourse, PA: Good Books, 1981.

———. *Why Do They Dress That Way?* Revised Edition. People's Place Book #7. Intercourse, PA: Good Books, 1997.

——— and Kenneth Pellman. *Living Without Electricity*. People's Place Book #9. Intercourse, PA: Good Books, 2000.

Stoltzfus, Louise. *Amish Women: Lives and Stories*. Intercourse, PA: Good Books, 1994.

Umble, Diane Zimmerman. *Holding the Line: the Telephone in Old Order Mennonite and Amish Life*. Baltimore, MD: The Johns Hopkins University Press, 1996.

Weaver-Zercher, David. *The Amish in the American Imagination*. Baltimore, MD: The Johns Hopkins University Press, 2001.

Information Centers

Menno-Hof
P.O. Box 701
Shipshewana, IN 46565-0701
219-768-4117
www.mennohof.org

Mennonite Heritage Center
565 Yoder Rd.
P.O. Box 82
Harleysville, PA 19438-0082
215-256-3020
www.mhep.org

Mennonite Information Center (Ohio)
5798 County Rd. 77
P.O. Box 324
Berlin, OH 44610-0324
330-893-3192
http://pages.sssnet.com/behalt

Mennonite Information Center (Pennsylvania)
2209 Millstream Rd.
Lancaster, PA 17602-1494
717-299-0954
http://mennoniteinfoctr.com

Illinois Amish Interpretive Center
111 S. Locust St.
P.O. Box 413
Arcola, IL 61910
217-268-3599 or 1-888-45AMISH
www.ilohwy.com/i/illiamic.htm

Illinois Mennonite Heritage Center
P.O. Box 1007
Metamora, IL 61548
309-367-2551
www.rootsweb.com/~ilmhgs/

The People's Place
3513 Old Philadelphia
P.O. Box 419
Intercourse, PA 17534-0419
1-800-390-8436
www.thepeoplesplace.com

Amish Periodicals

The Budget
Sugar Creek, Ohio 44681

Die Botschaft
Brookshire Printing Inc.
200 Hazel Street
Lancaster, PA 17608-0807

The Diary
P.O. Box 98
Gordonville, PA 17529

Plain Communities Business Exchange
P.O. Box 328
Lampeter, PA 17537
717-295-7667

Young Companion
Pathway Publishers
Route 4
Aylmer, Ontario N5H2R3

or

2580N, 250W
LaGrange, IN 46761

Blackboard Bulletin
Pathway Publishers
Route 4
Aylmer, Ontario N5H2R3

or

2580N, 250W
LaGrange, IN 46761

Family Life
Pathway Publishers
Route 4
Aylmer, Ontario N5H2R3

or

2580N, 250W
LaGrange, IN 46761

Websites—Amish

Amish.Net
www.amish.net

Religioustolerance.org
www.religioustolerance.org/amish.htm

Amish Buggies
http://members.tripod.com/amishbuggy

Arthur, Illinois: "The Heart of the Illinois Amish Country"
www.arthurIL.com/home1.htm

Holmes County Ohio Chamber of Commerce and Tourism Bureau
www.visitamishcountry.com/

National Committee for Amish Religious Freedom
www.holycrosslivonia.org/amish/

Pennsylvania Dutch Welcome Center
www.800padutch.com/index.html

Websites—Mennonite

Canadian Mennonite Encyclopedia Online
www.mhsc.ca/encyclopedia/search.html

MennoLink
www.mennolink.org/

The Mennonite—Magazine
www.themennonite.org/

Mennonite Central Committee
www.mcc.org/

Mennonite Church USA Sites:

Home Page
www.mennonitechurchusa.org/

Historical Committee and MC USA Archives—Goshen
http://www.goshen.edu/mcarchives/

Links to other church agencies:

Mennonite Church USA—Ministries and Resources
www.mennonitechurchusa.org/ministries/index.html

Mennonite Library and MC USA Archives—North Newton
www.bethelks.edu/services/mla/

Mennonite Media
http://mennomedia.org/resources/

Peace and Justice Support Network
http://peace.mennolink.org/

Third Way Café
www.thirdway.com

Mennonite Connections on the WWW
www-personal.umich.edu/~bpl/menno.html

Mennonite Historical Society of Canada
www.mhsc.ca/

Mennonite Life—Quarterly Journal
www.bethelks.edu/mennonitelife/

Mennonite Publishing House
www.mph.org/pbs/pbsbest.htm

Mennonite World Conference
www.mwc-cmm.org/

Index

N

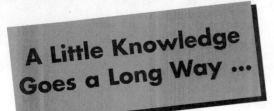
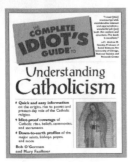

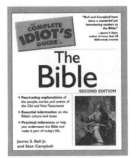

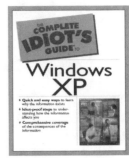